COMPARATIVE GREEK AND LATIN SYNTAX

Dr. S. Fritz Forkel
د. سليمان فريتس فوركل
ד"ר שלמה פריץ פורקל
Skénznen Rónznis

COMPARATIVE GREEK AND LATIN SYNTAX

BY

R.W. Moore

Published by Bristol Classical Press
General Editor: John H. Betts

This impression 2003
This edition published in 1999 by
Bristol Classical Press
an imprint of
Gerald Duckworth & Co. Ltd.
61 Frith Street, London W1D 3JL
Tel: 020 7434 4242
Fax: 020 7434 4420
inquiries@duckworth-publishers.co.uk
www.ducknet.co.uk

First published 1934 by
G. Bell and Sons, Ltd, London

All rights reserved. No part of this publication
may be reproduced, stored in a retrieval system, or
transmitted, in any form or by any means, electronic,
mechanical, photocopying, recording or otherwise,
without the prior permission of the publisher.

A catalogue record for this book is available
from the British Library

ISBN 1 85399 598 3

Printed and bound in Great Britain by
Antony Rowe Ltd, Eastbourne

"THE question is," said Alice, "whether you can make words mean different things."

"The question is," said Humpty Dumpty, "which is to be master—that's all."

Alice was too much puzzled to say anything, so after a minute Humpty Dumpty began again. "They've a temper, some of them—particularly verbs, they're the proudest—adjectives you can do anything with, but not verbs—however, I can manage the whole lot! Impenetrability! That's what I say!"

LEWIS CARROLL, *Through the Looking-Glass*

PREFACE

THE study of syntax is a study in the connexion of the units of human thought. It is the science that asks how, in the form of words, a man passes from one concept to another. But, as every other science, it must also ask why. What made X express himself in this or that particular form—when, perhaps, his auditor or his reader might have expected a different form ? It may be that in asking that question Syntax shows that as with so many other studies there is a shadowy margin where it merges into Psychology, past which it cannot be pursued. The suggestion need not be extended here, but the element of human mind needs vindication, and it must be recognized that Syntax admits the idiosyncrasies of individual thought. The point naturally raises the question of the right approach to syntax, of the right method of explanation of various constructions. Often these are departures from the ordinary usage, abnormalities of a central norm, and there is a strong temptation to regard them not as intentional variations but as reprehensible failures to comply with a rule. Ἐσθλοὶ μὲν γὰρ ἁπλῶς, παντοδαπῶς δὲ κακοί, says an unknown Greek poet ; it is a plausible aphorism, and human nature tends to re-echo the sentiment behind it. A more charitable approach must be taught ; a pupil confronted in a Critical Paper with half a dozen sentences must find in them, not so many howlers, but what are as often as not conscious adaptations used to express a particular shade of meaning or to produce a certain effect. A serviceable illustration may be recalled from Kenneth Grahame's *The Wind in the Willows* :

" I'll learn 'em to steal my house ! " he [Toad] cried.
" Don't say ' learn 'em ', Toad," said the Rat, greatly shocked. " It's not good English."

"What are you always nagging at Toad for?" inquired the Badger rather peevishly. "What's the matter with his English? It's the same what I use myself, and if it's good enough for me it ought to be good enough for you!"

"I'm very sorry," said the Rat humbly. "Only I think it ought to be 'teach 'em', not 'learn 'em'."

"But we don't *want* to teach 'em," replied the Badger. "We want to learn 'em! And, what's more, we're going to do it too!"

Like Rat, the modern commentator must learn to give his author credit for saying what he means and meaning what he says. He will then at least fall on the right side of presumption.

This short survey of the theory and practice of Greek and Latin syntax has three main objects, which may be symbolized by the epithets critical, historical and psychological. They are:

(i) To explain usages and their interrelations, labels and theories as thoroughly as possible and to get the student to require such explanation. The usual apprenticeship in Greek and Latin too often inoculates the reader to taking things on trust; syntactical rules are stated as indispensables to be taken or left as they stand; the critical instincts are not encouraged. But syntax should be regarded not as a tyrant whose caprices are to be meticulously recorded, but as a willing, if highly accomplished, servant. And if in these "dead languages" syntax has for many of its votaries assumed the menacing aspect of the tyrant, then at least unnecessary terror may be allayed by the reminder that after all he has risen from the ranks and not sprung into being fully armed like Athene from the head of Zeus. This leads to the second object—

(ii) To trace as clearly as possible within so small a book the lines along which syntax grows from the simplest utterance to the complex period. Why does the Accusative-and-Infinitive construction use an accusative and an infinitive? What is a Relative—how does it start? How does the Imperfect Subjunctive come to refer to present time? Or again, we are used to the dogma that the Greek Genitive represents both Genitive and Ablative: why should it? how are the two compatible? For these

PREFACE ix

random and many similar problems the historical approach suggests a solution.

(iii) To set about explaining usages, both normal and variations from the normal, as far as possible by asking what was the writer's purpose ; that is, in terms of the working of individual thought.

The logical method has rather been found convenient as a ground plan than followed as the ideal that it undoubtedly is. The book is on too small a scale for that. Its immediate object is to provide for the requirements of classical Critical Papers such as are set in the Higher Certificate and various University examinations, and it is therefore arranged so as to facilitate revision. Not that this somewhat narrow object is the only one ; the study of syntax should form part of any advanced classical course because of the training it can afford in the development of analytic thought.

There is another ideal (the method, as used by Roby, of contrasting various ways of expressing the same thought) which must, for similar reasons, remain beyond the horizon of the present work. Yet it is not wholly absent. In the interests of conciseness only a restricted number of instances is reproduced for each construction, but reference to works of the calibre of Goodwin's *Moods and Tenses of the Greek Verb* and Roby's *Latin Grammar* will provide additional examples where required.

Apart from these two famous works, in particular I must acknowledge indebtedness to the following : Monro's *Homeric Grammar* ; Donaldson's *Greek Grammar* (published 1859 and now very undeservedly forgotten) ; Thompson's *Attic Syntax* ; the *Latin Grammar* of Gildersleeve and Lodge; Lindsay's *Latin Language* and *Syntax of Plautus* ; the *Comparative Grammar of Greek and Latin* of King and Cookson ; Buckland Green's *Notes on Greek and Latin Syntax* ; the *Greek Grammar* of Hadley and Allen ; Riemann's *Syntaxe Latine* ; Wilamowitz's *Geschichte der griechischen Sprache*.

I include where possible the confirmation of Sanskrit usage, not that I can pretend to any real familiarity with the language or that the majority of my readers will appreciate it (for the same reason I give no transcription of Sanskrit words), but the student will find such mention comforting in view of the statements on the relations of the Indo-European languages, and I give references to Macdonell's *Sanskrit Grammar for Beginners* that the sceptical may verify.

I am very grateful to Professor T. B. L. Webster, of Manchester University, and to Mr. J. M. Street, Mr. H. N. Dawson and Mr. R. St. J. Pitts-Tucker, of Shrewsbury School, for much valuable help and encouragement.

R. W. M.

SHREWSBURY, 1934

CONTENTS

	PAGE
PREFACE	vii
THE LOGICAL SCHEME OF EXPRESSION	1
THE PARTS OF SPEECH	2
NOUNS AND PREPOSITIONS	4
THE CASES: HISTORY AND INTERPENETRATIONS	4
THE NOMINATIVE	6
THE VOCATIVE	9
THE ACCUSATIVE	10
PRELIMINARY NOTE ON PREPOSITIONS	12
THE DATIVE	29
THE GENITIVE	35
THE ABLATIVE	45
THE LOCATIVE	49
THE INSTRUMENTAL	52
SPECIAL PREPOSITIONAL USAGES	58
PRONOUNS. THE ARTICLE	61
VERBS	68
THE VOICES	68
THE TENSES	70
THE IDEAL REQUIREMENTS	71
THE PRESENT	72
THE IMPERFECT	74
THE FUTURE	76

CONTENTS

	PAGE
THE PERFECT	77
THE PLUPERFECT	78
THE FUTURE PERFECT	78
THE AORIST	79
THE MOODS	80
MEANINGS AND DEVELOPMENTS	80
THE INDICATIVE	81
THE SUBJUNCTIVE AND THE OPTATIVE	81
THE IMPERATIVE	85
THE INFINITIVE	85
VERBAL NOUNS AND ADJECTIVES	90
THE PARTICIPLE	92
THE SENTENCE	95
VARIATIONS FROM SIMPLE STATEMENT	95
JUSSIVE USAGES	95
POSITIVE COMMAND	96
NEGATIVE COMMAND	97
CONCESSION	98
WISH	98
DELIBERATION	99
PARATAXIS AND SYNTAXIS	101
THE COMPOUND SENTENCE	102
DEPENDENT CLAUSES	102
FINAL	103
CONSECUTIVE	107
DEFINITE RELATIVE AND TEMPORAL	111
CAUSAL	112
CONCESSIVE	116
CONDITIONAL CLAUSES PROPER	117
INDEFINITE RELATIVE AND TEMPORAL	131
OBJECT CLAUSES	137
MODAL CLAUSES	137

CONTENTS

	PAGE
OBJECT CLAUSES OF FEAR	138
ORATIO OBLIQUA	140
AN AND KEN	151
THE NEGATIVES	158
ATTRACTION AND ASSIMILATION	175
EXAMPLES FOR EXERCISE	181
INDEX	219

THE LOGICAL SCHEME OF EXPRESSION

§ 1. When we express an idea about the world around us, we do so by thinking of some object in it as a fixed point, which either is of a certain kind or acts (or is acted on) in a certain way. Our idea, in its essentials, is either of the type **The sky is blue** or of the type **The sky changes**. Thus the formulation of an idea depends upon these three concepts: (i) Thing or SUBSTANCE (i.e. that which " stands under " or underlies our idea, e.g. the sky), (ii) PROPERTY (i.e. that quality which " belongs " to the Substance, e.g. blue), (iii) EVENT (i.e. that which happens to the Substance, e.g. changes).

These three metaphysical concepts (i.e. concepts concerned with the nature of reality) give rise to the three logical forms (i.e. forms of human thinking)—SUBSTANTIVITY (the form of the Substance), ADJECTIVITY (the form of what is " added to " the Substance as a quality) and VERBALITY (the form of Event). These forms give grammar (the science that lays down the rules for the expression of human ideas in words) its Substantives (nouns and pronouns), Adjectives and Verbs. Grammar calls what you are speaking about the SUBJECT, and what you are saying about it the PREDICATE. The Subject is expressed by a Substantive and the Predicate either by a Verb or an Adjective; thus we have either **The sky/changes** (Verb) or **The sky/is blue** (Adjective). Adjectives may be used either predicatively or attributively (in which use they are used merely for incidental description and do not mark the main statement of a sentence, e.g. **The blue sky . . .**); some languages, as English, require a word to link the adjective to the substantive when it is used predicatively; this word is called the COPULA (" link ")—" The sky is blue "; Greek and Latin can, on occasion, dispense with it (καλὸς ὁ ἀνήρ, *optimus ille*). Plato (*Sophistes* 261 D) has a very interesting and simple account of predication.

Grammar distinguishes (i) Simple or Primary Predicates (such as are contained in every finite verb or copula + adjective)—*God is good, Man works*; (ii) Supplementary or Secondary Predicates (such as are contained in adverbs or the oblique cases of nouns)—*God is infinitely good, Man works the fields, I give it to him*, or further, *God is infinitely good to man, Man works the works of God.*

But N.B.—(i) Logically there is only one significant stress in a sentence, which can be understood only from the context. I may say " God is infinitely good " in answer to the question " Who is infinitely good ? " and then " God " is a predicate. In appropriate contexts any word in my sentence may represent the predicate.

(ii) On this score, too, the grammatical distinction between Subject and Predicate seems largely artificial : consider the statement " God is good " : what I am saying of God is not " good " but " that He is good." Thus it is better to say that the grammatical Predicate is the word or words which *represent* the new fact stated of the subject.

The Subject and Predicate may, in the simple sentence, be related to each other in any one of three manners ; we may say **The sky is blue** or **Is the sky blue ?** or **Sky, be blue.** Thus the sentence has three possible forms or tones, Statement, Question, Petition (this last containing the germ of all the oblique moods and their implications).

THE PARTS OF SPEECH

§ 2. The fundamental parts of speech are, then, nouns, adjectives, verbs. (And here it is interesting to see how readily the conventions of language depart from strict logic. See how these fundamentals overlap : we have such substantives as **change, nothing**, adjectives such as **parallel, unequal**, verbs such as **are at rest, conditions**.) Of the other parts of speech, interjections contribute nothing to logical meaning and suggest merely the tone with which the speaker speaks (compare underlinings and italics in printed

THE PARTS OF SPEECH

sentences); pronouns logically are not distinguished from nouns; adverbs are to verbs in the same relation as adjectives to substantives (compare " he runs swiftly " with " his running is swift "); both adjectives and adverbs are, as the name signifies, adjuncts, and in grammar play a subordinate part and will, therefore, not require a separate syntactical study. There remain prepositions and conjunctions: prepositions, in an inflectional language, as we shall see, are superfluous where there is a sufficient variety of cases; conjunctions would be superfluous if there were a similar variety of moods.

A word about cases: the Nominative is used both as Subject and Predicate; Accusative and Dative modify verbs and thus are used as supplementary Predicates; the Genitive qualifies a substantive and so is adjectival or attributive, but it also modifies a verb and in that capacity is a supplementary predicate.

Note.—The above remarks deal with only simple sentences; the development of compound sentences is considered in the course of the book under the various constructions.

NOUNS AND PREPOSITIONS

THE CASES

§ 3. Languages in their earlier times have more cases than they use in their later days when they have reached maturity. A possible reason for this phenomenon is that the more developed and systematized the language becomes the more it seeks to tidy up its devices; various types of expression are reduced more and more to common multiples, there is a gradual weeding-out of overlappings and an economizing in apparatus. A merging of cases is also in part the natural consequence of the operation of the phonetic laws of the individual language. Another consideration may be drawn from the usages of the cases; it does not make much difference whether we speak of " holding it in my hand " or " holding it with my hand "; but sooner or later one of these phrases will predominate. So the Instrumental may have merged into the Ablative-Locative in Latin. The tendency towards economy is seen particularly in the case-inflections; thus, as is seen in the next paragraph, the Instrumental case is swallowed up in the Dative in Greek, the Locative in the Genitive or Ablative in Latin. Consequently the Genitive, Dative and Ablative are **syncretistic** cases, that is, cases of mixed usage, the origins of which are difficult to unravel.

§ 4. Both Greek and Latin, like Sanskrit, are derived from a great common original language to which the name **Indo-European** (also Aryan, Indo-Germanic, Eurasian) has been given. The relations of these languages may be indicated thus:

THE CASES 5

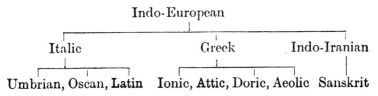

Thus it will be seen that Latin, Greek (i.e. Attic, which is for the most part the Greek we read) and Sanskrit all belong to the same stage of development. Where Latin has six and Greek five cases Sanskrit has eight, and it must be assumed that the parent language had these eight cases also. They may be tabulated thus :

Latin	Indo-European	Greek
Nominative	Nominative (subject)	Nominative
Vocative	Vocative (interjected name)	Vocative
Accusative	Accusative (object)	Accusative
Dative	Dative (conjunction)	
Ablative	Instrumental (accompaniment)	Dative
	Locative (" at ")	
	Ablative (separation)	
Genitive	Genitive (" belonging to ")	Genitive

Here is seen, for example, that in Greek the Genitive and Ablative are merged in the Genitive inflection, while the Dative inflection has to serve both for Instrumental and for Locative. Reasons for these fusions and the case-names will be considered under each case as it occurs.

§ 5. All cases may be regarded as **Limiting**, thus :
   (i) **Nominative** : *videt*—" sees "—who sees ?—*Caesar videt*—" Caesar sees ".
   (ii) **Vocative** : *vide !*—" look ! "—who are you talking to ?—*Caesar, vide !*—" Caesar, look ! "
   (iii) **Accusative** : *Caesar videt*—what ?—*Brutum*—" Caesar sees Brutus ".
     (But this though the commonest is not the only use of the case. This is the Grand Limiting Case,

the case *par excellence* (notice that this is the case that has survived pure and without prepositional support in the modern non-inflectional languages). The accusative in Latin and Greek expresses a variety of limitations: *vixit tres annos*, μάχην μάχομαι, *domum abii, nuda genu,* τὰ μετέωρα φροντιστής, etc.)

(iv) **Genitive** : *horti amoeni sunt*—which ? whose ?— *horti Caesaris amoeni sunt.*

(v) **Dative** : *hortos dedit*—to whom ?—*hortos Caesari dedit.*

(vi) **Ablative** : *nuper profectus est*—where from ?— *Roma profectus est.*

(vii) **Instrumental** : *Caesarem occidit*—how ?—*sica Caesarem occidit.*

(viii) **Locative** : *Caesarem occidit*—where ?—*Romae Caesarem occidit.*

It will be seen that the cases each supply an answer to a special question concerning the action of the verb.

§ 6. *Caution.*—In the living language an idea may be looked at in half a dozen ways and may therefore be expressed in as many case-usages. Hence all the overlappings in modern attempts to reduce such variety to a hard and fast scheme. But classification is possible because certain modes of expression become more usual than others. But throughout it must be remembered that usage and idiom develop not in the single-mindedness of theory but in the variety of practice, and obey the laws not of grammar but of natural growth and human needs.

THE NOMINATIVE

§ 7. The name (ἡ ὀνομαστικὴ πτῶσις) means the naming case, that which names the subject of the sentence. The Stoics called it the ὀρθή or εὐθεῖα πτῶσις in distinction from the rest, which were called πλαγίαι, " oblique ", being supposed to be deviations or **fallings-away** (πτώσεις, *casus*) from the nominative. All cases including the nominative are now considered extensions of the stem, which presents the unapplied, inarticulate concept of the noun.

THE CASES

The normal use of the nominative is to express the subject of the sentence. It has two abnormal uses : **The Whole and Part Construction** and **The Nominativus Pendens**.

§ 8. The Whole and Part Construction (Σχῆμα καθ' ὅλον καὶ μέρος), as the words imply, is the construction in which the part is put in apposition to the whole or vice versa. (For its use with the Accusative see § 37.) The following are straightforward examples :

1. Οἱ Ἀθηναῖοι καταπλεύσαντες, ἀπήγγειλαν οἱ στρατηγοὶ τὰ ἐπεσταλμένα. (Thuc. iii. 4)
 "The Athenians having sailed in, the generals announced . . ."
2. Ἀμφὼ δ' ἑζομένω, γεραρώτερος ἦεν Ὀδυσσεύς. (Hom. *Il.* iii. 211)
 "Both seated, Odysseus was the statelier."

We may compare in Latin (though, since there is no participle with *interfectores*, the construction is more normal) :

Interfectores, pars in forum, pars in Syracusas pergunt. (Liv. xxiv. 7)
"The murderers proceed,—some to the forum, some to S."

More difficult examples are :

1. Αἱ Ἀττικαὶ νῆες μάχης οὐκ ἦρχον, δεδιότες οἱ στρατηγοί . . . (Thuc. i. 49)
 "The A. ships did not begin the action, the generals fearing . . ."
2. Λόγοι δ' ἐν ἀλλήλοισιν ἐρρόθουν κακοί, φύλαξ ἐλέγχων φύλακα. (Soph. *Ant.* 257)
 "And evil speech began to surge among them, guard reviling guard."

The explanation of these examples lies along similar lines. The key is still Apposition. In 1. οἱ στρατηγοί appear in the Nominative because they are part of the fleet, in fact the controlling part. In 2. we have φύλαξ ἐλέγχων instead of φύλακος ἐλέγχοντος because the individual φύλακες are a part of the subject λόγοι as contributors to the noise. (See § 179.)

But N.B.—There is no real difficulty; the transition is easy and shows the natural flexibility of the language.

§ 9. Nominativus Pendens.

There are, further, examples of sentences which have two distinct nominatives one of which has no predicate, where the one nominative cannot be said to be in apposition to the other, but is left hanging without grammatical support. Examples :

"Wishing to see the Cathedral, donkeys were brought round at an early hour."

1.   Ὁ δ' ἀγλαΐηφι πεποιθώς,
ῥίμφα ἑ γοῦνα φέρει.   (Hom. *Il.* vi. 510)
"He, trusting in his pride—lightly his knees bear him."

2. Διαλεγόμενος αὐτῷ ἔδοξέ μοι . . .   (Plat. *Ap.* 21 c)
"Talking with him—it seemed to me . . ."

3. Καὶ ἄδεια ἐφαίνετο αὐτοῖς . . . τὸ πλέον βουλήσει κρίνοντες ἀσαφεῖ ἢ προνοίᾳ ἀσφαλεῖ.   (Thuc. iv. 108)
"There seemed to them to be no danger . . . being guided in their judgement by blind wishing rather than by sound forethought."

In these sentences a change in the writer's intentions seems visible. The thought is begun in one construction and carried on in another, i.e. there is a slight anacoluthon (grammatical inconsequence). In 2. ἔδοξέ μοι is the equivalent of ἐνόμισα ("I thought"). In all we may distinguish between the psychological subject and the grammatical.

§ 10. In **Latin** sometimes the nominative is used instead of the accusative with the infinitive in Oratio Obliqua, when the subject of the infinitive is the same as the subject of the principal verb. This is solely in imitation of the regular Greek construction (see § 259)—a natural attraction.

1. *Quas . . . Diabolus ipsi daturus dixit.*
                                                  (Plaut. *As.* 634)
". . . which D. said he was going to give . . ."

2. *Phaselus ille quem videtis, hospites,*
Ait fuisse navium celerrimus.   (Catull. iv. 1)
"That cutter which you see, my friends, avers that it has been the fleetest of craft."

§ 11. Finally the nominative (which in many nouns is

identical in form with the vocative) is sometimes found in place of a vocative in nouns which have separate forms for the two cases. This may be called the Interjectional Nominative: cp. the Homeric σχέτλιος! νήπιος! N.B. the similar English in 1.

1. Δημοβόρος βασιλεύς, ἐπεὶ οὐτιδανοῖσιν ἀνάσσεις.
   (Hom. Il. i. 231)
   "You folk-devouring king!—seeing you rule men of nought."
2. Ὦ φίλος εἰπέ . . . (Aesch. P.V. 546)
3. Audi tu, populus Albanus. (Liv. i. 24)
4. Agedum, pontifex publicus populi Romani, praci verba quibus me pro legionibus devoveam. (Liv. viii. 9)
   "Come, high priest of the Roman commonwealth, say before me the words with which I am to sacrifice myself for the legions."

These admit of various shades of explanation. That they are mere oversights is incredible. In 2. "O!—you are my friend—tell me" is a sort of anacoluthon; the use of φίλος (not φίλε) shows that the speaker has had a predicate ("you are my friend") in mind and not an interjection ("Friend!"). In 3. probably *populus* is written as a vocative and *Albanus* is attracted into the *-us* ending. (Gildersleeve, p. 16, says "In solemn discourse *-us* of the Nominative is employed for the Vocative".) See next section.

THE VOCATIVE

§ 12. The name (κλητικὴ πτῶσις) means the summoning, i.e. the case indicates a call to the person addressed. In inflection many nouns do not distinguish between Nominative and Vocative (it hardly survives except in e.g. *Aenea* and masculines of the second declension, and there Plautus's *puere* has become *puer*), and, since it never forms an integral part of the construction of the sentence with which it is used, the Vocative is hardly a case at all. (The Sanskrit grammarians do not include it in their list of cases.)

§ 13. There is only one abnormal use of the Vocative and

that is its use by attraction in a predicate in place of a nominative. Examples :

1. Ὦ πολύκλαυτε φίλοισι θανών. (Aesch. *Pers.* 674)
 " O greatly lamented by thy dearest in thy death."
2. Ἰὼ ἰὼ δύστηνε σύ,
 δύστηνε δῆτα διὰ πόνων πάντων φανείς. (Soph. *Ph.* 761)
 ". . . revealed indeed unhappy in all afflictions."
3. Σύ τ', ὦ ποτ' οὖσα καλλίνικε, μυρίων
 μῆτερ τροπαίων . . . (Eur. *Tro.* 1222)
 " And thou, once glorious in triumph, mother of countless memorials of victory . . ."
4. *Quo, moriture, ruis ?* (V. *Aen.* x. 810)
 " Whither dost thou rush to die ? "
5. *Macte nova virtute, puer.* (*ibid.* ix. 641)
 " Blest be thou for thy young valour, my son."

In these examples it will be seen that the abnormal vocative goes closely with the verb so as to form part of the predicate. It would, indeed, be possible to translate 4. " Whither dost thou rush, O thou fated to die ? " but the sense would be the poorer. The attraction would seem due to a mental shifting of the writer's : e.g. in 2. the speaker begins with an unrestrained cry of pity, and in intensity of feeling in the second line adds the reason : " O ill-starred ! (I say that ' ill-starred ' with conviction) because ' ill-starred ' is proved by your afflictions." In 5. the writer wants to say, " Boy, may you be happy ", but incorporates the more direct " O happy boy ", thus interrupting himself, but gaining in vividness. This last is possibly derived from the exactly similar Ὄλβιε, κῶρε, γένοιο (Theocr. xvii. 66). Cp. *Sic venias, hodierne* (Tib. i. 7. 53)—" Come—to-day ! "

THE ACCUSATIVE

§ 14. The name αἰτιατικὴ πτῶσις is not quite clear. Αἰτιατική may be taken in a passive sense, i.e. the case of τὸ αἰτιατόν (*casus effectivus*) ; or in an active sense, " the causing case " (*casus causativus*). In the traditional translation Varro's " *casus accusativus* " represents an error : Varro took

THE CASES 11

αἰτιατική as coming from αἰτιάομαι "I accuse". The Accusative is obviously a poor name. It is an **Adverbial Case** and, as we have seen (§ 5), is the **Grand Limiting Case**. Its work is to limit the application usually of a verb, sometimes of an adjective, rarely of a noun, to a particular extent.

§ 15. **Conspectus of the Accusative.**

I. The Internal Accusative—that which is **effected** by the verb.
    (a) Extent of action of verb—
        (i) Internal limiting,
        (ii) Cognate,
        (iii) Accus. in apposition to the sentence,
        (iv) Limitative of Purpose,
        (v) Of Manner or Description ;
    (b) Part concerned ;
    (c) Extent in Space and Time—
        (i) Space,
        (ii) Time,
        (iii) Accusative "Absolute".

II. The External Accusative—that which is **affected** by the verb.
    (a) Variations of the Direct Object—
        (i) With Internal Accus. added,
        (ii) Accus. after passive verbs,
        (iii) Whole and Part construction,
        (iv) After strictly intransitive verbs,
        (v) Accus. after a phrase,
        (vi) Accus. dependent on noun or adjective,
        (vii) Dependent on verb unexpressed.
    (b) Accus. of the End of Motion—
        (i) Literal Place,
        (ii) Metaphorical Place.

All these uses of the Accusative are accounted for under the name **Limiting**. The commonest use of the case is for the object of transitive verbs : here it limits the action of the verb to the particular object : " I see " is limitless, in " I see you " my seeing is limited. So with verbs of motion : " I go " is limitless, " I go home " gives the limit (see II.b). Used with all verbs, and even sometimes with adjectives and nouns, the accusative limits their application to some definite extent. Thus limitations in Space and Time are expressed by the accusative. The fundamental distinction is between the **External** and the **Internal** Object ; in the External the action is directed to an object outside ; in the Internal the action does not go outside itself. " Fight the foe " embodies an External Accusative, " Fight the good fight " an Internal Accusative. " The foe " limits the working of the verb " fight " by means of an outside object ; " the good fight " limits the working of the verb within that working itself (i.e. " the good fight " is essentially in conception a subdivision of fighting). We find in Antiphon τύπτει τὸν ἄνδρα πληγάς—" He strikes the man blows ", where τύπτει has two objects : τὸν ἄνδρα (external limitation) and πληγάς (internal limitation). Similarly Aeschines has τὴν μάχην τοὺς βαρβάρους ἐνίκησεν.

§ 16. **Preliminary Note on Prepositions.**

As various accusative-usages are used with prepositions and as it is important to remember that prepositions are merely additions to the case-meaning, it will be well to introduce them at this point.

Prepositions are adverbs which have become attached to (i) verbs, (ii) certain cases of nouns. The origin of the preposition is seen in such a sentence as σίτου τε γλυκεροῖο περὶ φρένας ἵμερος αἱρεῖ (Il. xi. 89), " desire of sweet food seizes his heart round about ". Here περί is an adverb. So in early Latin there are many adverbs which later become prepositions, e.g. *quae coram me incusaveras* (Ter. *Ph.* 914).

The next step is seen in the figure known as *Tmesis*, e.g. ἐν δ' αὐτὸς ἐδύσατο νώροπα χαλκόν (Il. ii. 578), " and he himself put on the shining bronze ", where the compound verb is necessary to the sense ; similarly in ὑπὸ δ' ἔσχετο μισθόν, where the simple verb could not give the required meaning " he promised ". Here, then, we see the adverb losing its original strength and coming to depend on the verb. " Tmesis " is a misnomer, for in early Greek it is not the separation but the combination that is significant. The transition from adverb to preposition is seen in such phrases as εἰσῆγον θεῖον δόμον (*Od.* iv. 43) and ἐκ δ' ἄγαγε κλισίης (*Il.* i. 346).

Even in Attic prose we have πρός still used as an adverb in πρὸς δέ . . ., καὶ πρός . . . Also in such a phrase as δι' ἄρ' ὀλώλαμεν (Eur. *I.T.* 1371) we can detect the survival of διά as an adverb meaning "thoroughly". Further evidence of the adverbial origin of prepositions is found in such words as ἐγγύς, ἔξω, *contra, iuxta*, which are regularly used both as adverbs and as prepositions.

§ 17. Prepositions are merely additions to the case-meaning (as they remain in Sanskrit—M. 176). The case constructed with the verb expresses a certain relation to which the preposition gives precision. The simple *domos abierunt* underlies *in domos abierunt*, and the addition of a preposition adds precision—*in domos abierunt, intra domos*, etc.; compare εἰσῆγον δόμον above. It is rather the case which determines the meaning of the preposition, as we see in the instance of παρά which in itself means "sideways"—with the accusative "sideways to", with the ablative-genitive "sideways from", with the locative-dative "sideways at"; so too *sub* means "under", with the accusative "up to under", with the locative-ablative "under at". Often the preposition may be dispensed with: ἀγαθοῦ ἀνδρός ἐστί = " it is the mark of a good man ", just as well as πρὸς ἀγαθοῦ ἀνδρός ἐστί. (But, N.B., by the time that the language had reached its maturity it is probable that writers had come to treat prepositions as determining cases, just as the Greek grammarians could regard ὑπὸ δ' ἔσχετο μισθόν as a Tmesis.) See Monro, pp. 163 ff.; Lindsay, *Histor. Lat. Gramm.* pp. 144 ff.

§ 18. THE INTERNAL ACCUSATIVE.

This is the function of the case in its simplest form—the addition of limiting detail or precise information.

§ 19. **Accusative of Extent of Action of the verb**: expressed by a neuter adjective or by a noun of the same meaning as the verb. The accusative simply limits the action of the verb, often in a descriptive way. The noun thus discharges the functions of an adverb :

1. Ἠγωνίζοντο στάδιον, πάλην καὶ πυγμήν. (X. *An.* iv. 8)
"They were contending in running, wrestling, boxing."
2. *Quid prodest ? Quid me ista laedunt ?* (Cic. *Agr.* ii. 13)
"What is the advantage ? What harm does that do me ? "

Laedunt has two objects, *me* external, *quid* internal. Cp. English, " I strike him a blow ". Cp. our " play cricket ", " fight ten rounds ", " dance a foxtrot ", (dialect) " he sang a treat ".

§ 20. Therefore the accusative exemplified by *quid* is usually called the **internal limiting accusative**. Naturally the distinction between internal and external accusatives is more clearly seen in sentences which contain one of each. The point is clearer, e.g., in " I strike him a blow " than in the expression " to hit a six " ; but a moment's thought will show that " a six " is not a genuine object ; what the batsman really hits is the ball, but he hits it in a six-sort-of-way, in-a-way-worth-six-runs, i.e. the accusative " a six " is an adverbial limitation of "to hit". Cp. in Greek Ὀλύμπια νικᾶν, " to win an Olympic victory " ; what the man " defeats " (νικᾶν) is his fellow-competitors.

1. Πάσας νόσους κάμνουσι. (Plat. *Rep.* 408 E)
"They are sick with all diseases."
2. Λίην ἄχθομαι ἕλκος, ὅ με βροτὸς οὔτασεν ἀνήρ.
(Hom. *Il.* v. 361)
"Overmuch am I afflicted with a wound wherewith a mortal man smote me."
3. *Dulce ridentem Lalagen amabo.* (Hor. *C.* i. 22. 23)
"... the sweetly smiling L." (cp. "laughing a good'un ").
4. *Asper, acerba tuens, retro redit* . . . (V. *Aen.* ix. 794)
"Back he comes, enraged, fierce-eyed."

Cp. Shakespeare's " He speaks holiday, he smells April and May " (*Merry Wives*, Act III, Sc. 2). Aristophanes, perhaps for comic effect, pushes this idiom to an extreme, e.g. κάβλεψε νᾶπυ (*Eq.* 631), " And he looked mustard " (as we say ". . . daggers "). (Sanskrit—M. 197.)

THE CASES

§ 21. When the accusative in this usage is of a kindred formation with the verb it is called a **Cognate Accusative** (e.g. " Fight the good fight ").

1. Συνέφυγε τὴν φυγὴν ταύτην. (Plat. *Apol.* 21 A)
"He shared in this exile."
2. Μέλητός με ἐγράψατο τὴν γραφὴν ταύτην. (*ibid.* 19 B)
"Meletus brought this suit against me."
3. *Hanc, oro, sine me furere ante furorem.* (V. *Aen.* xii. 680)
" Grant me, I pray, ere that to be mad with this madness."
4. *Tam te basia multa basiare* . . . (Catull. vii. 9)
". . . to kiss thee with so many kisses."

(N.B.—There is a temptation to connect these usages with those in § 38 (Direct Object after verbs which are strictly intransitive). There may be no rigid line of demarcation, and much must depend on the individual author's purpose, but in such examples as the above the Internal Limiting Accusative is the better explanation.)

§ 22. We may consider here as a species of the Internal Accusative the **Accusative in Apposition to the Sentence.** This may modify either the verb of the sentence or the idea of the phrase built round the verb. " Half way down hangs one that gathers samphire, dreadful trade ! " (Shakespeare).

1. Εὐδαιμονοίης, μισθὸν ἡδίττων λόγων. (Eur. *El.* 231)
" May happiness be thine in recompense for thy good words ! "
2. Ἑλένην κτάνωμεν, Μενελέῳ λύπην πικράν.
(Eur. *Or.* 1098)
" Let us slay Helen, (a slaying that will be) a bitter blow to Menelaus."
3. *Marcellum insimulabat sinistros* . . . *sermones habuisse, inevitabile crimen.* (Tac. *Ann.* i. 74)
" He accused M. of defamatory talk, a charge from which there was no escape."

The rationale of this use is best seen in 1. Εὐδαιμονοίης εὐδαιμονίαν μισθόν . . ., " be happy with a happiness that is reward ", may easily be contracted to εὐδαιμονοίης μισθόν.

In 3. *insimulabat crimen* = " he brought a charge ", which is hardly more difficult than ἐγράψατο γραφήν. The Accus. is the object *effected* by the whole action of the sentence.

Quod si (" but if ") is probably an example of accusative in apposition to the sentence. (It is not obvious at first sight. Think it out.)

The following are similar developments of the limiting Accusative.

§ 23. Accusative Limitative of Purpose (Greek).

1. Ἀλλ' αὐτὰ ταῦτα καὶ νῦν ἥκω.   (Plat. *Prot.* 310 E)
  " That is the very object of my coming now."
2. Ἀγγελίην ἐλθόντα σὺν ἀντιθέῳ Ὀδυσῆϊ.
  (Hom. *Il.* xi. 140)
  ". . . coming on an embassy with godlike Odysseus."

Cp. Shakespeare's " As well appeareth by the cause you come " (cp. " to run a message ").

§ 24. Accusative of Manner and Extent expressed by such phrases as τὴν ταχίστην (sc. ὁδόν), τοῦτον τὸν τρόπον, δίκην (" after the way of "), ἀρχήν (" in the beginning ", " to begin with ", " at all "), πρόφασιν (" in excuse "), προῖκα (" gratis "), . . . χάριν (" for the sake of "), τἄλλα, and in Latin (where the use is not so common) by *cetera, partem, vicem* (" instead of ", rarely " after the way of "), also *quam* = " as " etc. ; see § 218. Similar are the interrogatives τί; quid? Almost always with verbs.

1. Πεπληρῶσθαι δίκην ἀγγείου.   (Plat. *Phaedr.* 235 E)
  " To be filled like a pail."
2. . . . ἐλέγομεν τρόπον τινὰ αὐτό.   (*id., Rep.* 432 E)
  ". . . we were speaking of it in a manner."
3. *Inde bonam partem in lectum maerore dabuntur.*
  (Lucr. vi. 1249)
  " Then for a great part they will take to their beds for sorrow."
4. *Vos respondetote istinc istarum vicem.*   (Plaut. *Rud.* 814)
  " Do you from where you stand answer instead of them."

Similar is the **Accusative of Description in Latin** found in the words *genus* and *secus*. *Genus* is found qualified by the

THE CASES

words *hoc, quod, id, omne* ; *secus* (" sex ") by *muliebre* or *virile*. It is used to qualify nouns.

1. *Scis me antea orationes aut aliquid id genus solitum scribere.* (Cic. *Att.* xiii. 12)
  " You know that before I used to write speeches or something of that sort."
2. *Liberorum capitum virile secus ad X milia capta.*
  (Liv. xxvi. 47)
  " Of the free population about 10,000 males were taken."

A genitive of description would be the normal construction.

§ 25. **Accusative of Part concerned.** This accusative, usually dependent on an adjective, limits the description contained in the adjective. The old-fashioned name for this accusative was the Accusative of Respect ; a better name perhaps is the Accusative of Specification.

1. Τυφλὸς τά τ' ὦτα τόν τε νοῦν τά τ' ὄμματ' εἶ.
  (Soph. *O.T.* 371)
  " Thou art blind—ears, mind, eyes alike."
2. Εἶδος μὲν κάλλιστος, ψυχὴν δὲ φιλανθρωπότατος . . .
  (X. *Cyr.* i. 2. 1)
  ". . . handsome of body, kind of heart."
3. *Os humerosque deo similis* . . . (V. *Aen.* i. 589)
  ". . . in face and shoulders like unto a god."
4. *Feminae lineis amictibus velantur, nudae bracchia et lacertos.* (Tac. *Germ.* 17)
  " The women are dressed in linen smocks, with both forearm and upper arm bare."

This use is clearly an Internal Accusative and very near to the accusative of extent of space : cp. τὰ περὶ τοὺς θεοὺς εὐσεβοῦμεν (Isoc. iii. 2) (N.B. the neuter pronoun instead of noun, and it limits not an adjective but a verb) and *nigrantes terga iuvencos* ("black-backed bulls") (V. *Aen.* v. 97). But it is possible that this is an External Accusative of Part *affected*, especially when an *action* is implied, e.g. in *latus praefixa* (i.e. someone *stabbed* her side).

THE CASES

Extent in Space.

§ 26. **Accusative of Space over which, along which.**

1. Ἀπέχει ἡ Πλάταια τῶν Θηβῶν σταδίους ἑβδομήκοντα.
   (Thuc. ii. 5)
   "Plataea is seventy stades distant from Thebes."
2. *Caesar iter tridui processit.* (Caes. *B.G.* i. 38)
   "Caesar advanced a three days' march."
3. Φιλτάταν ὁδὸν ἐπαξιώσας ὧδέ μοι φανῆναι.
   (Soph. *El.* 1274)
   "... thus having deigned to reveal thyself to me in this sweet coming."
4. Πᾶσαν πλανηθεὶς τήνδε βάρβαρον χθόνα.
   (Eur. *Hel.* 598)
   "Having wandered over all this foreign land."
5. (*Negavit Marcellus*) *e republica esse vestigium abscedi ab Hannibale.* (Liv. xxvii. 4)
   "Marcellus said that it would be to the detriment of Rome if he left Hannibal by so much as a single step."

(It will be seen in Example 3. that the usage approximates somewhat to the accusative in § 19, where the accusative is closer to the verb; ὁδὸν φανῆναι is near to a cognate expression—"to come a coming". But this is only another branch of the Internal Accusative.)

Compare English, "to walk the earth", "to run a mile".

§ 27. Sometimes by a looseness of expression **space traversed** is written instead of the point reached.

1. *Caesar milia passuum tria ab Helvetiorum castris castra ponit.* (Caes. *B.G.* i. 22)
   "C. pitched camp about three miles from the H. camp."
2. *Quadringentos inde ferme passus constituit signa.*
   (Liv. xxxiv. 30)
   "... at about 400 paces from that point."

The irregularity is intelligible: in 1., e.g., Caesar writes with his mind rather on the extent of the distance (*milia passuum tria aberant castra*) than on his action (*ponit*); the accusative is constructed on this implicit idea.

§ 28. **Accusative of Time throughout which** (N.B. **throughout**). (Sanskrit—M. 197.)
  1. Αἱ σπονδαὶ ἐνιαυτὸν ἔσονται.   (Thuc. iv. 118)
   "The truce shall be valid for a year."
  2. *Dies noctesque omnia nos fata circumstant.*
   (Cic. *Phil.* x. 10)
   "Always, by day and night, all chances wait upon us."

§ 29. Irregularities are found here, too :
  1. *Quos id temporis venturos esse praedixeram.*
   (Cic. *Cat.* i. 4)
   "Whom I had previously indicated as likely to arrive at that hour."
  2. *Quaestor fuisti abhinc annos quattuordecim.*
   (Cic. *Verr.* i. 12)
   "You were quaestor fourteen years ago."

(*Abhinc*, "ago", expressing time **when**, not time **how long**, is normally constructed with the accusative.)

§ 30. In Greek an accusative with ordinal numbers means **how long since**.
  Ἐξήλθομεν τρίτον ἔτος τουτί.   (Dem. liv. 3)
  "We went out two years ago."

This may be the result of a conflation : "we went out—this is the third year "="the fact that we went out has now held for three years". All that can be said is that in these examples the time definition, instead of being expressed in the usual Locative construction, is given merely as an adverbial modification in the Accusative of Extent.

§ 31. **Prepositions defining Accusative of Extent :**

ἀμφί, " around "
ἀνά, " up ", " throughout "
διά, "through", "because of"
κατά, " down upon ", etc.
μετά, " after "

παρά { " alongside of "
       " contrary to ", etc.
περί, " around ", " about "
πρός, " with regard to "
ὑπέρ, " beyond ", " over "

ante, " before "
apud, " among "

circa (-um), " around "
cis, citra, " on this side of "

20   THE CASES

contra, " against "   praeter, " beside ", " except "
extra, " outside "   prope, " near "
inter, " between "   propter, " near ", " on account
intra, " within "   of "
iuxta, " near "   secundum, " after "
ob, " against "   super, " above "
per, " through "   trans, " across "
pone, post, " behind "   ultra, " beyond "

§ 32. Accusative Absolute in Greek.

This is an accusative of extent, the action of the main verb being modified in a particular circumstance (just as the Genitive "Absolute" strictly expresses time during which). Εὖ παρασχόν (Thuc. i. 120) = "when an opportunity is afforded"; οὐ προσῆκον (Thuc. iv. 95) = "when it is unfitting". Generally, it may be said, the accusative here indicates the circumstances during the prevalence of which something else is done.

(i) Participles of Impersonal Verbs, e.g. παρόν; also passive participles used impersonally, e.g. δεδογμένον; also such phrases as ἀδύνατον ὄν.

1. Ἁπλᾶς δὲ λύπας ἐξὸν οὐκ οἴσω διπλᾶς.   (Eur. *I.T.* 688)
   " I will not bear a double sorrow, when I may bear but one."

2. Παρεκελεύοντο, . . . ἀδύνατον ὂν ἐν νυκτὶ ἄλλῳ τῳ σημῆναι.   (Thuc. vii. 44)
   " They were cheering each other on, it being impossible by night to communicate by any other means."

(ii) Less commonly, Participles of Personal Verbs preceded by ὡς, ὥσπερ with their nouns.

1.   φόνῳ φόνον πάλιν
   λύοντας, ὡς τόδ' αἷμα χείμαζον πόλιν.
                                      (Soph. *O.T.* 100)
   " Atoning in turn blood with blood, since it is this blood-guilt that shakes the city."

2. Τῶν δ' ἀδελφῶν ἀμελοῦσιν, ὥσπερ ἐκ πολιτῶν μὲν γιγνομένους φίλους, ἐξ ἀδελφῶν δ' οὐ γιγνομένους.
                                      (X. *Mem.* ii. 3. 3)
   " But brothers they disregard, on the ground that

THE CASES

friends are made from among their fellow-citizens, not from brothers."

(iii) Rarely, Participles used personally without ὡς, ὥσπερ.

1. Ταῦτα δὲ γινόμενα, πένθεα μεγάλα τοὺς Αἰγυπτίους καταλαμβάνει. (Hdt. ii. 66)
"When this happens great distress comes upon the E."

2. Ἀμφοτέροις μὲν δοκοῦν ἀναχωρεῖν, κυρωθὲν δὲ οὐδέν, ... οἱ Μακέδονες ἐχώρουν ἐπ' οἴκου.
(Thuc. iv. 125)
"While both divisions had decided to retire, but there was no definite arrangement, the M. started off home."

§ 33. THE EXTERNAL ACCUSATIVE.

The ordinary use of the External Accusative as the case of the object of a transitive verb requires no illustration. But the following extensions of this use require notice.

Variations of the Direct Object.

External Object with Internal Accusative added.

Some verbs as a result of their own *double meaning* are able to take two direct objects, one a person, one a thing. In this class are verbs of asking, hiding, teaching, and in Greek of depriving, putting on or off (of clothes). In this usage the action of the verb is doubly limited. Usually one of these accusatives is external, the other internal; e.g. in 1. πολλά is an internal accusative, με is external. (Sanskrit—M. 198.)

1. Πολλὰ διδάσκει μ' ὁ πολὺς βίοτος. (Eur. *Hipp.* 252)
"Long life teaches me many things."

2. Χρόα νίζετο ἅλμην. (Hom. *Od.* vi. 224)
"He washed off the sea-salt from his flesh."

3. *Forte meum si quis te percontabitur aevum.*
(Hor. *Ep.* i. 20. 26)
"If by chance anyone shall ask you my age."

4. *Consules causam Sthenii senatum docent.*
(Cic. *Verr.* ii. 39)
"The consuls inform the senate of Sthenius's case."

In the passive construction one accusative is lost in the subject, the other (the internal) remains.

1. Ὅσοι . . . ἵππους ἀπεστέρηνται ταχὺ ἄλλους . . . κτήσονται.   (X. *Cyr.* vi. 1. 12)
"All who have been deprived of their horses . . ."

2. *Scito primum me non esse rogatum sententiam.*
(Cic. *Att.* i. 13)
"You must know that I was not the first to be asked for an opinion."

§ 34. This naturally leads to the consideration of the accusatives used after passive verbs in Latin in imitation of the Greek constructions. Greek regularly uses the accusative after both middle and passive verbs; we have both τὰ ἄλλα ἐπιτρέψονταί μοι (Hdt. iii. 155) and ἐπιτετραμμένοι τὴν φυλακήν (Thuc. i. 126). In the phrase from Thucydides φυλακήν may be called an object accusative, but it is not the object of ἐπιτετραμμένοι, but would be the object of the verb if the idea were expressed in the active voice (ἐπιτρέπειν τινὶ φυλακήν), and φυλακήν is retained in the passive probably by analogy, though in the passive version φυλακήν is nearer to the accusative of extent. The subject of the passive verb would be an indirect object in the active version ἐπιτρέπειν τινὶ φυλακήν. In fact we must distinguish between two passive versions:

1. Ἡ φυλακὴ ἐπιτρέπεταί τινι.
2. Ἐπιτρέπεταί τις τὴν φυλακήν.

§ 35. In Latin middle constructions are found with passive forms: all deponents are strictly middles. In the following examples the participles are genuinely **passive**:

1. *Inscripti nomina regum Nascuntur flores . . .*   (V. *Ecl.* iii. 106)
"Flowers spring up inscribed with names of kings."

2. *inductaque cornibus aurum Victima vota cadit.*   (Ov. *M.* vii. 161)
"With gilded horns the promised victim falls."

THE CASES

§ 36. In the following the passive form represents a middle use :
1. *Consurgit senior tunicaque inducitur artus.*
(V. *Aen.* viii. 457)
"The old man rises and draws on his tunic."
2. *Arma . . . circumdat . . . umeris et inutile ferrum Cingitur.* (*ibid.* ii. 511)
"His harness he sets about his shoulders and girds himself with useless blade."

§ 37. **Accusative of Whole and Part.**
This, so called, is a direct object with subordinate accusatives :
1. Τρῶας δὲ τρόμος αἰνὸς ὑπήλυθε γυῖα ἕκαστον.
(Hom. *Il.* vii. 215)
"Dread quaking gat hold on each of the Trojans in his limbs."
2. *Sed Latagum saxo . . . occupat os faciemque adversam.*
(V. *Aen.* x. 698)
"Smites L. with a boulder, full in mouth and face."

All three nouns are of the same kind, the second and third being in a sort of corrective apposition, i.e. "Quaking seizes on (i) the Trojan army, (ii) each individual, (iii) the limbs of each ", just as in *Il.* xi. 11 Ἀχαιοῖσι δὲ μέγα σθένος ἔμβαλ' ἑκάστῳ | καρδίῃ, where all three datives may be Datives of the Indirect Object in local relation. Cp. our ". . . smote the Philistines hip and thigh ", ". . . bound him hand and foot ".

§ 38. **Accusative after strictly Intransitive Verbs** as direct object : "This music mads me " (Shakespeare).
1. Χορεύω θεόν. (Pind. *I.* i. 7)
"I worship the god in dance."
2. Πορευόμενον αὐτὸν Μῆδοι . . . ἐδορυφόρουν.
(Thuc. i. 130)
"Medes escorted him on his march."
3. *Illum deperit impotente amore.* (Catull. xxxv. 12)
"She loves him distractedly with a helpless love."

4. *Sic et Europe . . . pontum mediasque fraudes*
Palluit audax. (Hor. *C.* iii. 27. 26)
"So for all her daring Europe grew pale at the sea and the dangers in its midst."

Here intransitive verbs are used transitively by a stretch of meaning. In 4. the accusative is governed by the idea of fear that occasions and is contained in Europe's paleness. It must be observed that this accusative resembles the class in § 21, e.g. *itque reditque viam.*

§ 39. Accusative after a Phrase equivalent to a Transitive Verb.

The phrase is usually complete in itself, e.g. ψήφους ἔθεντο (=ἐψηφίσαντο).

1. Ἰλίου φθορὰς ψήφους ἔθεντο. (Aesch. *Ag.* 814)
"They voted the ruin of Ilium."

2. Τίν' ἀεὶ τάκεις οἰμωγὰν Ἀγαμέμνονα; (Soph. *El.* 123)
"With what melting lamentation dost thou ever bewail Agamemnon?"

Cp. *Mea causa causam hanc iustam esse animum inducite.*
(Ter. *Haut.* 41)
"Persuade yourselves for my sake that this plea is just."

In 2. τίνα τάκεις οἰμωγάν; must be taken as the equivalent of, e.g., τί οἰμώζεις;
In the passage from Terence *animum inducite = credite.*
There are some interesting extensions of this usage, e.g.

Λέγ', ὡς τὸ μέλλον καρδία πήδημ' ἔχει. (Eur. *Bac.* 1288)
"Speak, for my heart jumps-in-foreboding-of the future."

§ 40. Accusative of Direct Object dependent on Adjective or Noun.

1. Καί σ' οὔτ' ἀθανάτων φύξιμος οὐδείς... (Soph. *Ant.* 789)
"And none of immortals is able to escape thee."

2. Ἐκ δόμων ἔβαν χοὰς προπομπός. (Aesch. *Cho.* 22)
"I have come from the house escorting the libations."

3. *Haec prope contionabundus circumibat homines.*
(Liv. iii. 47)
"With words to this effect he walked round his men."

4. *Quid tibi hanc digito tactio est ?* (Plaut. *Poen.* 1308)
  " What is the meaning of your touching her ? "

Cp. English gerund with a direct object : " Nothing in his life became him like the leaving it " (Shakespeare).

The adjectives so used are like participles, having a strong verbal quality. The noun used thus is of a verbal character and is used like the regular verbal noun, the gerund, which is regularly constructed with a direct object. 4. = " Why is there this touching her with your finger ? " (Cp. Plaut. *Asin.* 919.)

Some of the examples of this usage, as the following, suggest a nearness to the accusative of extent.

1. Σωκράτης τὰ μετέωρα φροντιστής. (Plat. *Apol.* 18 B)
  " Socrates, a student of things above the earth."
2. Ἐπιστήμονες τὰ προσήκοντα. (X. *Cyr.* iii. 3. 9)
  ". . . versed in fitting accomplishments."

§ 41. **Accusative dependent on a Verb unexpressed.**

This is best seen in the Accusative of *Exclamation*. The speaker's mind in excitement expresses only the object of his sensation, the object of some verb not distinctly conceived but implied. It is common in Latin ; in Greek the regular exclamatory case is the genitive, but what would appear to be an accusative of exclamation is found in oaths and in the use of τό with the Infinitive. So too we are using an accusative in saying " Thanks ! " or " A sail ! " as is the small child who says " Horse ! "

1. Νὴ τὸν Δία, ναὶ τὸν Δία.
  " Yes, by Zeus ! "
2. Οὗτος, ὦ σέ τοι. (Ar. *Av.* 274)
  " You there, ho ! you, I mean."
3. Τῆς μωρίας· | τὸ Δία νομίζειν ὄντα τηλικουτονί.
  (Ar. *Nub.* 819)
  " What folly ! To believe in Zeus at your age ! "
4. *O fortunatam natam me consule Romam !*
  (Cic. *ap.* Juv. x. 122)
  " O happy fate of Rome to date
   Her birthday from my consulate ! "

5. *Di magni, horribilem et sacrum libellum !*
(Catull. xiv. 12)
"Great gods ! an appalling and accursed book !"

Similarly in the following examples the verb that governs the accusative is left implied, and usually not distinctly conceived. Cp. Example 2, of Accusative of Exclamation.

1. Ποῖ λευκὸν ἵππον;   (Ar. *Lys.* 193)
"Why (should we take . . .) a white horse ?"

2. *Quo mihi fortunam, si non conceditur uti ?*
(Hor. *Ep.* i. 5. 12)
"To what purpose have I means, if I may not use them ?"

3. *Quo tibi formosam, si non nisi casta placebat ?*
(Ov. *Am.* iii. 4. 41)
"Why had'st thou a beautiful love, if none but a modest pleased thee ?"

The Accusative of the End of Motion.

§ 42. **Literal Place.**

This usage expresses the goal at which the action of the verb points ; the expression of this goal limits that action by giving a *terminus ad quem*. A particularized form of the case in Greek had for this purpose a suffix -δε ; Ἀθήναζε = Ἀθήνασδε, "to Athens". In Latin the use is regular with names of towns, small islands, and in *domus, rus, foras*. (Sanskrit—M. 197.)

1. Ἔρχεσθον κλισίην Πηληϊάδεω Ἀχιλῆος.
(Hom. *Il.* i. 322)
"Go ye to the hut of Achilles, son of Peleus."

2. Ἔβαν Πριαμίδαν.   (Eur. *Andr.* 287)
"I went to the son of Priam."

3. *Italiam fato profugus Lavinaque venit Litora.*   (V. *Aen.* i. 2)
"A fugitive by fate he came to Italy and the Lavinian shores."

4. *Ministerium restituendorum domos obsidum mihimet deposco ipse.*   (Liv. xxii. 22)
"I claim for myself the duty of restoring the hostages to their homes."

THE CASES

N.B.—This use must not be divorced from the regular prepositional construction, where the accusative is still limitative (see under " Prepositions "). In Greek without a preposition this accusative is poetical. (See § 44.)

§ 43. **Metaphorical Place.**

A similar accusative is found in Latin in (i) the use of the supine in -*um* (the accusative of the verbal noun) to express the end of motion in terms of action ; (ii) in such nouns as *infitias* (" denial "), *suppetias* (" assistance "), *exsequias* (" funeral "), combined with *ire*. Also *venum* (" selling "), *pessum* (" perdition "), with either *dare* (in an active sense) or *ire* (in a passive sense). (See Roby, 1114.)

N.B.—*Infitias ire* and *pessum dare* being equivalent to a single transitive verb (" deny ", " ruin ") take an accusative of the direct object, and *infitias ire* is found with the Accusative and Infinitive.

For these expressions cp. English, " I was going to say ".

1. *Spectatum veniunt, veniunt spectentur ut ipsae.*
 (Ov. *A.A.* i. 99)
 " They come to look on, they come to be looked at."

2. *Ne tibi suppetias temperi adveni modo.*
 (Plaut. *Men.* 1020)
 " By Jove, I came to your help just in time ! "

3. *Multos etiam bonos pessum dedit.* (Tac. *Ann.* iii. 66)
 " Many worthy men also he destroyed."

N.B.—Sometimes an accusative of this class is found dependent on a preposition compounded in the verb, e.g.

1. *Provinciam omnem in sua verba iusiurandum adigebat.*
 (Caes. *B.G.* ii. 18)
 " He compelled the whole province to swear allegiance to him."

2. *Hic tibi rostra Cato advolat.* (Cic. *Att.* i. 14)
 " At this point, if you please, C. dashes up to the platform."

§ 44. Prepositions defining Accusative of End of Motion:

εἰς, " into "
ἐπί, " against "
κατά, " down to "
μετά { " into the midst of "
       " in search of "

παρά, " to the side of "
πρός, " towards "
ὑπό, " up to under "

ad, " to ", " towards "
adversus, " towards ", " against "
erga, " towards " (of feelings)

in, " into ", " to "
sub, subter, " up to under "
usque, " as far as "
versus, " towards "

§ 45. Anticipatory Cases.

(The Greek term is ἀντίπτωσις.) As the use is all but confined to the Accusative, it will be best considered here. The type may be represented by the English " I know thee who thou art ", where " thee " anticipates " thou ". Both in Greek and Latin, for purposes of emphasis, the subject of a dependent sentence is brought out of its natural place into a new relation with the verb of the main sentence ; or, alternatively, it may be said that the " anticipatory " case is there, to start with, in its own right, and that the dependent clause is added as an afterthought for greater clearness. Often the use amounts to little more than a change of order for the sake of stressing a particular word (e.g. *Marcellum nosti quam tardus sit* for *nosti quam tardus Marcellus sit*).

This use is similar to that of the Double Accusative (§ 33)—e.g. τοῦτον is an External Accus. and the dependent clause represents an Internal Accus.—" Do you know *him*, do you know *this* about him ? "

1. Τοῦτον οἶσθ' εἰ ζῶν κυρεῖ; (Soph. *Ph.* 444)
" Dost thou know about him, if he is living ? "

2. *Marcellum nosti quam tardus sit.*
(Cic. *Fam.* viii. 10. 3)
" You know how slow M. is."

So with the genitive :

Θαυμάζω τῶν δυναστευόντων, εἰ ἡγοῦνται . . .
(Isoc. 76 B)
" I am surprised that those in power think . . . "

THE DATIVE

§ 46. The name ἡ δοτικὴ πτῶσις shows that the Dative is the case of that to which something is given. The name shows the essential working of the case—for a giving to take place there must be something given and somebody to whom it is given: in " I give gold to Caesar " the verb, being transitive, has both a direct object (accusative) and an indirect object (dative). But the case-name " giving " gives merely an example and not a definition.

There are two main uses of the true dative: I. To express the remoter object of the verb which requires two objects to define its application, e.g. " to give ", " to owe "; or, when the remoter object is not a thing but a person, to express the object indirectly affected by the working of a verb. II. To express Purpose or Result, i.e. one action is given as the indirect object of another. (Sanskrit—M. 200.)

N.B.—The word put in the dative belongs strictly to the whole predicate and not, as with the genitive, to some particular word; e.g. *Caesaris horti* forms a coherent phrase, not so with *Caesari horti* taken from *Caesari horti dantur*. But Greek with the help of the article can write, e.g., ἡ ἐμὴ τῷ θεῷ ὑπηρεσία; and in Latin we occasionally find such self-contained phrases as *exprobratio cuiquam* (Livy xxiii. 35).

Conspectus of the Dative.

I. Dative expressing a *Necessary* Complement:
    (a) Person as Indirect Object;
    (b) Place as Indirect Object.

II. Dative of Interest—expressing an *Added* Complement:
    (a) Ethic;
    (b) Possessive;
    (c) Agent;
    (d) Of special Limitation.

III. Dative of Destination—expressing Purpose or Result.

§ 47. DATIVE EXPRESSING A NECESSARY COMPLEMENT:

Of Person—Indirect Object proper: e.g. " Render to Caesar the things that are Caesar's . . ."

1. . . . ὀφείλειν θεῷ θυσίας. (Plat. *Rep.* 331 B)
   "To owe sacrifices to heaven."
2. *Debemus morti nos nostraque.* (Hor. *A.P.* 63)
   "Ourselves and our possessions we owe to death."

So with a noun in Greek: rare in Latin (see § 46, N.B.).

1. Ἡ ἐμὴ τῷ θεῷ ὑπηρεσία. (Plat. *Apol.* 30 A)
   "My service to the god . . ."
2. . . . καταδούλωσις τῶν Ἑλλήνων Ἀθηναίοις.
       (Thuc. iii. 10)
   "The servitude of the Hellenes to Athens."
3. . . . *ne qua exprobratio cuiquam veteris fortunae discordiam sereret.* (Liv. xxiii. 35)
   ". . . lest anyone's being reproached . . . should produce discord." (*Exprobrare alicui fortunam.*)

Similar is the dative with such intransitive verbs as δοκεῖ, πιστεύω, φθονῶ, *placeo, prosum, accido.* So ἀρέσκω σοι = (lit.) "I am fitting to you", λυσιτελεῖ μοι = "pays dues to me".

§ 48. **Of Place—Indirect Object in Local Relation.** If I direct or send something to some place, I may be said to *give it to* that place.

1. . . . κυνέῃ βάλε. (*Il.* vii. 187)
   ". . . threw the tokens into the helmet."
2. Ἔτυχον προσελθὼν Καλλίᾳ. (Plat. *Apol.* 20 A)
   "I happened to come up with C."
3. *Facilis descensus Averno . . .* (V. *Aen.* vi. 126)
   "Easy is the descent to Avernus."
4. *It caelo clamor . . .* (*ibid.* xi. 192)
   "The shout goes up to heaven."

Similar is the dative frequently found after *impono* and similar compound verbs in Latin.

1. *Eo ferocius adequitare Samnites vallo.* (Liv. ix. 22)
   "Therefore with all the more spirit did the S. ride against the rampart."
2. *Tecto adsuetus coluber succedere et umbrae. . . .*
       (V. *Georg.* iii. 418)
   "The serpent that is wont to creep under the shaded roof."

THE CASES 31

The Dative is also used after verbs and adjectives which express **contact, equality, resemblance**, which require an indirect object for their meaning to be complete, e.g. πλησιάζω, ὁμιλῶ, *misceo, haereo,* ὁμοῖος, *similis*: it is also found *by analogy* with their opposites, e.g. μάχομαι, *certo, dissimilis.* Seneca has (*Ep.* xx. 2) *orationi vita dissentiat.*

§ 49. DATIVE OF INTEREST—i.e. of the person to or *for* whom. Sometimes this dative is used of a person who is *not* strictly an object, even an indirect object, of the verb; but he is somehow involved in the action (or in the expression of it) and the action is said to be *directed towards* him. The action is regarded as *belonging to* the person in the dative.

This class is wide and loose (it is sometimes called the Dative of Advantage and Disadvantage), but the following divisions may be made. It will be seen how closely they are related.

Dative of the Person interested: the so-called Ethic Dative. Cp. Shakespeare—" She's a civil modest wife, one, I tell you, that will not miss *you* morning nor evening prayer"; " Knock *me* at that door, sirrah ! "

1. Ὦ τέκνον, ἦ βέβηκεν ἡμῖν ὁ ξένος; (Soph. *O.C.* 81)
   " Tell me, my child, has the stranger gone ? "
2. Ἐμμείνατέ μοι οἷς ἐδεήθην ὑμῶν μὴ θορυβεῖν.
   (Plat. *Apol.* 30 c)
   " Please remember not to interrupt."
3. *Ecce tibi qui rex populi Romani esse concupiverit.*
   (Cic. *Off.* iii. 21)
   " There's your man who wanted to be king of Rome ! "
4. *Hic tibi rostra Cato advolat.* (Cic. *Att.* i. 14)
   (See § 43.)

N.B. the use of this dative in a **predicative** sense.

1. Οὐκ ἂν ἔμοιγε | ἐλπομένῳ τὰ γένοιτο. (Hom. *Od.* iii. 228)
   " These things would not find me hoping for them."
2. *Quibus bellum volentibus erat probabant exemplum.*
   (Tac. *Agr.* 18)
   " Those who wanted war . . .'

Cp. Soph. *O.T.* 1356 ; Plat. *Gorg.* 448 D.

THE CASES

§ 50. Dative of the Person possessing : Roby suggests (1152) that the dative is used when the gist of the question relates to the thing possessed, the genitive when it refers to the possessor. 2. and 3. suggest a Dative of Person Interested.

1. Τῷ πατρὶ Πυριλάμπης ὄνομα ... (Plat. *Parm.* 126 B)
"His father's name was Pyrilampes."

2. *Militanti in Hispania pater ei moritur.*
(Liv. xxix. 29)
"While he was serving in Spain his father died."

3. *Olli dura quies oculos et ferreus urget
Somnus : in aeternam clauduntur lumina noctem.*
(V. *Aen.* x. 745)
"His eyes ungentle rest and iron sleep oppress, and their lids are closed on an eternal night."

§ 51. Dative of the Agent : the dative implies that the person has the thing done for himself. This is regularly found with verbal adjectives and pass. part. in Greek with gerunds and gerundives in Latin. In Latin not infrequently it is found with passive participles and adjectives in *-bilis*.

This dative should not express the same shade of meaning as *a* + Abl. : *eum numquam a me esse accusandum putavi* (Cic. *Har. resp.* 5) = " . . . that the accusation should come *from me* " ; *mihi accusandum* would mean " that it was my *duty* to accuse him " (Riemann, p. 103 ; but see Roby, 1147).

1. Τὰ τούτῳ πεπραγμένα. (Dem. xxix. 1)
"His achievements."

2. Τἀληθὲς ἀνθρώποισιν οὐχ εὑρίσκεται. (Men. *Mon.* 511)
"Truth is not found by mortals."

3. *Multis ille bonis flebilis occidit.* (Hor. *C.* i. 24. 9)
"He has died—to be lamented by many good men."

4. *Carmina quae scribuntur aquae potoribus.*
(Hor. *Ep.* i. 19. 3)
"Songs written by teetotallers."

4. may, however, be considered as an instrumental ablative, used contemptuously (see § 82, 4). Sometimes this dative appears to express the person *from whom* the action

proceeds as well as the person *to whom* it is directed. But ταῦτα λέλεκταί μοι = either " the words are given to me the hearer " or " . . . to me the speaker " ; τὰ ἐμοὶ πεπραγμένα means " the actions which stand to my credit ". When Homer writes δέξατό οἱ σκῆπτρον (*Il.* ii. 186), the idea must be " took the sceptre for him " or " . . . with a gesture to him ". For the meaning of the dative is essentially that of conjunction, and it cannot express separation.

§ 52. **Dative of Special Limitation** : often preceded by ὡς in Greek; e.g. Μακρὰν γάρ, ὡς γέροντι, προὐστάλης ὁδόν (Soph. *O.C.* 20) " . . . a long way for an old man ". So in Latin *Sp. Maelius, ut illis temporibus, praedives* (Liv. iv. 13)—" a very rich man for those days ". With this dative should be classed the *Dative of the Person judging* (which is similarly limitative). Cp. " To my mind he has made a mistake ".

1. Καίτοι σ᾽ ἐγὼ 'τίμησα, τοῖς φρονοῦσιν, εὖ.
   (Soph. *Ant.* 904)
   " And yet, in the eyes of the discerning, I did thee full honour."
2. Ὡς συνελόντι εἰπεῖν . . . (X. *An.* iii. 1. 38)
   " In short " (lit. " for one summing up ").
3. *Vere reputantibus Gallias suismet viribus concidisse* . . .
   (Tac. *H.* iv. 17)
   " . . . on a true estimate, the Gauls had fallen a victim to their own strength."
4. *Est oppidum primum Thessaliae venientibus ab Epiro.*
   (Caes. *B.C.* iii. 80)
   " It is the first town in T. for travellers from E."

§ 53. THE DATIVE OF DESTINATION, PURPOSE OR RESULT is an extension of the ordinary dative of the indirect object. One action is directed towards another ; e.g. " They devoted the day to sleeping ". Here should be included the use of the infinitive (originally a verbal noun in the dative or locative case, see § 162) to express purpose and result (the *epexegetic* infinitive). With ordinary nouns both in Greek and Latin the use is rare. In Latin with the gerund and gerundive the use is common. Generally nouns so used have a strong verbal character. Riemann quotes

French, e.g. " Le magistrat, tenant à mépris et irrévérence cette réponse . . ." (La Fontaine).

N.B.—Distinguish such a usage as *locum castris cepit* = (simply) " . . . for the camp "; but such an example shows how close the dative of Purpose is to that of Interest.

1. Οὐ γὰρ μετὰ τῶν κειμένων νόμων ὠφελίας αἱ τοιαῦται ξύνοδοι, ἀλλὰ παρὰ τοὺς καθεστῶτας πλεονεξίᾳ.
(Thuc. iii. 82)
"Such associations were formed not with the advantage given by the law, but, contra y to convention, for greed." (*Sic* MSS., but read ὠφελίᾳ, "for a salutary end" to balance πλεονεξίᾳ: *sic* Poppo.)

2. *Q. Fabius comitia censoribus creandis habuit.*
(Liv. xxiv. 11
"Fabius held an assembly for the election of censors."

3. *Receptui canere.* (Caes. *B.G.* vii. 47)
"To sound (for) the retreat."

Xviri legibus scribundis.
". . . for the compilation of laws."

The adjectival *frugi* ("good", "worthy") is such a dative; *ager frugi est* implies, e.g., *agrum frugi habemus*, which will illustrate the transition to § 54.

§ 54. **The Predicative Dative** in Latin is a certain stereotyped usage of this Dative of Purpose, usually with a dative of the object affected (indirect object) attached. It expresses that which something serves as or results in: e.g. "With me walking stands for exercise", "Retreat stands for disaster" are very rough English parallels. In meaning the predicative dative is an alternative to the predicative nominative: Cicero has *est turpitudo* . . ., Nepos has *fuit turpitudini* with precisely the same sense.

It is hardly distinct from the Dative of Purpose, except that it is used in nouns not necessarily of a verbal character, but more or less abstract. The use is confined to the dative singular of a limited number of nouns, usually unqualified (except quantitatively, e.g. by *magnus, tantus, nullus*), and is used only with the verbs *esse, ducere, vertere, dare, habere* and a few others; but *praesidio, auxilio, subsidio* are used with verbs of motion.

THE CASES 35

Some scholars have suggested that the usage may be due to attraction, *est mihi auxilium* becoming *est mihi auxilio*, as in *Huic item Menaechmo nomen est* (Plaut. *Men.* 1096).

Some examples of this dative suggest a locative use, e.g. in *argento faenori* (sc. *dato*) (Plaut. *Most.* 532), *postulare id gratiae apponi sibi*, but the explanation is inadequate if applied to the whole class.

N.B.—Usually a dative of the person or object affected (indirect object) is attached.

1. *Nemini meus adventus labori aut sumptui fuit.*
(Cic. *Verr.* i. 6. 16)
" My arrival caused no one trouble or expense."

2. *Quinque cohortes castris praesidio relinquit.*
(Caes. *B.G.* vii. 60)
" He left five cohorts as a guard for the camp."

THE GENITIVE

§ 55. As the accusative is the adverbial case, so the Genitive is the *adjectival* case: it limits a noun—by defining it as belonging to a certain class or description or as a part of a certain whole; e.g. " the gardens of Caesar ", " the bravest of the Greeks ", " the land of Ausonia ", " night of stars ", " a pearl of great price ". The genitive is also used as the object of verbs whose working affects only a part of the object.

The Greek name of the case, ἡ γενικὴ πτῶσις, means the case of the γένος, i.e. the larger whole to which the noun belongs. But the Latin name is not so satisfactory; *genetivus* translates not γενική but γεννητική, and seems to mean the case of origin. Now the Ablative is the case of origin; this in Greek is submerged in the Genitive, and the Latin name may be the result of a confusion.

Conspectus of the Genitive.

I. Belonging to a person—Possessive.

II. Belonging to a class—Partitive:
    (a) Simple;
    (b) of Place;
    (c) of Time—Genitive Absolute;
    (d) as Object of Verb.

III. Belonging to a particular class—Descriptive :
  (a) Defining ;
  (b) of Material or Quality ;
  (c) of Value ;
  (d) of Purpose.

IV. Belonging to a special reference—of Relation :
  (a) of Object ;
  (b) of Cause.

The thread of connexion is easily traced ; these are all different sorts of description : " the gardens of Caesar " describes the gardens by saying to whom they belong ; " garden of gardens " by relating the one garden to the whole world of gardens ; " a garden of roses " by defining its contents ; " a garden of great value " by describing its worth ; " a garden of rest " by giving its purpose ; similarly the objective genitive defines in terms of an object—" the love of pleasure ".

§ 56. POSSESSIVE GENITIVE—Belonging to a person.
  1. Ἡ πόλις ἁπάντων τῶν πολιτῶν κοινή ἐστίν. (Andoc.)
    " The city is the joint property of the citizen-body."
  2. *Patria est communis omnium nostrum parens.*
    (Cic. *Cat.* i. 7)
    " Our country is the common mother of us all."

Under this head falls the " predicative " genitive with meaning " it is the part of . . ."
  3. Τοῦτό ἐστι παίζοντος.   (Plat. *Apol.* 27 A)
    " This is the conduct of a jester."
  4. *Cuiusvis hominis est errare.*   (Cic. *Phil.* xii. 2)
    " Any man may sin."

N.B.—(i) Just as in, e.g., *Caecilia Metelli, uxor* may be understood, so sometimes we find such ellipses as ἐν Ἅιδου, " in (the house) of Death ", and *ventum erat ad Vestae,* " we came to Vesta's shrine ".

(ii) Distinguish this subjective genitive from the objective : *odium bonorum* may mean " the hatred felt *by* good men for something ", and it may also mean " hatred *for* good men ".   (See § 71.)

THE CASES

§ 57. The genitive used regularly *with certain verbs* is the ordinary possessive genitive. For example, verbs of ruling and leading in Greek and *potior* in Latin take this genitive (though *potior* often takes an ablative). These verbs are strictly intransitive : βασιλεύω = βασιλεύς εἰμί, *potior* = *potis fio*. Thus Περσῶν βασιλεύει means "He is the Persians' king ". (It is possible, however, that βασιλεύω's genitive is a genitive of comparison on the analogy of κρατῶ.)

Also, occasionally, in Greek a verb of speaking or hearing is constructed with a possessive genitive, which defines rather the thing heard or known than the verb. (The first example below means " What-news-belonging-to-your-brother do you bring ? " but, in ἀκούω ταῦτα σοῦ, σοῦ = " from you " and is not a true genitive but an ablative.) See § 79.

1. Τοῦ κασιγνήτου τί φῄς; (Soph. *El.* 317)
2. Εἰπὲ δέ μοι πατρός τε καὶ υἱέος. (Hom. *Od.* xi. 174)
   " Tell me both of father and son."

PARTITIVE GENITIVE—Belonging to a greater whole. Here the *fact* of belonging is stressed.

§ 58. **Simple Partitive** : giving the whole of which the noun defined is a part—*Phocidis Elatea* (" E. in Phocis ").

1. Ἀνὴρ τῶν ῥητόρων. (Ar. *Eq.* 425)
   Fortissima Tyndaridarum. (Hor. *Sat.* i. 1. 100)
2. Ποῦ ποτ' εἶ φρενῶν; (Soph. *El.* 390)
   " Where in thy wits art thou ? "
3. *Quicquid huius feci causa virginis feci.* (Ter. *Haut.* 202)
   " Whatever of this I did, I did it for the girl's sake."

§ 59. **Partitive of Place** : (Greek) gives the space within which something happens, i.e. the place to which it belongs. The use is poetical and common in Homer : common with adverbs in Greek and in colloquial Latin—ποῦ γῆς ; *ubi gentium ? Interea loci* (Ter. *Haut.* 257).

1. Τὰ μὲν γὰρ ἑστίας μεσομφάλου
   ἕστηκεν ἤδη μῆλα. (Aesch. *Ag.* 1056)
   " The victims stand already at the midmost hearth."

2. Ἐπετάχυνον τῆς ὁδοῦ τοὺς σχολαίτερον προσιόντας.
(Thuc. iv. 47)
"They hastened on the way those who approached too slowly."

§ 60. **Prepositions defining Partitive genitive** (of place, or field of action):

διά, " through "
ἐπί, " on "
μετά { " among ", " with " / " in front of " }
πρό, " before " (" in presence of ")
πρός, " belonging to "
ὑπέρ { " over " / " on behalf of " }

The adverbs ἄχρι, μέχρι(" up to "), μεταξύ (" between "), ἐγγύς (" near "), ἔνδον (" within "), ἔξω (" outside ") are similarly constructed; also the Latin *causa* (" for the sake of ") and *tenus* (" as far as "), which are really substantives (*tenus* (adverbial neut. acc.) = extent, *causa* = effect).

§ 61. **Partitive of Time**: (Greek) gives the period of time *within* which something happens (whereas the accus. expresses the time *throughout* which something lasts); e.g. νυκτός, " by night ", νηνεμίης (Homer), " in (time of) windless calm ". In Latin this is expressed by the locative ablative of time. (Sanskrit—M. 202. 5.)

1. Δέκα ἐτῶν οὐχ ἥξουσι. (Plat. *Legg*. 642 E)
"They will not come for ten years (i.e. at any time in . . .)."
2. Δίκη | μέτεισιν οὐ μακροῦ χρόνου. (Soph. *El*. 477)
"Within no long time justice pursues."

§ 62. **The Genitive Absolute** is usually explained under the heading of *time within which*, extended from time-conditions to cause-conditions, etc. (For the Latin Ablative Absolute see § 93.)

N.B.—(i) The secondary predicate is contained in the *participle*.
(ii) The genitive absolute like the ablative absolute may

THE CASES 39

well be explained differently in different contexts, e.g. it may often be a genitive of cause.

1. Οὔ τις ἐμεῦ ζῶντος σοὶ βαρείας χεῖρας ἐποίσει.
   (Hom. *Il.* i. 88)
   " None shall lay heavy hands on you in my lifetime."
2. Ἀνηγάγετο ἐπὶ τὴν Κύζικον ὕοντος πολλῷ.
   (Xen. *Hell.* i. 1. 16)
   " He put out for Cyzicus in the midst of a heavy rain."

§ 63. **Partitive Object of Verb** : where the action affects only part of the object, or affects it only tentatively.

1. . . . ὄφρα πίοι οἴνοιο. (Hom. *Od.* xxii. 11)
   " That he might drink of the wine " (cf. French *du vin*).
2. Ἀφίεις τῶν αἰχμαλώτων. (Xen. *An.* vii. 4)
   " Letting go some of the prisoners."

Also many verbs, especially in Greek, which are said to govern a genitive are really transitive and the genitive is partitive : in Greek such verbs as ἐσθίω, κοινωνῶ, γεύομαι, ἔχομαι, τυγχάνω, μεθίεμαι, μέμνημαι, ἐπιλανθάνομαι, μετέχω, συλλαμβάνω, κυρῶ : in Latin, *memini*, *obliviscor*, and in such sentences as *venit mihi Platonis in mentem* (= memineram) (Cic. *Fin.* v. 1). (Sanskrit—M. 202.)

Also a partitive genitive of the *material used* is found with verbs of " filling ", " supplying ", and the like. (Sanskrit—M. 202.) It is interesting to note a half-way stage between Possessive and Partitive in, e.g., μέτεστιν ὑμῖν τῶν πεπραγμένων μέρος.

1. Ἐσπάνιζον τροφῆς τοῖς πολλοῖς. (Thuc. iv. 6)
   " They lacked sustenance for the majority."
2. Παροίξας τῆς θύρας . . . (Ar. *Pax* 30)
   " Partly opening the door."
3. *Cum completus mercatorum carcer esset.*
   (Cic. *Verr.* v. 147)
   " . . . prison full of merchants."

Similarly with adjectives:

N.B.—(1) Verbs of touching, holding, etc., e.g. ἔχομαι, ἅπτομαι, are sometimes said to be constructed with a partitive genitive. That this is doubtful is shown by, e.g., ἐλάβοντο τῆς ζώνης τὸν Ὀρόντην (X. *An.* i. 6. 10) and μου ἐλάβετο τῆς χειρός (Plat. *Parm.* 126), where ζώνης and χειρός represent the part where the whole is also stated. We must refer these genitives to §§ 72-3.

(2) The fusion between ablative and genitive is well illustrated by the use of the genitive with ἀπολαύω ("to derive enjoyment *from* "), which suggests at once a partitive and an ablative. Cp. the use of *fruor, vescor*; and the genitive after *indigeo* is temptingly like the Greek ablative genitive.

DESCRIPTIVE GENITIVE—Belonging to a particular class.

§ 64. **Definition Proper** : expressing the whole contents (more normally expressed by apposition). Latin normally says *urbs Roma*, rarely *urbs Romae*, which seems to be an extension of the use in, e.g., Cicero's *cognomen habebat sapientis* (*Sen.* 6)—the name that belongs to a wise man, i.e. "wise" : in *nomen Latinum* the adjective stands for a genitive *Latii* : so we may have *urbs Romae* for *urbs Romana*.

1. Ὗς χρῆμα μέγα. (Hdt. i. 36)
   "A great monster of a boar."

2. *Aliis virtutibus continentiae, gravitatis, iustitiae, fidei te consulatu dignum putavi.* (Cic. *Mur.* 23)
   "I thought you deserved the consulate because of your qualities of self-control, dignity, impartiality and reliability."

§ 65. To this usage belongs the genitive used with many verbs of " accusing " and " condemning ", e.g. διώκω, γράφομαι, ἁλίσκομαι, *arguo, damno*. The genitive defines the noun implied in the verb. It may be well referred to the Genitive of Relation (" sphere within which ") § 71.

1. Διώκω μὲν κακηγορίας, τῇ δ' αὐτῇ ψήφῳ φόνου φεύγω. (Lys. xi. 12)
   "I am prosecuting for libel and in the same trial defending on a charge of homicide."

2. *C. Verrem insimulat avaritiae et audaciae.*
   (Cic. *in Verr.* i. 49)
   "He accuses V. of greed and effrontery."

THE CASES

§ 66. Prepositions governing Genitive of Definition or Class:

ἀντί { " in place of "   ἀμφί, " about "
      { " in return for "   περί, " concerning "

So too the adverb ἕνεκα (" on account of ").

§ 67. Genitive of Material: expressing some class, material or head under which a thing falls.

1. Οἱ στέφανοι ῥόδων ἦσαν.   (Dem. xviii. 70)
 " The garlands were of roses."
2. Ἔστιν ὁ πόλεμος οὐχ ὅπλων ἀλλὰ δαπάνης. (Thuc. i. 83)
 " . . . not a matter of arms but of money."
3. *Est fons aquae dulcis cui nomen Arethusa est.*
                             (Cic. *in Verr.* iv. 53)
 " There is a fountain of fresh water called A."
4. . . . *flumine sanguinis intercludendum.*
                             (Cic. *post Red.* 14)
 " . . . barred by a river of blood."

§ 68. Genitive expressing Quality: sometimes called Genitive of Quality: with an adjective common in Latin; in Greek frequently with numerical adjectives.

1. Γαμεῖν δεῖ ἐπειδὰν ἐτῶν ᾖ τις τριάκοντα.
                             (Plat. *Legg.* 721)
 " Marriage should come when a man is thirty years old."
2. *Ingenui voltus puer ingenuique pudoris.* (Juv. xi. 154)
 " A boy of gentle look and gentle modesty."

§ 69. Genitive of Value (the so-called Genitive of Price): this falls naturally under the Genitive of Definition. It defines a thing in terms of value, answering the question " Of what value is it ? " The usage developed thus: in *hoc nihili est* (= " it is worth nothing "), *nihili* (descriptive genitive) is equivalent to an adjective, e.g. *vanum est*: then it is just as natural to transfer the *nihili* predicate to a transitive verb as it is to transfer the adjective: e.g. *nihili facere aliquid* is as natural as *vanum facere aliquid.* So we get *aliquid tanti emere.* N.B.—St. Matthew xiii. 46, " And having found one pearl of great price . . . he bought it ", where the *magni pretii* goes with the noun, a descriptive genitive.

THE CASES

The Latin genitive, e.g. *parvi, magni, flocci aestimare*, is sometimes discussed as a locative—" to assess *at* a straw's worth "; but when we have both the true genitive of value in Greek and also in Latin such phrases as *boni consulere* and *lucri facere*, it seems unnecessary to regard this Latin genitive as other than a real genitive. (For Locative see § 85.)

1. Πόσου διδάσκει; Πέντε μνῶν.   (Plat. *Apol.* 20 B)
   "What do his lessons cost?"   "Five minae."

2. Προπέποται τῆς παραυτίκα χάριτος τὰ τῆς πόλεως πράγματα.   (Dem. iii. 22)
   "The city's interests have been gambled away for the moment's popularity."

3. *Rumoresque senum severiorum*
   Omnes unius aestimemus assis.   (Catull. 5. 3)
   "The murmurs of the greybeard puritans let us assess at one farthing's worth."

4. *Est mihi tanti, Quirites, huius invidiae tempestatem subire.*   (Cic. *Cat.* ii. 7)
   "It is worth that to me—to undergo this storm of hatred."

(Both in Greek and Latin *price* is also expressed by an instrumental usage, i.e. the buying is said to be done by means of the price.)

§ 70. **Genitive of Purpose**: here the genitive defines an action by expressing it as belonging to a purpose. Greek uses τοῦ with the infinitive, Latin the genitive of the gerundive agreeing with its noun. It will be clear from 2. below that the genitive is one of quality depending on a substantive or substantival idea understood and *not* on the verb: *cepit arma—libertatis—subvortendae* is extended to *cepit arma* (*libertatis subvortendae*).

1. Περιεσταύρωσαν αὐτούς, τοῦ μηδένα ἐπεξιέναι.
         (Thuc. ii. 75)
   "They fenced them in to prevent escape."

2. *Arma cepit . . . legum ac libertatis subvortundae.*
         (Sall. *Or. Phil.* 11)
   "He took up arms for the subversion of law and liberty."

THE CASES

3. *Unum vinciri iubet magis usurpandi iuris quam quia unius culpa foret.* (Tac. *H.* iv. 25)
   "He orders one of them to be jailed rather to assert authority than because one man was to blame."

GENITIVE OF RELATION—Belonging to a special reference.

This is a somewhat loose section expressing the sphere or relation within which a predicate falls. But all usages within it are at root *possessive*. Τοῦ κασιγνήτου τί φής; is near it as is (Soph. *O.C.* 355) μαντεῖα ἃ τοῦδε ἐχρήσθη σώματα. (Sanskrit—M. 202. 2.)

(a) **Objective Genitive**: here the special reference is to a noun that would be the object of a verb.

§ 71. This genitive is used with nouns (and in Latin with adjectives also) which have a verbal flavour and corresponds usually to the direct accusative after a verb. It defines the noun or adjective qualified by assigning it to a particular object.

1. Οἱ ἄνθρωποι διὰ τὸ αὐτῶν δέος τοῦ θανάτου καταψεύδονται. (Plat. *Phaed.* 85)
   "Men through their fear *of* death misrepresent the matter."

2. Τὸ Ἀθηναίων κράτος τῆς θαλάσσης. (Thuc. viii. 76)
   "The Athenian command *of* the sea."

3. *Atheniensium populi potestas omnium rerum.* (Cic. *Resp.* i. 28)
   "The sovereignty of the Athenian democracy in all things."

With adjectives we have, e.g.:

1. *Tempus edax rerum.* (Ov. *Met.* xv. 234)
   "Time the consumer of things."

2. *Amnis navium patiens.* (Liv. xxi. 31)
   "A river admitting of navigation."

Sometimes the objective genitive expresses an indirect, remoter object.

1. Ἡ τῶν κρεισσόνων δουλεία. (Thuc. i. 8)
   "Subserviency to the stronger."

   Θεῶν εὐχαί. (Plat. *Phaedr.* 244 c)
   "Prayers to the gods."

2. *Contentio honorum.* (Cic. *Off.* i. 25)
"Rivalry for office."

§ 72. (b) This section is best represented by a usage of the **genitive after adjectives** in Latin to denote, in Roby's cumbersome phrase, " the point in which a term is applied ". It is like the objective genitive, but the difference is that here the adjective is not verbal. No. 3. below seems to fall half-way between the two usages and should mark the transition : *disertus (dissero)* is half verbal, as is *rectus (rego)*.

Yet this genitive is also partitive—cp. Thuc. ii. 90 ὡς εἶχε τάχους ἕκαστος.

1. Τέλειος τῆς ἀρετῆς. (Plat. *Legg.* 643 D)
"Perfect in point of virtue."
2. Θέλω δ' ἄϊδρις μᾶλλον ἢ σοφὸς κακῶν | εἶναι.
(Aesch. *Sup.* 468)
"Better unversed than skilled in woes."
3. *Leporum disertus puer et facetiarum.* (Catull. 12. 9)
"A boy fluent in graceful speech and jest."
4. *Integer vitae scelerisque purus* . . . (Hor. *C.* i. 22. 1)
"Pure *of* life and free from crime."

(N.B. in Ex. 4. the *sceleris* is not a true genitive but an ablative-genitive in imitation of the Greek ; see below, § 77.)

So with an adverb + ἔχω—ξένως ἔχω τῆς ἐνθάδε λέξεως (Plat. *Ap.* 17 D) " a stranger to your ways of speech ". So the genitive after ἄξιος and the like and possibly the genitive of comparison, ἀμείνων ἄλλων—" in relation to others " ; but see § 80.

§ 73. Cp. the Latin genitives *discruciari animi, angi animi, desipiebam mentis* (Plaut. *Epid.* 138) (referring to an internal part, not an external object). These are not locatives : the genitive is still with 3rd declension nouns and it corresponds to the genitive in Greek. So *falsus animi* is related to *nec me animi fallit* (Lucr. i. 136). (Roby, 1321 ; Riemann, p. 131.)

§ 74. Similar is the genitive after *paenitet, taedet, piget* and other impersonals ; which illustrate the use of the Genitive of Relation to express **Cause**.

THE CASES

1. Ζηλῶ σε τοῦ νοῦ, τῆς δὲ δειλίας στυγῶ. (Soph. *El.* 1027)
  "I envy thee for thy sense, and hate thee for thy cowardice."
2. *Iustitiaene prius mirer, belline laborum ?*
  (V. *Aen.* xi. 126)
  "Shall I marvel first at thy righteousness or thy toils in war ?"

So (Isoc. *Nic.* 27 A) Θαυμάζω τῶν ταύτην τὴν γνώμην ἐχόντων. But the Latin is not necessarily a Graecism.

§ 75. The Genitive of **Exclamation** falls under this causal head.
1. Φεῦ τοῦ ἀνδρός. (X. *Cyr.* iii. 1. 39)
  "What a man !"
2. *Di immortales, mercimoni lepidi !* (Plaut. *Most.* 912)
  "Heavens, what a smart bit of goods !"

THE ABLATIVE

§ 76. The Ablative survives as a distinct case in Sanskrit (see M. 201) and Latin. The Latin name implies that it is the case of separation, and the name is a tolerable indication of its uses. In Greek the ablative has become a department of the genitive. Indications of the reasons for this fusion are to be seen in the partitive genitive which is equally well conceived as ablative—a part taken *from* the whole (see § 61): similarly the genitive of cause is very near to the ablative of cause (ζηλῶ σε τοῦ νοῦ may be " my envy proceeds from your wit ").

Conspectus of the Ablative.
  I. The Fact of Separation.
  II. The Result of Separation—Origin.
  III. Of Comparison.
  IV. Metaphorical Origin—
    (a) Cause ;
    (b) Agent.

The connexion of these usages should be clear from the following paragraphs.

§ 77. **The Fact of Separation** : expressing the point from which motion or separation takes place. In Latin the simple ablative of "motion from" is regular with names of towns, etc., and in certain words—*domo, humo, rure*; in Greek the simple genitive is rare in prose unless helped by a preposition in the verb as in Ex. 2. Usually prepositions are used with this case in this use, e.g. ἀπό, ἐκ, παρά, *a, ex*.

1. Τᾶς πολυχρύσου Πυθῶνος . . . ἔβας. (Soph. *O.T.* 152)
"From Pytho rich in gold . . . hast thou come."
2. Ξυνέβη Θασίους τῶν Ἀθηναίων ἀποστῆναι.
(Thuc. i. 100)
"It happened that the Thasians revolted from the A."
3. *Caelo venere volantes.* (V. *Aen.* vi. 191)
"They came flying from heaven."
4. *L. Brutus civitatem dominatu regio liberavit.*
(Cic. *pro Planc.* 25)
"Brutus freed the state from the tyranny of kings."

Horace and others sometimes imitate the Greek construction in using a genitive instead of an ablative:

Tempus desistere pugnae. (V. *Aen.* x. 441)
"Time to cease from battle."

§ 78. **Prepositions defining Ablative** (i.e. Genitive in Greek):

ἀπό "from"
ἐκ, "out of"
κατά, "down from"

παρά {"from"
       "from the side of"}
ὑπό, "from under"

a, ab, abs, "from"
absque, "without"
de, "away from"

e, ex, "out of"
procul, "far from"
sine, "without"

So too the adverbs ἄνευ, ἄτερ, χωρίς, δίχα ("apart from", "without") and πλήν ("except"); so also Latin *tenus* ("as far as") sometimes with ablative.

Ablative dependent on Verbs: in Greek this ablative-genitive is used with verbs and adjectives expressing "deprivation" and "deficiency", giving the object from which the subject is removed. (Sanskrit—M. 201.)

(N.B.—The genitive that follows certain verbs of "wanting" in Latin is a true genitive; see § 63.)

THE CASES

Also used after verbs of removing, freeing, repelling, ceasing.

1. Οὐ πόνων κεχρήμεθα. (Eur. *Med.* 334)
   "We have no lack of troubles."
   ... ὀρφανὸς ἀνδρῶν. (Lys. ii. 60)
   "Bereft of men."
2. ... πολλοῦ δέω ... ἀπολογεῖσθαι ... (Plat. *Apol.* 30 D)
   "I am far from defending ..."
3. ... *dicitur oculis se privasse.* (Cic. *Fin.* v. 57)
   "He is said to have deprived himself of eyesight."

N.B.—For the Ablative Absolute in Latin see under "Instrumental".

§ 79. **The Result of Separation**: one thing to be *produced out of* another must be *separated from* it. Therefore the connexion between these ablatives is obvious. The Ablative of Origin is commonly used of parentage, e.g. *nate dea*. The Greek genitive with verbs of sense-perception is really this ablative of origin, which expresses the source of the sensation; κρομμύων ὀσφραίνομαι = "the smell I notice comes from onions".

1. Δαρείου καὶ Παρυσάτιδος γίγνονται παῖδες δύο.
   (Xen. *An.* i. 1. 1)
   "Two children were born of D. and P."
2. Ἥδομαι ἀκούων σου φρονίμους λόγους.
   (*ibid.* ii. 5. 16)
   "I am glad to hear sensible words from you."
3. *Apollo Iove natus est et Latona.* (Cic. *N.D.* iii. 23)
   "Apollo was born of Jupiter and Latona."
4. *L. Domitius Cn. f. Fabia Ahenobarbus.*
   (*S. C. ap.* Cic. *Fam.* viii. 8)
   "Lucius Domitius Ahenobarbus son of Gnaeus, from the Fabian tribe."

§ 80. **Ablative of Comparison**: this expresses the *source* of the comparison by giving an object from which the subject is apart: i.e. every comparison expresses a contrast or *difference*, i.e. a motion away from. (Sanskrit— M. 201.)

N.B.—It is the Ablative which accompanies the adjective

that provides the comparison. The so-called comparative in itself is merely an intensive : *melior, ἀμείνων* = " rather good ", " especially good " (*senectus natura loquacior* = " . . . rather talkative ").

This Ablative use is earlier than the *quam* construction which strictly should express *equality* : *melior est quam Traianus* = *tam melior est quam T. est* = " he is as outstandingly good as T."

1. Δόξα κρείττων τῶν φθονούντων . . . (Dem. iii. 24)
   " A reputation stronger than the forces of envy."
2. *Nihil est virtute amabilius.* (Cic. *Lael.* viii. 28)
   " Nothing is more lovable than goodness."
3. . . . *neve putes alium sapiente bonoque beatum.*
   (Hor. *Ep.* i. 16. 20)
   " And do not think any other than the wise and good is happy."

Occasionally in Greek this usage is found loosely used without an explicit comparative, e.g. in

   Νικᾷ γὰρ ἀρετή με τῆς ἐχθρας πολύ.
   (Soph. *Aj.* 1357)
   " Valour weighs far more with me than enmity."

Here the genitive is dependent upon the idea of comparison implied in νικᾷ πολύ (" sways me *more* ").

§ 81. **Metaphorical Origin** : *Cause* as the source of action. Here Latin follows rather the instrumental ablative of manner and attendant circumstances (see § 86). (Sanskrit —M. 201.) But the Greek use may be referred to § 71.

1. Χωόμενος . . . γυναικός . . . (Hom. *Il.* i. 429)
   " Being wroth because of a woman."
2. *Oderunt peccare boni virtutis amore.* (Hor. *Ep.* i. 16. 52)
   " Because of their love of virtue the good hate to sin."

§ 82. **Metaphorical Origin** : *the agent* as the origin of action, usually with a preposition, e.g. ὑπό, *a*.

1. Πληγεὶς θυγατρὸς τῆς ἐμῆς. (Eur. *Or.* 497)
   " Struck by my daughter."
2. Οὕτως ἄτιμός εἰμι τοῦ τεθνηκότος. (Soph. *El.* 1214)
   " Thus am I unhonoured of him who is dead."

THE CASES

3. . . . *assiduo ruptae lectore columnae.* (Juv. i. 13)
"Pillars shattered by the incessant reader."

4. *Paenula inretitus, raeda impeditus, uxore paene constrictus erat.* (Cic. pro Mil. 20)
"Entangled in his cloak, impeded by his carriage, all but tied down by his wife."

Without a preposition this usage is rare and is probably limited to agents when no intention or motive is implied, i.e. when the agent is no more than a passive instrument. In 4. above *uxore* may be assimilated to *paenula, raeda,* but more probably the simple case is used just because the wife was as much a mere encumbrance as cloak and carriage. 3. is sometimes explained as an instrumental ablative of attendant circumstances ("the reader being incessant"), but this gives a less satisfactory sense than ". . . by the reader".

THE LOCATIVE

The name is modern and signifies adequately the point of place or time to which an action is limited.

§ 83. LOCATIVE OF PLACE. In Greek and Latin the locative as a separate case disappeared. But χαμαί, οἴκοι, Πυθοῖ, Σφηττοῖ, Ἀθήνησιν, Ὀλυμπίασι, *domi, humi,* are old locatives. In Greek the locative is lost in the dative form, not unnaturally since the dative is the circumstantial case (see § 89) : similarly in Latin in the ablative—*terra marique* may be regarded as partly instrumental, just as, say, "by land and sea", "*par* terre et mer". In singular names of the first and second declensions originally the locatives were *Romai, Corinthei,* like the genitives and slipped with them into the -*ae,* -*i* forms, and the genitive was no doubt considered as a partitive of place. In Sanskrit the locative (M. 203-205) is a very important case and can express circumstance and even object.

Usually the use is supported by prepositions, e.g. ἐν, ἐπί, *in, sub.* In Latin towns and small islands are used without prepositions, as also *domi, humi, foris, loco, dextra, laeva, medio, terra marique, militiae, parte, regione* (the last two both qualified), and expressions compounded with *totus* or *medius*. In poetry, especially in Virgil, a locative-ablative without a preposition is not uncommon.

§ 84. Literal Place.

1. Ἔτι μέγας οὐρανῷ Ζεύς. (Soph. *El.* 174)
   "Zeus is still great in heaven."
2. Τὰ τρόπαια τά τε Μαραθῶνι καὶ Σαλαμῖνι καὶ Πλαταιαῖς.
   (Plat. *Menex.* 245 A)
   "The trophies at Marathon, on Salamis and at Plataea . . ."
3. *Seniores medio aedium eburneis sellis sedere.* (Livy v. 41)
   ". . . on ivory chairs in the space before the houses."
4.   *Cernis custodia qualis*
   Vestibulo sedeat. (V. *Aen.* vi. 575)
   "Thou seest what guardian sits in the porch."

Often the ablative-locative borders indeterminately on the instrumental where the place is also the means.

    Vix arma humeris gestabant. (Liv. xxvii. 48)
    "Scarcely could they carry their shields on their shoulders."

Class here the "ablatives" after *sto, nitor, confido, pendo* ("ponder"), and the "datives" after ναίω, ἵστημι, κτλ.

§ 85. Metaphorical Place, as with *loco, numero*:

    Illi se iudicum numero haberi volunt. (Cic. *T.D.* i. 41)
    "They wish to be included in the body of judges."

There is also the metaphorical Locative of Value (or Price): as we say in English, "to buy at ten shillings, to sell at a pound". The underlying idea is that of a scale of values; the particular article *stands at* a certain mark in the scale (just as a temperature stands at a certain point in a thermometer scale). N.B.—There is also an Ablative expressing price in Latin which must be regarded rather as Instrumental: there is an obvious difference, e.g., between *emit morte immortalitatem* (Quint. ix. 3. 71) and the examples of the Locative use below. So *quo mihi . . . ?* ("What is it worth to me?")—see § 41. See also § 69.

1. *Magno illi ea cunctatio stetit.* (Liv. ii. 36)
   "That hesitation cost him dear."

THE CASES

2. *Probitatis impendio constat.* (Quint. vi. 3. 35)
"It stands at the price of honesty."

§ 86. LOCATIVE OF TIME. This may be distinguished in Greek from the dative only in a few words such as ἀεί, ἀντί, ἀμφί, περί, which are old locatives, and from the ablative in Latin only in such words as *pridie, postridie, quotidie.* The regular construction for *Time when* in Greek is the dative with a preposition, which is dispensed with only when the time mentioned is a particular date or occasion. In Latin the simple ablative is regular.

1. Τῇ ὑστεραίᾳ. Τῷ ἐπιόντι μηνί. Τετάρτῳ ἔτει.
2. Ἀλλ' ὡσπερεὶ Θεσμοφορίοις νηστεύομεν.
 (Ar. *Av.* 1519)
"But we are fasting as we do at the Thesmophoria."
3. *Pyrrhi temporibus iam Apollo versus facere desierat.*
 (Cic. *Div.* ii. 56)
"Apollo had already stopped writing verses in the days of P."
4.   *Tibi vota quotannis*
Agricolae facient. (V. *Ecl.* v. 79)
"Each year to thee the farmers will make their prayers."

§ 87. The ablative-locative is also used in Latin to express *Time within which* (expressed in Greek by the partitive genitive).

1. *S. Roscius multis annis non venit.* (Cic. *Rosc. A.* 27)
". . . for many years."
2. *Cui viginti his annis supplicatio decreta est . . . ?*
 (*id., Phil.* xiv. 11)
"To whom for the last twenty years has a thanksgiving been decreed . . . ?"

In Sanskrit it is the locative which is used as the equivalent of the Latin "ablative absolute" construction (M. 205); which suggests that the "ablative absolute" may be in origin a locative and even used as such in the mature language—e.g. *sciant bono imperatore haud magni fortunam momenti esse* (Livy xxii. 25) = ". . . *when* there is a good general".

THE CASES

§ 88. **Prepositions defining Locative** (i.e. Dative in Greek, Ablative in Latin) : expressing point of place or time :

ἀμφί, " about "
ἀνά, " upon " (poet.)
ἐν, " in "
ἐπί, " on "
μετά, " among " (poet.)

παρά, " at the side of "
πρός, " at ", " in addition to "
σύν, " with ", " inclusive of "
ὑπό, " underneath "

cum, " with "
prae, " in front of "

pro { " in front of "
" instead of "
" on behalf of " }

Here may be included the adverbs *coram* (" in the presence of "—an adverbial feminine accus. of an adjective *corus** compounded of *co* (*cum*) and *os, oris* = face), *simul* (" with "—poetical) and *tenus* (" *at* the extent of ").

THE INSTRUMENTAL OR CIRCUMSTANTIAL CASE

§ 89. The (modern) name implies that it is the case of the object *by means of which* it is said that something is done. The name is not full enough : *circumstantial* would be more satisfactory. Only in Sanskrit it remains an independent case ; it is included in the Dative in Greek and in the Ablative in Latin.

Why these fusions took place is suggested by certain usages noted above under Dative, Ablative, Locative (see §§ 51, 80, 83, 87 ; also Monro, p. 138).

This is its primary use, but it is extended to cover other ways of answering the question How ? In answer to this question an action may be said to be done, e.g., by means of some tool or help, or from certain causes, or in a certain manner, or in certain circumstances ; e.g. " she killed him *with* an axe ", " *with* assistants ", or " *with* good cause ", " *with* cruelty ", " *with* a loud cry " or " in the prevailing disorder " (and compare the colloquialism " What with one thing and another I can't . . .").

For Instrumental the name Sociative is sometimes used, indicating that the case expresses what accompanies the action.

The original termination of the case in Greek was -φι

THE CASES

which survives in some words in Homer as ἧφι βίηφι ("with all his might"—expressing means), αὐτοῖσιν ὄχεσφιν ("chariots and all"—sociative), ἅμ' ἠοῖ φαινομένηφι ("with the appearing of dawn"—attendant circumstances).

Conspectus of the Instrumental.
I. Instrumental Proper :
   (a) of Means ;
   (b) of Cause.
II. Circumstantial :
   (a) Persons—Sociative
   (b) Things—Attendant Circumstances ;
   (c) Manner ;
   (d) Defining Circumstances—Measure, Part.

§ 90. **Instrumental of Means :** " by means of . . ." Dative in Greek, Ablative in Latin without prepositions.

1. Ἔσθ' ὅτῳ ἂν ἄλλῳ ἴδοις ἢ ὀφθαλμοῖς; (Plat. *Rep.* 352 E)
   " Is there any organ but the eye by which you could see ? "
2. *Amicos neque armis cogere neque auro parare queas.*
   (Sall. *Jug.* 10)
   " You cannot make friends by force or buy them with gold."

The ablatives regularly used in Latin with *fruor, utor, fungor, vescor, nitor*, which are strictly reflexives, i.e. " I enjoy myself ", " I employ myself ", etc., are instrumental. *Victoria potiri* (Caesar), " to make one's self powerful by means of victory." So too are the ablatives after *fretus* (lit. " supported "), *contentus* (" satisfied "). Similarly with Greek χρῶμαι.

Price is often expressed as means both in Greek and Latin (Sanskrit—M. 199) :

1. . . . Πρίατο κτεάτεσσιν ἑοῖσιν.   (Hom. *Od.* xv. 483)
   " . . . bought with his substance."
2. *Vendidit hic auro patriam.*   (V. *Aen.* vi. 621)
   " This one sold for gold his country."

§ 91. **Instrumental of Cause :** obviously this is closely

related to the Instrumental proper; both express that which is the *medium* between the doer and the deed; the one expresses that *by means of* which, the other that *because of* which; unlike the Instrumental proper this causal Instrumental cannot strictly express intention. N.B.—Without prepositions both in Greek and Latin. (Sanskrit—M. 199.)

1. Οὐκ εἰμὶ τοῖς πεπραγμένοις δύσθυμος. (Soph. *El.* 549)
"I am not despondent because of what has happened."
2. Ἡγοῦνται ἡμᾶς φόβῳ οὐκ ἐπιέναι. (Thuc. v. 97)
"They think that we are not advancing because we are afraid."
3. *Multi homines officia deserunt mollitia animi.*
(Cic. *Fin.* i. 10)
"Many neglect their duty through slackness."
4. *Macte nova virtute, puer* . . . (V. *Aen.* ix. 641)
"Blest be thou for thy young valour, my son."

The dative-instrumental of cause in Greek is joined to many verbs of emotion, e.g. ἥδομαι, ἄχθομαι, χαλεπαίνω, θαυμάζω, κάμνω. Similar is the Latin ablative with *confido*, *fido*.

§ 92. **Circumstantial of Persons—Sociative** : expresses that which accompanies the working of the verb. The simple case (without *cum*) is rare in Latin; not uncommon in Greek.

Example 1. will show how this usage may overlap with the Instrumental proper; whereas the dative in 4., which cannot possibly mean "by means of the men", overlaps with the Instrumental of Attendant Circumstances. (Sanskrit—M. 199.)

1. Ἵπποισι καὶ ἅρμασι πέμπε. (*Od.* iv. 8)
"Sent him on with chariots and horses."
2. Αὐτῇ κεν γαίῃ ἐρύσαιμ' αὐτῇ δὲ θαλάσσῃ. (*Il.* viii. 24)
"I would drag you up, earth and sea withal."
3. Ἐφοβοῦντο μὴ μείζονι παρασκευῇ ἐπέλθωσιν.
(Thuc. iv. 1)
"They feared that they might come against them with a larger force."

THE CASES 55

4. Μίαν ναῦν ἔλαβον αὐτοῖς ἀνδράσιν. (Thuc. iv. 14)
"They took one ship with the entire crew."

Monro (p. 138) has a good note on the αὐτός use: the precise sense of an epithet often gives the clue to the particular meaning of the case-form—τοίχου τοῦ ἑτέροιο suggests Genitive of Place; μέσσου δουρὸς ἑλών a partitive Genitive: so αὐτός (= "as before", "itself without change") suggests the sociative case—"with the men there as before."

5. *Albani ingenti exercitu in agrum Romanum impetum fecere.* (Liv. i. 23)
"The Albans made an attack on Roman territory with a huge army."

The Dative after such verbs as ὁμιλῶ, ἕπομαι (especially = "go *with*"), μίγνυμι may be a sociative case (but see § 48). So in Latin we find, e.g., *mendicitas aviditate coniuncta* (Cic. *Phil.* v. 20).

§ 93. **Attendant Circumstances.** Here the Instrumental expresses merely the conditions that accompany an action: it is often very close to the Instrumental of Manner, as, e.g., in ζῶσαν ἀβλαβεῖ βίῳ above. Under this heading falls the so-called Ablative Absolute in Latin, to which a Greek equivalent may be noted in Examples 1 and 2 below. But usually Greek prefers a Genitive Absolute (see § 62).

N.B.—The Ablative Absolute may be put under this heading, though it can often according to the context be explained by other uses of the Ablative, e.g. those expressing cause and manner. But see under Locative and N.B. 2. below. 3. again is near the Locative and suggests the way in which cases were combined.

1. Οἱ Ἀθηναῖοι ἀτελεῖ τῇ νίκῃ ἀνέστησαν.
(Thuc. viii. 27)
"The Athenians withdrew while their victory was still incomplete."

2. Τί μοι . . . περιτελλομέναις ὥραις ἐξανύσεις χρέος;
(Soph. *O.T.* 156)
"What thing wilt thou work for me in the fullness of years?"

3. *Tabulas in foro summa hominum frequentia exscribo.*
(Cic. *Verr.* ii. 77)
"I draw up the documents in public in the midst of a great crowd."

4. *Nec auspicato nec litato instruunt aciem.* (Liv. v. 38)
"Without consulting either auspices or sacrifice they draw up their line."

N.B. the occasional use in Latin of this ablative in a passive participle with a sentence for subject, e.g.

Est progressus, nondum comperto quam regionem hostes petissent. (Liv. xxxi. 39)
"He marched forward, it not being yet known which quarter the enemy had made for."

§ 94. **Manner.** This is merely the Attendant Circumstances construction used descriptively : the two usages are scarcely distinguishable. When the noun is qualified by an adjective, as in the examples below, usually no preposition is used ; unqualified nouns take μετά, *cum*. Latin uses this ablative, much as the genitive of description, to qualify nouns.

1. Κραυγῇ πολλῇ ἐπίασι. (X. *An.* i. 7. 4)
"They advance with a great shout."

2. Ἀλλ' ὧδέ μ' ἀεὶ ζῶσαν ἀβλαβεῖ βίῳ. (Soph. *El.* 650)
". . . thus living ever with unscathed life."

3. *Polliceor hoc vobis, Quirites, bona fide.*
(Cic. *Agr.* ii. 37)
"I make this promise, gentlemen, in all good faith."

4. *Agesilaus statura fuit humili et corpore exiguo.*
(Nep. *Ages.* 8)
"A. was of short stature and slender body."

Under this heading come the adverbials σπουδῇ ("carefully"), σιγῇ ("silently"), *casu* ("accidentally"), *ratione* ("rightly"), etc.

§ 95. **Defining Circumstance or Relation** (cp. the Genitive of Relation, § 71). This expresses the respect in which a term is applied or a statement made (sometimes called the Dative (Gr.) or Ablative (Lat.) of Respect) ; e.g. "I

THE CASES

can beat him at running ", " Vane, young in years, but in sage counsel old " (Milton). (Sanskrit—M. 199.)

1. Τὸ πράττειν τοῦ λέγειν ὕστερον ὂν τῇ τάξει πρότερον τῇ δυνάμει ἐστίν. (Dem. iii. 15)
   " Action is posterior to speech in point of time, but in significance it comes first."

2. *Totidem annis tum mihi aetate praestabat Crassus.*
   (Cic. *Brut.* 43)
   " At that time C. surpassed me in age by a like number of years."

3. *Ennius ingenio maximus, arte rudis.*
   (Ov. *Trist.* ii. 424)
   " Ennius foremost in genius, but rough in craft."

Perhaps such expressions as *capite damnati* ("condemned to death"), *capite censi* (lit. "reckoned by heads," i.e. the lowest property-class) are best included here; cp.

Frusinates tertia parte agri damnati . . . (Liv. x. 1)
" The people of Frusino were condemned to forfeit a third of their territory."

§ 96. Under this heading comes the **Instrumental of Measure** which is *Quantitative* (whereas § 95 concerns Qualitative reference). Example 3. above illustrates both uses. It will be seen that there is in the Instrumental of Defining Circumstances a strong resemblance to the Locative; so here in the Instrumental of Measure which specifies amount of difference, etc., and expresses the *point* rather than the *manner* (see e.g. Example 3.). It is commonest with comparatives and superlatives, with such verbs as ἀπέχω, *disto*, and in such phrases as ὅσῳ . . . τοσούτῳ . . . and *quanto . . . tanto . . .*

1. Τῇ κεφαλῇ μείζων. (Plat. *Phaed.* 101 A)
   " A head taller."

   Πολλῷ χείρων.
   " Much worse."

2. Πολλαῖς γενεαῖς ὕστερα τῶν Τρωικῶν . . . (Thuc. i. 14)
   " Many generations later than the Trojan war . . ."

3. *Quo plures erant Veientes eo maior caedes fuit.*
   (Liv. ii. 51)
   "The more numerous the people of Veii the greater the slaughter."

4. *Voverat aedem X. annis ante Punicum bellum.*
   (Liv. xxxiv. 53)
   "He had vowed a temple ten years before the Punic war."

SPECIAL PREPOSITIONAL USAGES

§ 97. (For the development of prepositional constructions and normal usage see §§ 16, 17, 31, 44, 60, 66, 78, 88.) Generally the special usages which it is possible to consider here may be classed under the term *Proleptic*, or pregnant, i.e. the prepositions vary from the normal usage because they look forward beyond their own phrase to another, usually the main, clause.

Sometimes such usages can be explained by understanding a clause which was in the writer's mind but was suppressed in writing.

In Greek such uses are not infrequent; in Latin they are rarer.

1. Ἡ μάχη ἐτελεύτα ἐς ὀψέ.   (Thuc. iii. 108)
   "The fight . . . ended late (went on till late and then ended)."

2. Προηγόρευε στὰς ἐς μέσον.   (Hdt. iii. 62)
   "He came into their midst and began to speak (came into the midst and stood there . . .)."

3. *Obsistens ad prima signa . . . repressit.* (Livy xxv. 37)
   ". . . went to their front, blocked their way and held them back."

§ 98. With some examples the prepositional phrases, if their true significance is to be appreciated, have to be taken with a verb-form other than that with which they would appear to go. In such instances a mental re-punctuation will make clear the construction and the thought behind it.

1. . . . Ὅσα εἰκὸς ἐν τοιούτῳ χωρίῳ ἐμπεπτωκότας κακοπαθῆσαι. (Thuc. vii. 87)
2. . . . ταῖς ἐν τῇ γῇ καταπεφευγυίαις (sc. ναυσίν).
(Thuc. iv. 14)

In 1. the thought is ". . . to suffer in such a place, being cast into it ", and so ἐμπεπτωκότας may be construed, as it were, in parenthesis. So 2.—" the ships that were on the shore, having fled there ". In both instances it is the *presence in* a certain place rather than how they came there which is stressed : the perfect denotes state rather than action.

§ 99. Most instances of "proleptic" prepositions, then, arise from brachylogy (i.e. a shortened form of expression), two thoughts being run together into one. It is unnecessary to classify such uses with different types of prepositions, as this principle virtually applies to all. But there is one use which calls for special notice, as the same idiom is found in Greek and Latin. This is the use of prepositions indicating *motion from* with verbs of *rest*.

1. Καθήμεθ᾽ ἄκρων ἐκ πάγων ὑπήνεμοι. (Soph. *Ant.* 411)
   " We sat on the topmost peaks under the wind."
2. *Gallia attingit ab Sequanis et Helvetiis flumen Rhenum.*
   (Caes. *B.G.* i. 1)
   " In the territory of the S. and H. Gaul borders on the Rhine."
3. *Erat e regione oppidi collis.* (Caes. *B.G.* vii. 36)
   " There was a hill opposite the town."

Of these far-fetched explanations have been given, as that of Jebb (on Soph. *Ant.* 411), but the explanation is simple as before : 1. " We sat being sheltered by the top of the hill " ; 2. " Gaul borders on the Rhine (stretching) from the country of . . ." ; 3. is more difficult: the *e* of *e regione* is metaphorical—" in accordance with (lit. proceeding from) a ruling," i.e. a ruled line, and the sentence means " The hill was in a straight line with the town ". Something, too, may be said for the suggestion that when we have *e regione* for " *in* the line of " it indicates the quarter from which the impression came from Caesar's scouts.

Similar to 3. are the uses in *a tergo, a laeva,* etc., and in the phrases expressing the function of a slave or official, e.g. *servus a rationibus, a libellis, ab epistolis*—as we might say " my right-hand man from the point of view of finance ", meaning " in financial matters ".

PREPOSITIONS AND THE DEVELOPMENT OF LANGUAGE

§ 100. Three main stages can be marked in the use of prepositions in an inflexional language.

I. We have seen how in the early language the case-endings are enough : prepositions are not needed.

II. As language became more precise, case-meanings were subdivided into more particular meanings by the addition of certain adverbs. As the language grows these prepositions are used more and more (even *de vino* for *vini* and *ad patrem* for *patri*).

III. The preposition absorbs all emphasis from the case-meaning, with the result that the case-endings become unimportant and, like some atrophied part in a living organism, gradually disappear : *vinum -i -o* becomes the Italian *vino* and the French *vin*, but the prepositions still live. (A similar development in the Romance languages is that by which the tense inflexions break down before the use of auxiliaries—*vidi eas* becomes *visas habeo*—French *je les ai vues*.)

PRONOUNS

The Article.

§ 101. Originally Greek, like Sanskrit and Latin, had no article either definite or indefinite. But, as in Sanskrit, certain words came to be used in such a way that they may be translated by " a " and " the ". So in Latin *ille, illa, unus,* etc., came to be used in such a way that they gave rise to the articles in modern Romance languages.

The article in Greek is strictly a **pronoun** (ἀντωνυμία), and was originally the Third Person pronoun.

Further it was used as a relative (i.e. referring back) and as a demonstrative pronoun.

§ 102. *The Homeric Article.*

(i) As a true pronoun, used especially at the beginning of a clause : often resumptive (i.e. picking up a thread from a previous clause) : often marking a contrast.

1. Αὐτῷ γὰρ ἑκάεργος Ἀγήνορι πάντα ἐοικὼς
ἔστη πρόσθε ποδῶν· ὁ δ' ἐπέσσυτο ποσσὶ διώκειν.
(*Il.* xxi. 600)
" For the far-darter in all the likeness of Agenor stood before his feet : and *he* hasted to pursue . . ."

2. Σύν τε δύ' ἐρχομένω, καί τε πρὸ ὃ τοῦ ἐνόησεν. (*Il.* x. 224)
" When two go together, the one sees before the other."

3. Τὴν δ' ἐγὼ οὐ λύσω. (*Il.* i. 29)
" But her I will not let go."

(ii) As pronoun with nominative in apposition :

Ὁ δ' ἔβραχε χάλκεος Ἄρης. (*Il.* v. 859)
" But he, bronzen Ares, shouted . . ."

Here we can see the process by which the use of the

ordinary definite article was developed—ὁ Ἄρης = Ares. But in Homeric usage, as in Latin, nouns stand without the article, which serves as a *joint* (which is what the Greeks called it—ἄρθρον).

(iii) Used to point a contrast:
Ὥστε λέων ἐφόβησε . . .
πάσας· τῇ δ' ἰῇ ἀναφαίνεται αἰπὺς ὄλεθρος.
(*Il.* xi. 174)
"(Cows) the lion affrights all, but to one is doom revealed."

(iv) As a demonstrative adjective:
1. Ὁ μολοβρός. (*Od.* xviii. 26)
"That glutton!"
Τὴν ὀλοήν. (*Od.* xii. 113)
"That curse!"
2. Ποῖον τὸν μῦθον ἔειπες; (*Il.* i. 552)
"What is this word that thou hast spoken?"

(v) As relative pronoun, i.e. its use when later Greek would have used a relative pronoun. Strictly Homer has no relative pronoun, e.g.
. . . οὐλήν, τήν ποτέ μιν σῦς ἤλασε. (*Od.* xix. 393)
". . . a wound; a boar once gave it him."

For this parataxis see § 212.

§ 103. *Traces of Older Usage in Attic.*

(i) Article as Demonstrative Pronoun: especially with adversative particles as ὁ μέν . . . ὁ δέ . . .; in the phrase ἦ δ' ὅς = "said he" (ὅς is an older form of ὁ); in phrases like ἐν τοῖς πρῶτοι (Thuc. i. 6) with superlatives (possibly due to an ellipse, for ἐν τοῖς πρώτοις πρῶτοι), and in πρὸ τοῦ = "before this", "in old times".

1. Ἔδει γὰρ τὸ καὶ τὸ ποιῆσαι καὶ τὸ μὴ ποιῆσαι.
(Dem. ix. 68)
"This and that should have been done, and not so-and-so."
2. Ἰνάρως Ἀθηναίους ἐπηγάγετο· οἱ δὲ ἦλθον.
(Thuc. i. 104)
"Inaros appealed to the Athenians, and they came."

PRONOUNS

3. Καὶ τὸν κελεῦσαι δοῦναι (λέγεται).   (X. *Cyr.* i. 3. 9)
"And it is said that he ordered him to give . . ."

(ii) Article as Relative Pronoun : only in the tragedians.

. . . διπλῇ μάστιγι τὴν Ἄρης φιλεῖ.   (Aesch. *Ag.* 642)
". . . with the double scourge which Ares loves."

§ 104. *The Article in Attic.*

The following are interesting and familiar uses :

(i) Generally the article denotes something known and definite whether individuals or classes :

ὁ Σωκράτης = " our old friend Socrates ".
οἱ σοφοί = " the wise ".

(ii) It is used with possessive and demonstrative adjectives : ἐκεῖνος ὁ τόπος = " that there " place.

(iii) Instead of a possessive adjective : ἔλαβον τῆς ζώνης τὸν Ὀρόντην = (as we say) " they took O. by the belt " (X. *An.* i. 6. 10).

(iv) N.B.—The Predicate does *not* take the article, where the subject does : if the subject is defined it is unnecessary for the predicate to be defined again.

§ 105. *Idioms of the Article* to be noted :

(i) It is used before phrases to make them substantival, especially with infinitive, participle, adjective, adverb (τὸ ἀδικεῖν, τὸ προσῆκον, τὸ ἀγαθόν, τανῦν) : also to mark a word or phrase *quoted* (τὸ ἄλφα, Plat. *Crat.* 405 c) : this article hangs up inverted commas round its word (just as it may in English).

1. Ὑμεῖς, ὦ ἄνδρες Ἀθηναῖοι—τὸ δ' ὑμεῖς ὅταν εἴπω τὴν πόλιν λέγω.   (Dem. xxv. 54)
"You, gentlemen . . . and by ' you ' I mean the city."

2. Ὑπερέβη τὸ καὶ ἐὰν ἁλῷ φόνου.   (Dem. xxiii. 220)
"He has passed over the clause 'if he be convicted of manslaughter '."

(ii) With numerals : marking a definite whole or a definite part within a whole ; cp. Thuc. i. 10 τὰ δύο μέρη, " two-thirds ".

Τῶν πασῶν τριήρων τὰς διακοσίας ἡ πόλις παρέσχετο.

(iii) With the nominative to call someone familiarly :

Ὁ Ἀπολλόδωρος οὗτος, οὐ περιμενεῖς; (Plat. *Symp.* 172 A)
" Hi ! Apollodorus, won't you wait ? " Cp. Ar. *Ran.* 40

(iv) With ποῖος, πόσος, τί when the object of the question has already been mentioned :

Λέγεις δὲ τὴν ποίαν κατάστασιν . . . ; (Plat. *Rep.* 550 c)
" What's that constitution . . . ? "

Also with personal pronouns, for emphasis (accusative only), τὸν ἐμέ (Plato) :

Δεῦρο δὴ εὐθὺ ἡμῶν . . . παρὰ τίνας τοὺς ὑμᾶς;
(Plat. *Lys.* 203 B)
". . . to the you being whom ? " (lit.)

(v) The article in ironic emphasis :

Σὲ τὴν σκυθρωπὸν καὶ πόσει θυμουμένην
Μήδειαν εἶπον τῆσδε γῆς ἔξω περᾶν. (Eur. *Med.* 271)
" You the sullen, the husband-hater Medea,
I bid leave this land."

§ 106. (vi) *Omission of article* : this is common with familiar places, persons, things, i.e. which, being everyday expressions, have become so well known that they achieve the status of Proper Names (cp. our provincial " going up town ", " down street " ; also " on 'Change ", " Town " = London).

So we have ἔξω Ἰσθμοῦ, πρὸς ἄστυ (" to Athens "), familiar places ; βασιλεύς (= the Persian king), πρυτάνεις (Presidents of the Council), everyday expressions ; so with common phrases ἐπὶ δόρυ (" to the right "), ἐξ ἀριστερᾶς, ἅμ' ἡμέρᾳ.

N.B.—We also find the article *used* with such phrases, and with geographical names its use is particularly fluctuating. Thus we find in Thucydides :

1. Πίνδος ὄρος : τὸ ὄρος ἡ Ἰστώνη : τὸ ὄρος τῆς Ἰστώνης.
2. Ἅλυς ποταμός : ὁ ποταμὸς ὁ Εὐφράτης.

Also we find the article omitted in compound phrases, with a resultant gain in emphasis, e.g.

Οὔτε πατρὸς οὔτε μητρὸς φείδεται. (Plat. *Phil.* 15 E)
" He spares neither mother nor father."

PRONOUNS

(The article is omitted with θεός for divinity in general: ὁ θεός refers to a particular god.)

§ 107. (vii) Meaning is greatly affected by the *order* in which article and adjective occur; an adjective or qualifying phrase standing between the noun and its article is *attributive*: ἡ καλὴ πόλις, ἡ τῶν 'Αθηναίων πόλις: but τῶν 'Αθηναίων ἡ πόλις = "the city belongs to the A.".

When the attributive adjective follows the noun it takes another article: τὸ τεῖχος περιεῖλον τὸ καινόν (Thuc. iv. 51), "they threw down the wall—I mean the new one", where the attribute is added as an afterthought.

An adjective or qualifying phrase, without the article, standing after the noun, or outside the noun and its article, is *predicative*:

1. Τοὺς δε λόγους μακροτέρους μηκυνοῦμεν. (Thuc. iv. 17)
   "We shall extend our speeches to greater length."
2. . . . ψιλὴν ἔχων τὴν κεφαλήν. (X. *An.* i. 8. 6)
   ". . . with his head bare."

Notice how the position of the article affects the following phrases:

ἡ μέση πόλις = "the central city".
μέση ἡ πόλις = "the centre of the city" (or "the city is central").

Latin has *urbs media* for both.

ὁ αὐτὸς ἀνήρ = *idem vir*.
αὐτὸς ὁ ἀνήρ = *ipse vir*.
ὁ πᾶς χρόνος = "eternity" (Plat. *Ap.* 40 E).
πᾶς ὁ χρόνος = "all the time (a given period)".

§ 108. There is not much in the usage of **Pronouns proper** that need concern us here, but the following peculiarities are to be noticed.

Greek.

(i) The use of the Third Person reflexive for First and Second Persons:

1. Δεῖ ἡμᾶς ἀνερέσθαι ἑαυτούς . . . (Plat. *Phaed.* 78 B)
   "We must ask ourselves . . ."

2. Εἰ δ' ἐτητύμως
μόρον τὸν αὐτῆς οἶσθα . . .   (Aesch. *Ag.* 1296)
"But if truly thou knowest thine own doom . . ."

Also for the Reciprocal ἀλλήλους :

Βούλεσθε περιιόντες αὐτῶν πυνθάνεσθαι;   (Dem. iv. 10)
"Do you want to be running about and inquiring one of another ? "

Cp. St. Luke xxiii. 12 : "For before they were at enmity between themselves ".

(ii) An apparent anomaly of agreement in Plato's use of αὐτό, even with masculines and feminines, to denote the abstract idea of a thing :

Οὐκ αὐτὸ δικαιοσύνην ἐπαινοῦντες . . .
(Plat. *Rep.* 363 A)
"Praising not (the thing) Justice itself . . ."

Latin.

§ 109. (i) Extended use of reflexives, *se, suus.*

1. *Nunc, si ille huc salvos revenit, reddam suom sibi.*
(Plaut. *Tri.* 156)
"Now, if he comes back safe, I will restore his property to him."

2. *Id multos patrum, ipsos possessores, periculo rerum suarum terrebat.*   (Liv. ii. 41)
"That frightened many senators, themselves property-owners, by reason of the danger to their own property."

3. *A Caesare valde liberaliter invitor, sibi ut sim legatus.*
(Cic. *Att.* ii. 18)
"Caesar very generously suggests that I should join his staff."

Generally this use of reflexives is not found where there would be ambiguity. In the first two examples *suus* has taken on the meaning of *proprius* ; the first incorporates the everyday slogan "*suum sibi*"; in the other two examples the reflexives refer to the *logical*, though not the grammatical, subject of the sentence : "The senators were frightened, feared . . .", "Caesar asks me . . .".

PRONOUNS

§ 110. (ii) *Eum*, etc., instead of *se* :

> *An, quod a sociis eorum non abstinuerim, iustam querelam habent ?* (Liv. xxxii. 34)
>
> "Have they a justifiable plea in that I did not keep my hands off their allies ?"

In some places (e.g. Caes. *B.G.* i. 5) this is done to avoid ambiguity.

§ 111. (iii) *Se, suus* are found referring to a subject unexpressed :

> *Honestius est alienis iniuriis quam re sua commoveri.*
> (Cic. *Verr.* iii. 72)
>
> "It is finer to be stirred by another's wrongs rather than by one's own troubles."

Here, again, *suus* is used in the sense of *proprius* ; *suus* has, strictly, an individual reference ; its use here is in a way like saying "One should be stirred by another's troubles, not by his own " (as if the sentence had begun, " A man . . .").

VERBS
THE VOICES

§ 112. Originally there were two voices (διαθέσεις), Active (ἐνέργεια) and Middle (μεσότης), which were distinguished by inflection. So they remain in Sanskrit and Greek. The Passive (πάθος) was originally one of the uses of the Middle voice, though the Greeks did not recognize this, for they put the Middle, as the name shows, halfway between Active and Passive. In Latin the significance of the Passive and Middle is reversed : the Passive forms are rarely used in a Middle sense, but many of the deponents, Passive in inflexional form, are Middle in origin, e.g. *potior, utor*.

§ 113. THE ACTIVE VOICE (ὀρθὰ ῥήματα just as the Nominative case is the ὀρθὴ πτῶσις from which the others deviate) denotes that the action starts from the subject of the verb, e.g. " I hit " as opposed to " I am hit ". Active verbs are either

(i) **Transitive** (the Sanskrit for " Active " means " transitive ")—the name means that their action *goes over* to an object, i.e. they require, for their meaning to be complete, the addition of an object which the meaning presupposes, e.g. the statement " I found " inevitably raises first the question " Found what ? "—or

(ii) **Intransitive**—the name means that the action need *not* go over beyond the subject, i.e. they do not require an object, e.g. " I run ".

Sometimes an active verb may bear both transitive and intransitive meanings, e.g. πράσσω (trans. " I do ", intrans. καλῶς πράσσω, " I fare well "), ἐλαύνω (" I drive " or " I ride "), *ruo* (" I knock down " or " I rush "), *moveo* (" I move " both trans. and intrans.) ; so " break ", " turn ", " melt ", etc., still more commonly in English.

VERBS

§ 114. THE MIDDLE VOICE ("Reflexive" in Sanskrit) represents the subject as acting for or on self, i.e. more generally as affected by its own action. The following usages may be distinguished as common to Sanskrit, Greek and, to a small extent, Latin :

(i) **The Direct Reflexive**, where the subject is the direct object of the action of the verb, e.g. λούομαι, lavor, "I wash myself", "I bathe".

(ii) **The Indirect Reflexive**, where the subject is the indirect object of the verbal action, e.g. πορίζομαι χρήματα, "I get myself money"; purgor bilem, "I rid myself of bile".

(iii) **The Causative**, often very near (ii) : παρατίθεμαι δεῖπνον, "I have myself served a meal" (make others serve it for me); tondeor, "I have my hair cut".

(iv) **The Reciprocal** : each agent acts for himself and the action is reciprocal, e.g. ἀμειβόμενος, "taking my turn" (there is no Latin equivalent).

(v) **The Intransitive**, where the idea of self is so blurred that the Middle merely gives a slightly different meaning to the active, e.g. ἀγάλλω, "I adorn"; ἀγάλλομαι, "I pride myself"; often the self-meaning is faint : οἴομαι, "I think"; morior, "I die".

And we may add (vi) **The Passive** use: φιλοῦμαι, amor, "I am loved".

§ 115. THE PASSIVE VOICE denotes that the subject receives the action of the verb. As has been said, the Passive was originally one of the uses of the Middle. In Greek the "passive" voice consists to a large degree of certain tenses of the middle. The present, imperfect, perfect, and occasionally the future, middle are found in a passive meaning, e.g. ἀδικήσομαι, "I shall be wronged"; διδάξομαι, "I shall be taught" (διδάξω καὶ διδάξομαι λόγους, Eur. Andr. 739). The aorists in -ην and -θην, with their corresponding futures in -ήσομαι, -θήσομαι, are the only purely passive forms of the Greek verb ; and it should be noted that the person-endings of these aorists are active in form. The reason for this is probably that the passive sense has developed out of the intransitive use of certain stems. In Homer we have ἐχάρη, "he rejoiced"; and many aorists in -ην which are all intransitive in meaning.

The nearness of the passive to the intransitive may be seen from the existence side by side of ἀπέθανεν ὑπ' αὐτοῦ and ἐσφάγη ὑπ' αὐτοῦ for " he was killed by him " ; similarly Ovid can write *ne vir ab hoste cadat*. There was then probably a time in the prehistory of these languages when the work later done by the passive voice was performed by the active use of intransitive verbs, constructed, e.g., with instrumentals of cause, e.g. Πηλεΐωνι δαμείς (strictly an active form), " having fallen at the hands of the son of Peleus ", the dative supplying the attendant circumstances and cause of the action or, alternatively, the person for whom the action is said to exist. Other examples of active intransitive verbs commonly used as passives are φεύγω, ἐκπίπτω, εὖ πάσχω (" I am treated well "), *pereo, veneo*.

§ 116. In Latin, too, the passive grew out of the middle voice, but superseded it, and passive forms used in a middle sense are rare and poetical (see § 36), e.g. *tunicaque inducitur artus*, " he clothes his limbs ". Latin deponents are verbs which have abandoned their active forms and remain as a combination of passive and middle. This is indicated by the fact that in early Latin there existed in many instances active forms of verbs later known as deponents, e.g. there was *imito* side by side with *imitor*, *assentio* and *assentior*, *vago* and *vagor* ; and other deponents have in early Latin active forms with transitive meanings, e.g. *potior* had *compotio*. Further, the present and future participles of active form, e.g. *hortans, hortaturus*, point to the existence of an earlier active form. In classical times the past participle of deponents often, and gerundives always, appear in a passive meaning.

TENSE-MEANINGS

§ 117. The tense-stem indicates the time to which an action is assigned. Tenses may be classified in two ways :

I. With reference to *Time-Order*—Is it past, present or future ?

II. With reference to the *Kind of Action*—Is it incomplete, complete or expressing state of subject ?

§ 118. I. In some sentences the time is absolute, i.e. it has no relation to any definite moment of time, as e.g. in

"Honesty is the best policy", where "is" is the merest copula or link and stands for the timeless = of mathematics. Usually the time is relative, e.g. when I say "I am looking", "I have looked" or "I will look", I am using these tenses in reference to the time of speaking. But, again, an event may be present, past or future in reference to some point in past time, e.g. "I was looking", "I had looked", "I shall have looked". Sometimes the verb is relative not to the time of speaking but to the time of another verb in the sentence; e.g. if I say ὁρᾷ, then ὁρᾷ is relative to the time of my saying it, but if I say εἶπον ὅτι ὁρᾷ, ὁρᾷ is relative to the time of εἶπον as a past event. In Latin and Greek, as in Sanskrit, there are different tenses to express present, past and future in reference to the present time of speaking, but not to express all the relations of present, past and future to the time of other verbs in the sentence. These other relations if needed to be expressed with precision (which is not often) have to be expressed periphrastically.

§ 119. II. Besides expressing the time of an action, the tense-stems, e.g. λυ-, λυσ-, λυσα-, λελυ-, also express its character. Thus the present indicates an action now in progress, the perfect an action now completed, the aorist a momentary action: these distinctions may be expressed by these tense-stems, theoretically, in any mood.

§ 120. *The Ideal Requirements.*

Type	Past	Present	Future
Progressive	I was doing ἐποίουν *faciebam*	I am doing ποιῶ *facio*	I shall be doing ποιήσω *faciam*
Completed	I had done ἐπεποιήκη *feceram*	I have done πεποίηκα *feci*	I shall have done πεποιηκὼς ἔσομαι *fecero*
Indefinite	I did ἐποίησα *feci*	I do ποιῶ *facio*	I shall do ποιήσω *faciam*

In English, as in French, etc., we can by using auxiliaries express all these shades of time. In Latin and Greek usually the context will indicate the time with sufficient precision : ποιῶ, *facio* stand both for "I do" and "I am doing". In considering Greek we shall find differences in Kind of Act (II) rather more stressed than mere Time (I), whereas in Latin Time distinction (I) seems to be more important.

§ 121. **The Present Tense** (ὁ ἐνεστὼς παρατατικός or ἀτελὴς χρόνος—"present continuous") represents an action as *going on* at the time of speaking or writing : γράφω, *scribo* (I am writing). Latin and Greek have no separate form for the aorist present (i.e. a single act expressed as a mere act without limitation of continuance or completion) ; but as there are many ways of forming the present stem we may ask whether different formations had not originally different meanings, i.e. one form expressing the "I am doing" type, another the "I do" type. See King and Cookson, *Comparative Grammar*, pp. 129, 149, 189; so Sanskrit, *ibid.* p. 189.

Noteworthy uses of the Present :

§ 122. (i) Present of *Customary Action*, or general truth ; thus invariably used in English, e.g. "A rolling stone gathers no moss". So in Greek and Latin : τίκτει τοι κόρος ὕβριν, *fortes fortuna iuvat*.

(ii) *Conative* Present (Greek) denotes the continuance of an action without reference to its completion ; esp. with δίδωμι in the sense "I offer".

1. Νῦν δ' ἅμα τ' αὐτίκα πολλὰ διδοῖ. (Hom. *Il.* ix. 519)
   "And now straightway he offers many gifts at the same time . . ."
2. Πείθουσιν ὑμᾶς ἐναντία . . . τοῖς νόμοις . . . ψηφίσασθαι. (Isaeus i. 26)
   "They are trying to persuade you to vote contrary to the laws."

§ 123. (iii) Present of *Action continued from the Past*: present used with expressions denoting past time as a sort of present and perfect combined ; this is usual in Greek and Latin, but in English we say "I have been looking . . ."

VERBS

1. Κεῖνον ἰχνεύω πάλαι. (Soph. *Aj.* 20)
"I have been tracking (and still am tracking) him for a long time."

2. *Tibin' umquam quicquam postquam tuus sum verborum dedi ?* (Plaut. *Most.* 925)
"Have I ever cheeked you since I have been your slave ?"

§ 124. (iv) The *Historic* Present: when the time of the action is really past in relation to the time of writing, still the writer imagines it to be present; in some cases it may be called the *Annalistic* Present. (Sanskrit—M. 212.)

1. Βουλὴν ἐπιτεχνᾶται ὅπως μὴ ἁλισθεῖεν Ἀθηναῖοι.
(Hdt. i. 63)
"He schemes to prevent the Athenians from rallying."

2. *Disputatur in consilio : plerique censebant . . .*
(Caes. *B.C.* i. 67)
"It is discussed in council : most were of the opinion . . ."

N.B. the sequence in 1. because ἐπιτεχνᾶται is in meaning historic. This is the present regularly used with *dum* clauses. Cp. Ex. 1, § 79, which may be called a *tabular* present—we say, tracing a family table, " J. marries A.", as for our purposes the action is a present factor.

§ 125. (v) Present in *Future sense*: used graphically, where strictly a future is required, to express danger, strong intention, etc. (Sanskrit—M. 212.)

1. Εἰ αὕτη ἡ πόλις ληφθήσεται, ἔχεται ἡ πᾶσα Σικελία.
(Thuc. vi. 91)
"If Syracuse can be taken, all Sicily is in our hands."

2. *Itaque ni propere fit quod impero vinciri vos iam iubebo.*
(Liv. xxxvi. 28)
"If my orders are not quickly carried out, I shall have you at once imprisoned."

This is a very common English idiom, English being notoriously slack in point of tense accuracy.

In Greek εἶμι was commonly used as a future and was in Attic regularly used instead of ἐλεύσομαι as a future of ἔρχομαι. (Similarly other verbs, e.g. ἥκω, οἴχομαι, ἁλίσκομαι, acquired perfect meanings.)

§ 126. (vi) Sometimes, especially in poetry, the Present is used of an act which is past but which has a *permanent result* in the present : e.g. ἡ τίκτουσα = " the mother ", οἱ φεύγοντες = " exiles ", ἀδικῶ = " I am a criminal ", νικῶ = " I am victor " ; so in Latin we have *auctore Phoebo gignor* (Sen. *Ag.* 295), " I am a son of Phoebus ", and *salibus vincimus* (Quint. x. 107), " we are superior in wit " ; in some lines in Virgil a historic present suggests this use : e.g.

Hoc erat, alma parens, quod me per tela, per ignis Eripis? (V. *Aen.* ii. 664)

" Was it for this you are my deliverer through fire and sword . . . ? "

§ 127. **The Imperfect Tense** (παρῳχημένος παρατατικός or ἀτελής) represents an action as *going on in past time*, and retains most of the peculiarities of the present. It may represent an action as customary or attempted : further, where the present is used as a perfect (iii), the imperfect is used as a pluperfect. In narrative it shows an action not as an event but as in process of happening : it dwells upon the incident as though painting a picture, where the aorist hurries on.

In Sanskrit (M. 213) it was the regular tense of narration, and there are traces of such a use in Greek, e.g.

Εἰσιόντες οὖν κατελαμβάνομεν τὸν Σωκράτη ἄρτι λελυ-
μένον. (Plat. *Phaed.* 60 A)

" Well, we went in and found S. just freed from his chains",

where " were finding " is pointless. So too πῶς ἐτελεύτα ; " How did he die ? " (*ibid.* 57 A) and ἔπεμπον, ἐκέλευον in the historians.

§ 128. (i) The *Incipient* Imperfect : i.e. the action is begun but remains imperfect.

The ordinary use of the imperfect (e.g. " I was walking ") and the incipient use are complementary halves of the whole duty of the imperfect. The ordinary use expresses an action the beginning of which is blurred but which, at the time of speaking, is definitely regarded as past ; the incipient use

VERBS

shows an action whose beginning is clear-cut ("I began to walk"), but which has its other end trailing off indefinitely.

The Ordinary Imperf. . . . . ─────────
I was walking (and now it's all over).

The Incipient Imperf. ───────────── . . . .
I began to walk (and I say no more than that . . .).

Risu omnes emoriri; denique metuebant omnes iam me.
(Ter. *Eun.* 433)
"They all killed themselves with laughing; then they all began to be afraid of me."

§ 129. (ii) *Conative* Imperfect: as in the Incipient use here too the action is begun but left unfinished; but there is an added idea of deliberation—"I was trying to walk".

1. Ἐμισθοῦτο παρ' οὐκ ἐκδιδόντος τὴν αὐλήν. (Hdt. i. 68)
"He tried to hire the yard from one who would not let it."

2. *Consules incerti . . . sedabant tumultus, sedando interdum movebant.* (Liv. iii. 15)
"The consuls doubtful . . . tried to assuage the disturbance, but at times their very efforts stirred it up."

§ 130. (iii) Imperfect of *Fact just recognized*: a fact is stated which was previously unknown, e.g. "Then it was you after all!" (Compare Present use (iii).) Here, though the fact recognized is usually true of the present time, the speaker stresses the fact that it *was* so while he was ignorant of it. *Tempus erat* = " it is, and has long been, time . . ."

1. Ὦ πόποι, οὐκ ἄρα πάντα νοήμονες οὐδὲ δίκαιοι
ἦσαν Φαίηκες . . . (Hom. *Od.* xiii. 209)
"Out upon it, then not wholly wise and just were (are) the Phaeacians."

2. *Tempus erat iam te, Sosibiane, legi.* (Mart. iv. 33)
"It is high time you were read, S."

§ 131. (iv) *Philosophic* Imperfect (so called) expresses the conclusion of an earlier discussion which is still valid (Greek only).

> Ἦν ἡ μουσικὴ ἀντίστροφος τῆς γυμναστικῆς, εἰ μέμνησαι.
> (Plat. *Rep.* 522 A)
> "Music then, as we found, if you remember, corresponds to gymnastic."

§ 132. (v) *Epistolary* Imperfect is used in Latin, i.e. a man writing to a friend says "I was hoping you were well" because his hoping will be a past action to his correspondent when reading it. It is usually found at the beginning and end of the letter, to mark the time; it would be over-formal and perhaps stilted to write a letter wholly in the past tense.

> *Nihil habebam quod scriberem.* (Cic. *Att.* ix. 10. 1)
> "I've nothing to write about."

§ 133. The Future Tense (μέλλων) denotes that an action is to take place in time to come, whether the action is to be complete or incomplete. The tense has elements other than that of mere time, i.e. of purpose. Ἥκει εὑρήσων may mean (1) "He has come (in order) to find out" or (2) "He has come—so that he will find out", if the speaker's view is involved. Which was the original use of the future is in doubt. The future, being so dependent upon mental attitude, is rather a mood than a tense, and must be considered closely with the Subjunctive.

The Future has uses similar to that of the Present (i) in general truths (e.g. "He who fights and runs away, Will live to fight another day"), and of the Imperfect (iv) in expressing something which will hereafter be proved true.

§ 134. N.B.—*Future of Command.* Here the person giving the command confidently expresses it as a future fact: "You will do nothing of the sort", "Company will parade . . .", "Thou shalt not kill". (So Sanskrit—M. 214.)

> 1. Πρὸς ταῦτα πράξεις οἷον ἂν θέλῃς. (Soph. *O.C.* 956)
> ". . . Do just as you please."
>
> 2. Λέγ' εἴ τι βούλει, χειρὶ δ' οὐ ψαύσεις ποτε.
> (Eur. *Med.* 1320)
> ". . . Shalt never lay hands on me."

VERBS

3. *Si quid acciderit novi, facies ut sciam.*
(Cic. *Fam.* xiv. 8)
"If anything fresh happens, let me know."

Sometimes this future of command is found with negative μή, which is borrowed from the regular prohibition constructions.

Ταύτην, ἄν μοι χρῆσθε συμβούλῳ, φυλάξετε τὴν πίστιν
... καὶ μὴ βουλήσεσθε εἰδέναι ...
(Dem. xxiii. 117)
"If you follow my advice, hold on to this security and do not wish to know ..."

§ 135. The Perfect Tense (ἐνεστὼς συντελικός or παρακείμενος).

I. In Greek it represents an action as *finished at the present time, but with result continuing*: ὃ γέγραφα γέγραφα, says Pilate—"What I have written, I have written, and that's that": ἔγνωκα = "I have discovered and now know". Usually it is more accurate to use a present in English in translating a Greek perfect, e.g. τέθαπται, "he is buried" rather than "he has been buried". The perfect passive is more commonly found than the perfect active, the reason being that it is far more often necessary to indicate that the *subject* of *passive* action is still in an unchanged relation to the action than that the subject of the active action is.

In later Greek the perfect was sometimes used with less insistence on the completeness of the action, e.g.

Ἅ σοι τύχη κέχρηκε, ταῦτ' ἀφείλετο. (Men. fr. 598)
"Fortune has taken back what she lent to you."

§ 136. II. In Latin the perfect represents an action done in past time. As contrasted with the imperfect, it denotes, like the Greek aorist, a single act—*veni, vidi, vici*; as opposed to the present it denotes that the action is already completed — Cicero's *vixerunt* meant "they are dead". Usually it is the equivalent of the Greek aorist.

Noteworthy uses of the *Perfect*:

§ 137. (i) *Gnomic*: in generalizations:

Πολλοὶ διὰ δόξαν καὶ πολιτικὴν δύναμιν μεγάλα κακὰ
πεπόνθασιν. (X. *Mem.* iv. 2. 35)

The idea is "Up to the present many have suffered and many do suffer . . ."

For Latin examples see Gnomic Aorist (§ 143).

§ 138. (ii) *Periphrastic* Perfects are formed from the *active* aorist participle and ἔχω; similarly with *habeo* and the past participle passive in Latin (which produced the auxiliary tenses of the Romance languages; cp. our "For mine eyes have seen . . .", which means *literally* that the eyes *have* the object-which-is-seen).

1. . . . Ἑλλήνων τοὺς σὺ δουλώσας ἔχεις.   (Hdt. i. 27)
 ". . . whom you hold in slavery."

2. *Perfidiam Haeduorum perspectam habebat.*
(Caes. *B.G.* vii. 54)
i.e. "got their treachery all weighed-up."

This form has a slightly stronger effect than the ordinary tense: δουλώσας ἔχεις means "you have enslaved and keep enslaved", *perspectam habebat* means something like our slang "got it taped".

Compare perhaps the use of ἔχω with adverbs: καλῶς ἔχω = "I am in a good condition"; τελέσας ἔχω = "I am in a having-finished condition".

§ 139. The Pluperfect Tense (παρῳχημένος συντελικός or ὑπερσυντελικός) represents an action as finished at a given *past* time. In Greek its use is comparatively infrequent: ἐγεγράφειν, "I had written and my writing was finished at that time".

"When I had seen, I went away"—Latin says *ubi videram abii*, where Greek would say ἐπεὶ εἶδον, ἀπῆλθον. The Greek mind found it unnecessary to draw such a distinction.

§ 140. The Future Perfect Tense. In Greek the future perfect is rare (there is no distinctive inflexion for the future perfect active); in Latin it is regularly used to represent an action as complete in the future as contrasted with another future action: *ubi viderit ridebit,* "He will laugh when he sees . . ."; Greek would say ὅταν ἴδῃ γελάσεται. So, too, Greek can say ἂν τοῦτο νικῶμεν, πάνθ' ἡμῖν πεποίηται (X. *An.* i. 8. 11) for "If we win this battle, we (shall) have achieved everything". (Cp. § 125.)

§ 141. **The Aorist Tense.** The Aorist in Greek expresses the single occurrence of an action in past time, unlimited (ἀόριστον) in reference to completeness, continuance, etc. For this Latin uses the perfect. But the Greek aorist lays more stress on the singleness of the action than on its pastness: ἐσίγησα = " I ' shut up ' " (whereas ἐσίγων = " I was holding my tongue ").

Even where the action is recent and has effects reaching into the present Greek uses the Aorist where English has a Perfect: Νῦν δ' ἐνθάδε κάββαλε δαίμων (Hom. *Od.* v. 172). " Now has a god cast me up here ". (Cp. Sanskrit—M. 213.)

So, too, when the action occurred but a moment ago: πῶς ἔλεξας; "what do you mean?" This is sometimes called

§ 142. (i) The *Dramatic* Aorist:

1. Ἐδεξάμην τὸ ῥηθέν.   (Soph. *Phil.* 1314)
   i.e. "I received your word a moment ago when you said it in the last line."
2. Πῶς τοῦτ' ἔλεξας; οὐ κάτοιδ' ὅπως λέγεις.
   (Soph. *Aj.* 270)
3. Ἐπῄνεσ' ἔργον.   (*ibid.* 536)

§ 143. (ii) The *Gnomic* Aorist:

1. Κάτθαν' ὁμῶς ὅ τ' ἀεργὸς ἀνὴρ ὅ τε πολλὰ ἐοργώς.
   (Hom. *Il.* ix. 320)
   "They die alike, the man of no works and he who has wrought many works."
2. Ὅταν τις ὥσπερ οὗτος ἰσχύσῃ, ἡ πρώτη πρόφασις . . . ἅπαντα ἀνεχαίτισε.   (Dem. ii. 9)
   "When a man achieves power as he has, the slightest cause overthrows it all."

A likely explanation is that suggested by the English parallel " Faint heart ne'er won fair lady ", i.e. the notion that a certain thing *has* always turned out thus and always *does* turn out, the basis of the generalization being the observed instances in the past; so in Greek we find ἤδη, πολλάκις, οὔπω inserted. Cp. also our "Don't-Care was hanged".

Another view is that this aorist is a survival of the lost aorist-present. Common general truths are expressed, as in English and Latin, by the present: the gnomic aorist when used points to a single or sudden occurrence.

Latin sometimes copies the Greek use:

> *Omne tulit punctum qui miscuit utile dulci.*
> (Hor. *A.P.* 343)
> "He wins every vote who combines utility and pleasure." ("Full marks for him who . . .")

THE MOODS

§ 144. The mood of a verb shows the manner in which its message is given. The Greek term is ἔγκλισις = inclination.

The Greek verb has four moods, Latin three:

Greek	Latin
Indicative	Indicative
Subjunctive	Subjunctive
Optative	
Imperative	Imperative

Classical Sanskrit has no subjunctive (though it is found in Vedic, which is to classical Sanskrit as Homeric to classical Greek).

The Infinitive and Participle are not strictly moods, but are so closely related to the moods in various constructions (e.g. taking the same case and being modified, not qualified) that it is convenient to group them with the moods. The Infinitive is strictly a verbal noun, the Participle (as also the Latin gerundive and the Greek verbal in -τέος) a verbal adjective.

§ 145. *Note.*—We will now consider the syntax of each mood in turn. With each we must begin with simple independent sentences, for these must be the more primitive form of articulate expression, and from combinations of such simple sentences have developed the complex constructions of the mature language. Thus when in Homer we come across μή τι κακὸν ῥέξωσι as a main sentence in the sense "I fear they may do us some mischief", we must

VERBS 81

not attempt to explain it by saying that, e.g., φοβοῦμαι is left understood. That would be putting the cart before the horse: we should be explaining an early idiom by a later and making a complex sentence out of a simple. We must not suppose that moods have one meaning in main sentences and another in dependent clauses. Every mood had its own significance, and as time went on acquired in varying combinations varying shades of meaning. The indicative is the mood of simple fact, yet it comes to be used in final sentences and conditionals, etc.

§ 146. Homer is particularly valuable for the study of the growth of Greek syntax. There, as we shall see again and again, we find a wide use of the subjunctive and optative in independent sentences side by side with their use in dependent clauses. In Latin our knowledge of early language and growth is much smaller, as what must have been syntactically the most interesting stage of the language has left hardly any literature.

§ 147. The Indicative Mood (ὁριστική—" defining ", " pointing ") in all tenses, as the name implies, points to a plain fact (or asks a straightforward question which concerns such a fact). In Greek the historic tenses of the Indicative are used to express past wishes, past purposes, and in conditional clauses (even when unreal), the reason being that the subjunctive and optative make no distinction in their tenses between past and present in time.

§ 148. **The Subjunctive and Optative Moods**, their origin, development and significance have occasioned much controversy. The names (Subjunctive—ὑποτακτική, " subordinate "; Optative—εὐκτική, " wishing ") are no clue; the one name tells us nothing, the other less than half the truth. (For the use of ἄν and κεν with these moods see §§ 277 ff.)

The following seems to be the simplest account.

They both represent an action as *not a fact, but an idea*, e.g. as something that is *possible* or *likely* or *desired*.

The optative is roughly a *remoter* form of the subjunctive; where the subjunctive says " I may ", the optative says " I might ".

From this basic principle we may note the following uses:

§ 149. (i) In Homer the subjunctive appears to be used to express mere *futurity*:

    1. Καί ποτέ τις εἴπῃσι . . . (*Il.* vi. 459)
    "And thus will a man say . . ."
    2. Οὐ γάρ πω τοίους ἴδον ἀνέρας, οὐδὲ ἴδωμαι.
    (*Il.* i. 262)
    "Never yet have I seen such men, nor shall I see."

Here the only possible meanings for οὐδὲ ἴδωμαι are "I shall not see" or "I *may not* (i.e. *cannot*) see". N.B. the negative is οὐ, not μή, i.e. there is no wish or desire about it. Nestor knows that it is impossible.

All examples of this future use of the subjunctive admit the sense of *possibility*.

    1. Ὑμῖν δ᾽ ἐν πάντεσσι περίκλυτα δῶρ᾽ ὀνομήνω.
    (*Il.* ix. 121)
    "In the midst of you I may mention the excellent gifts."
    2. Οὐκ ἔσθ᾽ οὗτος ἀνὴρ οὐδ᾽ ἔσσεται οὐδὲ γένηται.
    (*Od.* xvi. 437)
    ". . . is not, will never be, may never be . . ."

The subjunctive, then, as contrasted with the future indicative, expresses possibility rather than certain futurity. To this subjunctive of possibility the optative supplies a *remoter variant*. (Sanskrit—M. 216.)

    Οὐ μὴν γάρ τι κακώτερον ἄλλο πάθοιμι.
    (*Il.* xix. 321)
    "Nor might I suffer anything more evil." (See Monro, p. 273.)

This remoteness may well be derived from the idea of pastness in the optative which its terminations suggest; they are parallel with the terminations of the historic tenses of the indicative rather than with those of the primary. (See B. C. F. Atkinson, *The Greek Language*, p. 154.)

§ 150. This optative is similarly used in Homer to express—

(a) *Polite Command* (as in the English idiom):
    1. Ταῦτ᾽ εἴποις Ἀχιλῆϊ. (*Il.* xi. 791)
    "You might tell Achilles this."

VERBS 83

2. Ἀλλά τις ὀτρηρῶς Δολίον καλέσειε γέροντα . . .
(Od. iv. 735)
" Would some one make haste to call the ancient Dolius . . . ? "

(b) *Concession*: cp. " I might come . . .", " you may go " :

1. Αὐτάρ τοι καὶ κείνῳ ἐγὼ παραμυθησαίμην. (Il. xv. 45)
" I might even counsel him . . .", i.e. " I am willing . . ."

2. Κτήματα δ' αὐτὸς ἔχοις καὶ δώμασι σοῖσιν ἀνάσσοις.
(Od. i. 402)
" Thou mightest keep thy substance and rule thine own house."

N.B.—In Homer the **Present Optative** may be used to express a *present unfulfilled* idea, and the **Aorist Optative** to express a *past unfulfilled*.

§ 151. (ii) *The Jussive Subjunctive*: here the future contingency is perhaps voiced in a more confident tone—" you may go ".

Ἡμεῖς δὲ φραζώμεθ', ὅπως ὄχ' ἄριστα γένηται.
(Od. xxiii. 117)
" Let us bethink us how this may be best."

To this class belongs the subjunctive used in final clauses— " We do this that we *may* . . ."

§ 152. (iii) *The Deliberative Subjunctive*: " what am I to do ? " i.e. " what may I do ? " " what is there a chance of my doing ? " Here the possibility is questioned.

Εἴπωμεν ἢ σιγῶμεν ἢ τί δράσομεν;   (Eur. *Ion* 758)
" Are we to speak or keep silence, or what shall I do ? "

Further classes of Optative use (remoter possibility) are :

§ 153. (i) Of *Wish*: perhaps this originated in the possibility stated as a hopeful question, e.g. especially to a god, " Might I have . . .? " (Sanskrit—M. 216.)

Αὐτίκα τεθναίην.   (Hom. *Il.* xviii. 98)
" Straight may I die ! "

These wishes are almost invariably for the future. Often

this optative is supported by εἰ γάρ, εἴθε, which probably led on to its use in conditional sentences.

§ 154. (ii) *The Potential Optative* : this is the use typified by the example above: οὐ μὴν γάρ τι κακώτερον ἄλλο πάθοιμι, i.e. to express an action that might take place in the future under certain conditions. When these conditions are not expressed the sentence is called Potential.

In Attic this optative is regularly strengthened by the particle ἄν.

Δὶς ἐς τὸν αὐτὸν ποταμον οὐκ ἄν ἐμβαίης.
(Plat. *Crat.* 402 A)
" You could not step into the same river twice."

§ 155. (iii) In dependent clauses after an Historic main verb as a remoter expression of the subjunctive with a Primary verb.

Also in Reported Speech when the action is stated as an *idea* in the mind of the speaker (see § 148).

The various classes of use, Final, Deliberative, Temporal, etc., will be later considered in their several sections.

§ 156. The optative in historic subordinate clauses (Sanskrit—M. 216) developed from the use of optative in independent sentences. It is not hard to see how it may have developed. " When I came " indicates a definite event ; but " whenever I came " indicates a group of comings, a number of events which though as a group stated as a fact are individually vague and indefinite, and therefore liable to be considered rather as possibilities than as facts. So " whenever I came " becomes " whenever I might come ", and similarly " I asked who he was " becomes ". . . who he might be ".

In late Greek the optative tends to disappear into the subjunctive and it is absent from modern Greek.

§ 157. In Latin the subjunctive expresses possible or imagined facts along the same lines as the Greek subjunctive + optative. A great point of difference is that Latin tenses of the subjunctive can express past time. (In some constructions the work of the optative is done by the Latin imperfect and pluperfect subjunctive and in others by the present subjunctive.)

VERBS

These and other differences will appear in the consideration of various constructions.

§ 158. **The Imperative Mood** (προστακτική) is an interjectional mood, expressing an exclamation. It ranks among the moods as the vocative ranks among the cases. For this reason the infinitive, which represents the mere concept of the verb, is sometimes used instead of the imperative (see § 167). For a milder form of command the subjunctive, especially in Latin, is used, representing the command rather as a suggested possibility than as an assumed fact, as e.g. we say " You might lend me a hand ".

Latin prohibitions except where the roundabout *noli* and infinitive is used are put into the subjunctive. In Greek, by an idiomatic convention, prohibitions are expressed by the present imperative, but not the aorist imperative; whereas if the subjunctive is used in prohibition it is the aorist, not the present : μὴ λῦε or μὴ λύσῃς.

§ 159. An interesting imperative usage in colloquial Attic (in a dependent clause) is of the type :

  Ἀλλ' οἶσθ' ὃ δρᾶσον; (Ar. *Av.* 54)
  " Do you know what you must—Do it ! "

δρᾶσον means, e.g., χρὴ δρᾶσαι. A syntactical irregularity such as this might well be used to give the effect of abruptness, and is easily understood. Plautus attempts an imitation—*Tange sed scin' quomodo?* (*Rud.* 797).

§ 160. N.B.—Similarly an imperative used in a deliberative question—Τί οὖν ; ὃ πολλάκις ἐρωτῶ, κείσθω νόμος ὑμῖν; (Plat. *Legg.* 801 D)—" . . . shall it be laid down ? " (So Sanskrit—M. 215.)

§ 161. **The Infinitive** (ἀπαρέμφατος—" not determining ") forms are derived from substantives, chiefly from the dative of a primitive verbal noun. Its sense as the dative of abstract nouns survives, e.g. in the epexegetic construction : λεῖπε φορῆναι, ". . . leave for carrying"; *ibat videre feras* (Prop.), ". . . went for the sight of beasts". This origin came to be forgotten and in both Greek and Latin it became assimilated to the verb, governing accusatives like other moods. But it regularly serves as a noun (in

Greek with the article), used in the nominative, accusative, and frequently dative case.

§ 162. *Infinitive as Dative.* This is its normal use. The Greek infinitive is in form a dative, as in Sanskrit. The termination -αι (= the first declension ᾳ) is widespread among the tenses : there is, e.g., εἶναι, στῆναι, λύεσθαι, ἱστάναι, λύσεσθαι, λύσασθαι, λῦσαι, λυθῆναι, λυθήσεσθαι, λελυκέναι, λέλυσθαι, and in Homer there is εἰπεμέναι for εἰπεῖν, ἔμμεναι for present infinitive, so sometimes with future infinitive. The Latin infinitive is probably of the same origin. (Sanskrit uses an infinitive wherever a dative of purpose may be used—M. 211.)

The uses of the Infinitive as Dative (of Purpose, see § 53) may be classified as follows :

§ 163. *General Infinitive of Purpose.* This dative use is the dative of purpose explained above, § 53. In Greek it is commonly used after verbs denoting *send, appoint, select, give, take, bring,* and the like ; but not usually in prose after verbs of motion. In Latin the use is rare, but is found in early Latin and is a natural growth. (Sanskrit —M. 211.)

1. Χέρνιβα δ' ἀμφίπολος προχόῳ ἐπέχευε φέρουσα
   νίψασθαι.   (Hom. *Od.* i. 136)
   " And a handmaid brought water in a ewer and poured—for the washing."

2. Τοὺς ἱππέας παρείχοντο Πελοποννησίους ξυστρατεύειν.
                    (Thuc. ii. 12)
   " They provided P. cavalry to join in the expedition."

3. *Ecquis currit pollictorem arcessere ?*
                    (Plaut. *Asin.* 910)
   " Is anyone running to fetch the undertaker ? "

§ 164. After verbs of *wishing, beginning,* verbs denoting *ability, duty, purpose, custom,* etc., e.g. ἐθέλω λέγειν, *coepi ire,* δύναμαι ὁρᾶν, *soleo scribere.* That these infinitives are not accusative uses is indicated by the fact that the verbs enumerated are usually in themselves intransitive : δύναμαι ὁρᾶν = " I have power for a seeing " (though it is just possible that the inf. may represent an internal acc., cp. δύναμαι δύνασιν).

The Dative is that of Purpose (see § 53). (Sanskrit— M. 200 B.)

So too with verbs of *preventing*.

§ 165. After *Nouns and Adjectives*, denoting, e.g., fitness, ability, readiness, sufficiency, and those bearing such meanings as those verbs above mentioned. In Greek this use is as common as with verbs; with adjectives in Latin it is a rare variant on the gerund (cp. § 172).

1. Μαλακοὶ καρτερεῖν. (Plat. *Rep.* 556 B)
"Weak in endurance."
2. Δέδοικα μὴ εἰς ἀνάγκην ἔλθωμεν ποιεῖν . . .
(Dem. i. 15)
"I fear we may reach the necessity of doing . . ."
3. *Ornare pulvinar deorum tempus erat.* (Hor. *C.* i. 37. 3)
"It is time to honour the gods' couch."

§ 166. *Explanatory and Limiting Infinitives.* This is the use typified by the English "This house is very good, to look at", where the attached infinitive both explains the speaker's meaning and limits his approval of the house. This use is distinguished from that in (2) in being rather an adjunct to the sentence than an integral part of it. (Cp. § 210.)

In Greek this use is common especially in the simple phrases ὡς εἰπεῖν, ὡς ἔπος εἰπεῖν, ἐμοὶ δοκεῖν, as also in ὀλίγου δεῖν κτλ. In Latin it is uncommon, and mostly an imitation of the Greek usage, but cp. the predicative dative, § 54.

The infinitive here is similar to that of Purpose, e.g. αἰσχρὸν ὁρᾶν = " disgraceful—for the eyes to see ".

1. Αἰσχρὸν γὰρ τόδε γ᾽ ἐστὶ καὶ ἐσσομένοισι πυθέσθαι.
(Hom. *Il.* ii. 119)
"Shameful is this even for them that shall be hereafter to hear of." (". . . for the hearing.")
2. Χῶρος ὅδ᾽ ἱρός, ὡς ἀπεικάσαι. (Soph. *O.C.* 16)
"This ground is holy—at a guess."
3. Μικροῦ δεῖν ὅμοιόν ἐστι τῷ ὀνειδίζειν.
(Dem. xviii. 269)
"It is almost like abuse." ("for, i.e., at, a small deficit.")
4. *Loricam donat habere viro.* (V. *Aen.* v. 262)
"He gives the breastplate to the man to keep."

VERBS

§ 167. *Infinitive of Command.* Sometimes in Greek the infinitive is used in the sense of the second or third person of the imperative. (Similarly in Sanskrit.) The explanation seems to be that there is an ellipse, i.e. of some finite part of the verb "to be", e.g. Ex. 2 "You for a rushing out" (§ 163). Or perhaps it is rather that the verb is here used in an unresolved form ; cp. the French *que faire?* The effect is one of vagueness : the object of the speaker's wish is stated in an undetermined way with explicit relation to a person who is to carry it out.

1. Οἷς μὴ πελάζειν.   (Aesch. *P.V.* 712)
   "Approach them not." ("Keep away" is the word).

2. Ὑμεῖς δ', ὅταν καλῶμεν, ὁρμᾶσθαι ταχεῖς.
                                                            (Soph. *Phil.* 1080)
   "And you, when we call, come quickly."

§ 168. When the infinitive represents the third person imperative, its subject is put into the accusative : here the tone is more often that of a wish than of a command.

1. Εἰ δέ κ' Ἀλέξανδρον κτείνῃ ξανθὸς Μενέλαος,
   Τρῶας ἔπειθ' Ἑλένην καὶ κτήματα πάντ' ἀποδοῦναι.
                                                          (Hom. *Il.* iii. 284-5)
   "But if M. slays A., let the Trojans give back Helen and all her possessions."

2. Ζεῦ πάτερ, ἢ Αἴαντα λαχεῖν ἢ Τυδέος υἱόν.
                                                               (*ibid.* vii. 179)
   "Father Zeus, let the lot fall on Aias or on the son of Tydeus."

§ 169. *Exclamatory Infinitive*: this is somewhat similar to the last. Again there is some sort of ellipse apparently required to complete the sense ; though often thus used without the article, the frequent occurrence with the article shows that it represents an accusative of exclamation (which see, § 41).

Ἐμὲ παθεῖν τάδε (Aesch. *Eum.* 837) suggests the thought τὸ ἐμὲ παθεῖν τάδε δεινόν ἐστιν, but such a thought need not have been consciously implied in the writer's mind. Again it is rather the infinitive used as an unresolved verb-form as, e.g., *que faire !*

1. Ὡς δυστάλαινα, τοιάδ' ἄνδρα χρήσιμον φωνεῖν.
   (Soph. *Aj.* 410)
   " Ah ! unhappy me ! that a good man should say such things ! "

2. *Mene incepto desistere victam !* (V. *Aen.* i. 37)
   " Me ! leave my enterprise, thwarted ! " (French *Moi, quitter . . . !*)

N.B.—Generally the infinitive with the article may be used as a noun in any case corresponding to the use of the gerund and gerundive in Latin (cp., e.g., τοῦ + infinitive to express purpose ; see § 70).

§ 170. The *Historic Infinitive* in Latin shows the unresolved verb-form used for vividness : in his excitement, as it were, or to suggest excitement, the writer dashes down the mere idea of the verb without thinking out the exact form required by the sentence. The verb is left *infinite*, i.e. undefined, not finite. Quintilian's explanation—supposing an ellipse, e.g., of *coepit*—is unconvincing.

Verres minitari Diodoro, vociferari palam, lacrimas interdum vix tenere. (Cic. *Verr.* iv. 39)
(As Jingle might say) " V.—D.—throats—loud shouts —brink of tears."

Usually to give the appropriate staccato effect a string of historic infinitives is used.

§ 171. *Infinitive as Nominative* : this is very common.

1. Σωφρονεῖν καλόν. (Soph. *Aj.* 586)
   " Discretion is a virtue."

2. *Displicet philosophari.* (Cic. *Fin.* i. 1. 1)
   " Philosophizing is a bore."

§ 172. *Infinitive as Accusative* :

1. Ἔπειθεν αὐτὸν πορεύεσθαι. (X. *An.* vi. 2. 13)
   " He was trying to persuade him to go."

2. *Cato servire quam pugnare mavult.*
   (Cic. *Att.* vii. 15. 2
   " Cato prefers submission to fighting."

In 1. the verb has a double object : " he persuaded him,

he persuaded a going " (internal acc.) ; though it is possible that πορεύεσθαι is here used as a dative—" he persuaded him for a going ".

It is even used with prepositions, especially in Greek, which with its article can turn it into a *gerund*.

1. Ἀντὶ τοῦ πόλις εἶναι φρούριον κατέστη.
(Thuc. vii. 28)
" Instead of being a city it became a fort."

2. *Multum interest inter dare et accipere.*
(Sen. *Ben.* v. 10)
". . . between giving and receiving."

Out of this use of the infinitive developed the Accusative and Infinitive construction ; *puto te insanire* strictly contains a double object (see § 258).

§ 173. The Verbal Adjectives in -τέος and -τέον, Gerund and Gerundive.

(The Latin names, though not particularly apt, might equally be applied to the Greek : " gerund " = *gerundum* (*gerendum*), " that which is to be done ", a mere instance of the form ; in " gerundive " the addition of the adjectival suffix indicates that *gerundus -a -um* is an adjective where the gerund is a noun.)

Both gerund and gerundive are in form passive verbal adjectives (though the gerund is active in sense). The gerundive is used personally—*res gerendae, amandi* ; but the gerund (= the neuter singular of the gerundive used as a noun, just as e.g. τὸ δίκαιον, *bonum*, are used as nouns) is used impersonally : *laudatur* = " he is praised ", *laudandus est* = " he is to be praised " ; so *pugnatur* = " it is fought ", *pugnandum est* = " there is to be a fighting ". *Pugno* is intransitive, but sometimes the gerund of a transitive verb is found, just as its passive may be used impersonally, e.g. *videtur, videndum est.*

The Greek verbal adjectives in -τέος and -τέον are similarly used, but the -τέον gerund is found with transitive and intransitive verbs alike.

Uses of the *Verbal Adjective* :

§ 174. Expressing *Necessity* or Obligation : *amandus est*, φιλητέος ἐστί = " he must be loved ", " he ought to be loved ". This use is regular in both languages, as is the impersonal *faciendum est, ποιητέον ἐστί* with the nominative of the verbal adjective (the accusative, of course, in Reported Speech). The agent is expressed in the dative (see Dative of Agent, § 51). This dative may be regarded as a possessive use : *faciendum est mihi*—the doing attaches, belongs, to me, i.e. *I* must do.

(a) N.B.—In Greek besides this dative of the agent there is found the accusative of the agent : this may have been constructed on the analogy of δεῖ + infinitive. Thucydides has both uses in one sentence :

Οὔτε μισθοφορητέον ἄλλους ἢ τοὺς στρατευομένους οὔτε μεθεκτέον τῶν πραγμάτων πλέοσιν ἢ πεντακισχιλίοις.
(viii. 65)
" None but those on active service are to draw pay and not more than 5000 are to have a share in administration."

(b) N.B. in Latin the accusative after the gerund of a transitive verb. This is rare except in earlier Latin (Cicero has it twice). Cp. Shakespeare's " Nothing in his life became him like the leaving it ".

1. *Quare monendum te est mihi.* (Catull. 39. 9)
" I must warn you."
2. *Tempora . . . animadvertendum et loca . . . providendum.* (Varr. R.R. iii. 16)
" You must watch the times and provide places."

N.B.—At other times a similar gerund is constructed with an objective genitive, in which use the gerund has *lost* its verbal character and has come to be regarded as an ordinary substantive, e.g. :

Ex maiore copia nobis quam illi fuit exemplorum eligendi potestas. (Cic. *Inv.* ii. 2)
" We had the opportunity of choosing our instances from a larger stock than he."

(It is possible, however, that Cicero, having written *exemplorum*, wished merely to avoid the cumbrous *-orum -orum* ending.) This instance properly belongs to (2).

§ 175. Expressing *merely passive verbal action* (only

in Latin) in any case. The rule of the usage is that the gerundive itself takes the requisite case and attracts the noun to its case, but it follows the gender and number of the noun, e.g. " concerning the taking of gifts ", *de donis capiendis*. Exceptions are found as in the example above quoted from Cicero.

Thus it is used to supply a present or future participle passive :

Plumbea glans . . . cursu volvenda calescit.
(Lucr. vi. 179)
" The bullet grows hot as it whirls in its flight."

Also to express possibility (only negative or virtually negative sentences) ; as we say, " not to be counted " :

Infandum regina iubes renovare dolorem. (V. *Aen.* ii. 3)
" You bid me relate a sorrow that cannot be told."

§ 176. The *Supines* in Latin : these are the accusative (in *-um*) and the ablative (in *-u*) of a verbal noun in *-us*.

(i) The *Accusative* is an acc. of action as the end of motion and is found in transitive verbs taking an object (cp. *infitias ire*, see § 43). It is very common in early, colloquial Latin, and Caesar has frequently *pabulatum ire*, *aquatum ire*, " to go foraging, watering ", etc.

Deos atque amicos it salutatum.   (Plaut. *Bac.* 347)

(ii) The *Ablative* form is used as a Locative or an Instrumental of the respect in which a statement is made or a description given (§ 95). A Separative Ablative of the Supine with verbs is rare.

1. *Pudet dictu.*   (lit. " in the saying ").   (Tac. *Agr.* 32)
2. (*Vilicus*) *primus cubitu surgat, postremus cubitum eat.*
(Cato, *Agr.* 5. 5)
" The bailiff must be the first to rise from his bed, the last to go to bed."

There is also a *dative* form—*lepida memoratui* (Plaut. *Bac.* 62), *sunt nobis quaestu* (predic. dat., cp. *usu = usui* in Lucret.) (Plaut. *Rud.* 294).

§ 177. **The Participle.**

The participle (μετοχή—explained by Dionysius Thrax

as μετέχουσα τῆς τῶν ῥημάτων καὶ τῆς τῶν ὀνομάτων ἰδιότητος), like an adjective, is used to qualify nouns and pronouns; but, unlike an adjective,

(1) it can in its active verbal character take an object in the accusative or in any other case peculiar to its verb (cp. χοὰς προπομπός, § 40);

(2) it expresses distinctions in time.

The participle plays a much bigger part in Greek than in Latin, which lacks particularly a past participle active and a present participle passive. We have considered the "absolute" participle constructions severally under their several cases. The other most conspicuous uses are:

§ 178. (i) The *Circumstantial Participle*, expressing the circumstances in which an action takes place. This use admits of many shades of meaning—of manner, cause, time, purpose, limitation, condition, e.g. εἰπὼν ἀπῄει may mean "when he had spoken", "although he had spoken", "as having spoken", etc.; λέξων ἀπῄει = "with the purpose of speaking"; εἰπὼν ἂν ἀπῄει = "if he had spoken . . ." These various meanings will be dealt with severally in the later sections.

§ 179. (ii) *Participle in function of verbal noun*: e.g. *terra mutata* for "the changing of land", i.e. the expression stresses not so much the thing or person acted upon as the *action* itself.

This use is common in Latin, less common in Greek. The result of this usage is to give a peculiar stress to the noun.

1. Ἔτει πέμπτῳ μετὰ τὰς Συρακούσας οἰκισθείσας.
   (Thuc. v. 3)
   "In the fifth year after the foundation of Syracuse."

2. . . . *cum Caesar occisus aliis optimum aliis pessimum facinus videretur.* (Tac. *Ann.* i. 8)
   ". . . the murder of Caesar seemed to some the noblest deed, to others the worst possible."

This example shows excellently the effect of the usage, i.e. that it can by no means be taken literally.

§ 180. (iii) The *Neuter Participle as verbal substantive* in

Greek with the article where the infinitive + article would be more normal : it is very near to the τὸ δίκαιον usage, and is poetical except in Thucydides. In Latin it is found chiefly in Livy.

1. Ἐν τῷ μὴ μελετῶντι ἀξυνετώτεροι ἔσονται.
(Thuc. i. 142)
"Through want of practice they will become more clumsy."

2. *Tentatum . . . ut ambo patricii consules crearentur rem ad interregnum perduxit.* (Liv. vii. 22)
"The attempt to obtain the election of two patrician consuls brought about an interregnum."

N.B. this use with a dependent indirect question in Virgil :

. . . dolores
. . . notumque furens quid femina possit
. . . pectora ducunt. (V. *Aen.* v. 6)
". . . and the knowledge what a woman's frenzy may achieve led their hearts . . ."

§ 181. (iv) *Participle in Periphrastic perfect.* (Periphrases of participles with ἔχω and *sum* for, e.g., the future are common.) In a few instances past participles (Greek aorist, Latin perfect) are used with ἔχω in a sense similar to that of the English perfect—" I have done " ; cp. *j'ai fait*. (See § 138.)

THE SENTENCE

Variations from Simple Statement.

The following Jussive usages cover such of these variations as need special syntactical study. The common variations contained in interrogative and negative forms are considered below (§§ 292 ff.) under " Negatives ".

JUSSIVE USAGES

§ 182. The varieties of Jussive construction show most clearly the transition from the simple to the compound sentence. As will be seen, these usages are primarily found in simple sentences.

These are the subdivisions of the Jussive type :

    I. Positive Command.
   II. Negative Command.
  III. Concession.
  IV. Wish.
   V. Deliberation.

The use of subjunctive and optative in jussive constructions will be clear from what has been already said about the general meaning of these moods. Both express some action as other than a fact, i.e. as a possibility, near or remote. Thus the present subjunctive πράσσῃς, *facias* means " you may do " : spoken in a certain tone this would be a command. (N.B.—In affirmative sentences Classical Greek retains this subjunctive of command only in the First Person.)

Similarly a wish is the voicing of a *desired* possibility, perhaps originally in the form of a question—" Oh, may I hear ? " Latin here uses the subjunctive in the same way as a command; but Greek keeps the politer, subtler form for wishes, i.e. the optative—" Might I hear ? "

§ 183. **Command.** Greek uses imperative and subjunctive in First Person exhortations; Latin uses both imperative and subjunctive generally.

1. Ἀλλ' εἰ δοκεῖ, πλέωμεν, ὁρμάσθω ταχύς.
(Soph. *Ph.* 526)
"If thou wilt, let us sail, and let him set forth with speed."

2. ... ἐπίμεινον, Ἀρήϊα τεύχεα δύω.   (Hom. *Il.* vi. 340)
"Wait, let me put on my war-harness."

3. *Iniurias fortunae quas ferre nequeas defugiendo relinquas.*
(Cic. *T.D.* v. 41)
"Flee from and leave behind you such blows of fortune as you cannot endure."

N.B. in 2. the *parataxis*, the germ of the complex sentence, where two simple clauses are placed side by side, grammatically co-ordinate, though one is logically subordinate; the writer says, "Wait—let me put on ...", but what he means is "Wait *until* I put on ...". Compare in Latin *di facerent sine patre forem* (Ov. *Met.* viii. 72)— lit. "O that the gods had brought it to pass—O that I were fatherless ! "

§ 184. In Latin a command relating to past time—"you should have"—may be expressed by the imperfect and pluperfect subjunctive.   (Roby, 1604.)

1. *At tu dictis, Albane, maneres.*   (V. *Aen.* viii. 643)
"But thou, Alban, shouldst have kept thy word."

2. *Civem Romanum in crucem egisti. Adservasses hominem.*
(Cic. *Verr.* v. 65)
"You crucified a Roman citizen. You should have kept him ..."

N.B.—In this usage the pluperfect, strictly, refers to an unfulfilled contingency in *past* time, the imperfect subjunctive to an unfulfilled contingency in present time (as in conditionals). *Maneres* in 1., however, expresses continuance: "Thou shouldst have remained and gone on remaining by thy word ! "   Contrast *vocasses* (*Aen.* iv. 678).

THE SENTENCE

Also in both Greek and Latin the future indicative may express command. This usage has already been considered (see § 134).

§ 185. **Negative Command.** In Greek prohibitions are conveyed by μή with the Present Imperative or Aorist Subjunctive (see § 158); in Latin by *ne* with (a) Imperative, especially in the Third Person in formal documents, (b) any tense of the subjunctive, though sometimes a periphrasis is used (e.g. *noli facere, cave ne facias*).

1. Μὴ θῆσθε νόμον μηδένα, ἀλλὰ τοὺς βλάπτοντας ὑμᾶς λύσατε. (Dem. iii. 10)
   "Don't *pass* any law, but repeal those which stand in your way."
2. *Abi, ne iura : satis credo.* (Plaut. *Pers.* 490)
   "Go on, don't swear : I believe you."
3. *Ne sis patruus mihi.* (Hor. *Sat.* ii. 3. 88)
   "Don't come the uncle over me!"
4. *Nihil gratiae concesseris.* (Cic. *Mur.* 31)
   "Make no concession to favouritism."

The old rule of *ne* + the perfect subjunctive in Second Person prohibitions is not stringent.

§ 186. As with positive commands the future indicative is sometimes used—in Greek usually with ὅπως. See § 197.

1. Λέγ' εἴ τι βούλει, χειρὶ δ' οὐ ψαύσεις ποτέ.
   (Eur. *Med.* 1320)
   "Speak if thou wilt, but never lay hands on me."
2. Πενθεὺς δ' ὅπως μὴ πένθος εἰσοίσει δόμοις.
   (Eur. *Bac.* 367)
   "See that Pentheus bring not within his house his namesake sorrow" (from "how may he not?" For μή see § 308.)
3. *Non me appellabis si sapis.* (Plaut. *Most.* 515)
   "Don't address me—if you've any sense!"

In Greek οὐ μή with the future indicative (and, alternatively, with the aorist subjunctive) expresses a strong Second Person prohibition. (See under Negatives, §§ 307 ff.)

§ 187. **Concession.** " Let it be (granted to be) true ; what then ? " i.e. there is a rhetorical assumption. Greek uses here the imperative ; Latin uses usually subjunctive (commonly with *quamvis, licet*, etc., in a complex sentence —see § 218).

1. Προσειπάτω τινὰ φιλικῶς ὅ τε ἄρχων καὶ ὁ ἰδιώτης.
(X. *Hier.* viii. 3)
"Suppose that both ruler and private citizen address one friendlily."

2. *Haec si vobis non probamus, sint falsa sane.*
(Cic. *Acad.* ii. 32)
"If we do not prove this to your satisfaction, then suppose it false."

Cp. the use in, e.g., Shakespeare's "Be he the fire—I'll be the yielding water".

§ 188. **Wish.**

(i) Wishes for the *future* (most common because there is a chance of their being fulfilled) :

Greek—*optative* (εἴθε, εἰ γάρ, εἰ may be prefixed).
Latin—*present subjunctive* (*utinam, o si* may be prefixed).

(ii) Wishes for *past* or *present* (i.e. for impossible contingencies) :

Greek—*historic indicative* tenses (εἴθε, εἰ γάρ, εἰ, etc.).
Latin—*historic subjunctive* tenses (*utinam, o si*, etc.).

In future wishes the optative in Greek and the subjunctive in Latin express their normal meaning, i.e. they give the action of the verb as other than a fact—here, as a desired possibility—"I might see", "O that I might see" says Greek ; "I may see", "O that I may see" says Latin (present subjunctive) : both expressions, the near and the remote, are natural in English.

In impossible wishes Latin still, quite rightly, uses the mood of other-than-fact in different tense-forms conveying different times (*utinam viderem, utinam vidissem*) ; and the optative is thus used in Homer. But in classical Greek the optative admits of no time-distinction ; only the indicative in Greek is capable of that, and so has to be used (εἰ γὰρ ἑώρων, εἰ γὰρ εἶδον) : the εἰ shows the unreality.

THE SENTENCE 99

It will be seen that the use of moods and tenses in both kinds of wishes with εἰ γάρ, *o si* is exactly the same as in the parallel forms of protasis in conditional sentences: εἰ γὰρ τοῦτο ποιοίη, *O si hoc faciat*; εἰ γὰρ τοῦτο ἐποίει, *O si hoc faceret*; εἰ γὰρ τοῦτο ἐποίησεν, *O si hoc fecisset*.

§ 189. (i) *Wishes for the Future.*
1. Ὦ παῖ, γένοιο πατρὸς εὐτυχέστερος. (Soph. *Aj*. 550)
 "My child, mayst thou be luckier than thy father!"
2. Εἰ γὰρ γενοίμην, τέκνον, ἀντὶ σοῦ νεκρός.
 (Eur. *Hipp*. 1410)
 "O might I be dead, my son, instead of thee!"
3. *Utinam ipse Varro incumbat in causam.*
 (Cic. *Att*. iii. 15)
 "If only Varro himself would apply himself to the cause!"

But the present optative in Homer may refer to present time:
 Νῦν μὲν μήτ' εἴης, βούγαιε, μήτε γένοιο.
 (*Od*. xviii. 79)
 "Now, braggart, would that thou wert not now, nor hadst ever been born."

§ 190. (ii) *Impossible Wishes.* Imperfect tense for *present* time: aorist in Greek, pluperfect in Latin for *past*. But see § 150.
1. Εἰ γὰρ τοσαύτην δύναμιν εἶχον. (Eur. *Alc*. 1072)
 "Had I but such strength!"
2. *Modo valeres!* (Cic. *Att*. xi. 23)
 "If only you were well!"
3. Εἰ γάρ μ' ὑπὸ γῆν ἧκεν. (Aesch. *P.V*. 152)
 "Would he had sent me under the earth!"
4. *Utinam ne . . . tetigissent litora puppes.*
 (Catull. 64. 171)
 "Would that their ships had never touched the shore!"

(Sometimes in exclamatory wishes in Latin the verb is omitted, e.g. *di meliora* (sc. e.g. *dent*) (Cic. *Phil*. viii. 3).)

§ 191. **Deliberation.** "What am I to do?" "What may I do?" "What might I do?" "What is there a chance of my doing?"

Here, again, the moods of other-than-fact are called into play, and such sentences are expressed in Greek by the subjunctive or, where remoteness is needed, the optative; in Latin by the subjunctive.

Past deliberatives (What *was* I to do ?) may be expressed in Latin by the imperfect and pluperfect subjunctive, but Greek must use a periphrasis, e.g. τί χρῆν ποιεῖν;

Some distinguish between *Deliberative* (First Person only) and *Dubitative* (other Persons, e.g. Ex. 2).

    1. Ὤμοι ἐγώ, πᾶ βῶ; πᾶ στῶ; πᾶ κέλσω;
(Eur. Hec. 1056)
"Ah me ! where shall I go ? where stand ? where find haven ? "

    2. Τεάν, Ζεῦ, δύνασιν τίς . . . κατάσχοι;
(Soph. Ant. 605)
"Thy power, O Zeus, who might restrain ? "

    3. *Mirer si vana vestra auctoritās . . . est ?*
(Liv. iii. 21)
"Am I to marvel if your authority is ineffectual ? "

    4. *Haec cum viderem, quid agerem, iudices ?*
(Cic. Sest. 19)
"When I saw this what was I to do, gentlemen ? "

The construction is also found, in Greek, in a loose parataxis with, e.g., βούλει;—βούλει ἐπισκοπῶμεν; (X. *Mem.* iii. 5. 1).

§ 192. All the above deliberative uses are in independent sentences; there are also rare instances of a deliberative optative ("What might I do ? ") in a *dependent* clause. Some editors prefer to believe that these are potential optatives with ἄν omitted. This is unnecessary. The speaker refers to a remote chance or hope. Plato has οὐκ ἔχω πῶς ἀμφισβητοίην (*Euthyd.* 296 D). The stock example is the cry:

    Ἔστ' οὖν ὅπως Ἄλκηστις εἰς γῆρας μόλοι;
(Eur. Alc. 52)
"Is there no way that Alcestis might reach old age ? "
  cp. Οὐκ ἔσθ' ὅπως λέξαιμι τὰ ψευδῆ καλά.
(Aesch. Ag. 620)
    i.e. "How might I ever call falsehood fair ? "

THE SENTENCE

§ 193. N.B. also the use of vivid present indicative in a deliberative sentence :

1. Ὦ δαῖμον, ὦ Φοῖβε, πῶς πείθομαι; (Eur. *Andr.* 1036)
"O God, O Phoebus, how am I to obey ?"
2. *Credimus ? an qui amant ipsi sibi somnia fingunt ?*
(V. *Ecl.* viii. 108)
"Are we to believe ? or do lovers fashion their own dreams ?"

(Cp. Catullus 1. 1.)   (So Sanskrit—M. 212.)

Parataxis and Syntaxis

§ 194. In the various forms of the jussive construction we have seen for the most part simple independent sentences, but we have also seen a number of examples in which two such simple clauses are placed *side by side* as if to form one sentence, e.g. βούλει ἐπισκοπῶμεν; and, in Latin, *di facerent sine patre forem*. Βούλει ἐπισκοπῶμεν; started life as βούλει; ἐπισκοπῶμεν; = " do you wish it ?— are we to consider it ? " and the Latin phrase as *di facerent— sine patre forem*.

Usually Latin would say *di facerent ut sine patre forem* ; but it would be quite fallacious to explain the usage by saying that *ut* is left out. The final use develops *out of* the jussive.

Grammatically *di facerent forem* is paratactic (where *facere ut forem* would be hypotactic, *forem* being subordinated) ; but logically it is hypotactic and forms a compound sentence. And however far we go back in the history of a language we find the subordination of some clauses to others an established use. Even in an aggregate of simple sentences, logically, there must be one or more which contain the most important information. Consider such sentences as :

1. "Seek and ye shall find."
2. "I bridled him and saddled him and took him out and rode him the way that I had meant to go alone."
(Belloc)
3. Ἔδοχσεν τῆι βουλῆι καὶ τῶι δήμωι. Ἱπποθωντὶς ἐπρυτάνευε, Λόβων ἐγραμμάτευε, Φιλιστίδης ἐπεστάτει, Γλαύκιππος ἦρχε, Ἐρασινίδης εἶπε.
(Dittenberger, *S.I.G.*² 50)

But, grammatically, in a phrase like *Rogo eum quid dicat* (standing for the *quid dicis?* of direct speech) it is obvious that we have something more than two clauses originally co-ordinate fused into one, and that mere parataxis will not necessarily explain the construction.

In Homer the structure of simple sentences predominates; though syntax is replacing parataxis, the simple sentence dies hard: there is less sophistication in the change of mood and tense in complex sentences, because everywhere the expression of the thought in its simplest fashion shines through. The same is true in a greater degree of all Sanskrit (M. 190) and in a lesser degree of early Latin.

§ 195. The following are interesting specimens of Parataxis in the mature language:

1. Ἐπίσχετον μάθωμεν. (Soph. *Phil.* 539)
   "Hush, that we may hear."

2. *Censeo ad nos Luceriam venias.* (Cic. *Att.* viii. 11 A)
   "I think you should come to us at Luceria."

3. *Date vulnera lymphis Abluam . . .* (V. *Aen.* iv. 683)
   "Give the wounds that I may wash them with water," or, "Grant that I may wash the wounds with water."

THE COMPOUND SENTENCE

§ 196. Dependent clauses may be divided into three main groups:

(i) *Amplifying* Clauses, i.e. which rather *add* extra information than give something necessary to the meaning of the sentence. Under this head falls—

Final Clauses proper.
Consecutive Clauses.
Definite Relative and Temporal Clauses.
Causal Clauses.
Concessive Clauses.

(ii) *Hypothetical* Clauses, i.e. which render the main clause only conditionally true: the main clause is dependent

THE SENTENCE 103

for its own truth upon the truth of the subordinate clause. Here fall—
Conditional Clauses proper.
Clauses of Stipulation, e.g. *dum* = " provided that ".
Indefinite Relative and Temporal.

(iii) *Object* Clauses, i.e. which supply the object of the action, without which the sentence would be incomplete.
Modal Clauses.
Object Clauses of Fear.
Reported Speech, etc.—Clauses which limit the action of verbs of saying and thinking by giving their object.

FINAL USAGES

Distinguish (see § 255)—
I. Final Clauses proper : " He sends me to report."
II. Modal (Object) Sentences : " See that you take care."

§ 197. The development of the final construction out of a parataxis has already been mentioned. Thus ἀπόστιχε, μή τι νοήσῃ (*Il.* i. 522), " Depart lest she notice anything ", shows a parataxis half-way towards the compound sentence; strictly it may be taken in two halves : " Depart ; let her not notice anything ". So, too, with verbs of fear : δείδοικα . . . μή τι πάθωσιν (*Il.* x. 538) was originally " I am afraid ; let them not suffer anything ". Similarly in Latin.

In the normal maturity of the languages we should have connecting particles in such Final Clauses—ἀπόστιχε ἵνα μή τι νοήσῃ, *date vulnera lymphis ut abluam* ; but it is just the wrong thing to say that Homer and Virgil have omitted these particles (see § 183). These particles suggest that there may be a *deliberative* element in the construction : ἦλθον ὅπως ἴδοιμι suggests an earlier ἦλθον· ὅπως ἴδοιμι; (" I came—how might I see ? ").

The particles (final) in Greek are : ἵνα (the normal particle in Attic) = literally " where ", ὅπως and ὡς both = " how ", ὄφρα (Epic) = " until ". " I am standing where I may see, how I may see, until I may see " are all specialized forms of " I am standing that I may see ", and it is easy to understand how they came to be merged in the general final use. So in Latin *ut* means " how ", and *ne* (standing for *ut ne* = ὅπως μή) "how not". Like ὄφρα, *dum, priusquam*, etc., are used of projected contingencies. *Quo* = " by which amount " (instrumental of measure), e.g. *sto quo facilius videam*. Other relative adjectives and adverbs are regularly used in Latin in final clauses generally, in Greek particularly in object-clauses.

§ 198. The moods used in the pure final clause are in *Greek*:
(i) *Subjunctive* in *Primary* sequence—" I stand that I may see ".
(ii) *Optative* in *Historic* sequence—" I stood that I might see ".
(iii) Historic *Indicative* tenses to express a *past unfulfilled* purpose—" I ought to have stood that I might have seen " (see § 147).

In *Latin* the subjunctive is always used : a primary main clause is followed by a present or perfect subjunctive, a historic by an imperfect or pluperfect subjunctive. As usual, the Latin tense is determined by the time of the action, but the Greek tenses reflect merely the completeness or incompleteness of the action.

Examples :
1. Τὸν κακὸν δεῖ κολάζειν ἵν' ἀμείνων ᾖ. (Plat. *Legg.* 944 D)
   " We must punish the bad man to make him better."
2. *Esse oportet ut vivas, non vivere ut edas.*
   (Auct. *ad* Her. iv. 28)
   " We must eat to live, not live to eat."
3. Ἔπεμψα ὡς πύθοιτο. (Soph. *O.T.* 71)
   " I sent him that he might learn . . ."
4. *Inventa sunt specula ut homo ipse se nosset.*
   (Sen. *N.Q.* i. 17. 4)
   " Mirrors were invented that man might know himself."

§ 199. Examples of past indicative in Greek to express a *past unfulfilled* purpose (see § 147):
1. Τί δῆτ' . . . οὐκ . . . ἔρριψ' ἐμαυτὴν τῆσδ' ἀπὸ . . . πέτρας, ὅπως . . . πάντων κακῶν ἀπηλλάγην;
   (Aesch. *P.V.* 747)
   " Why did I not cast myself from this rock, that I might have rid myself of all my woes ? "

THE SENTENCE 105

2. Ἔδει τὰ ἐνέχυρα τότε λαβεῖν, ὡς μηδ' εἰ ἐβούλετο ἐδύνατο ἐξαπατᾶν. (X. *An.* vii. 6)

"The securities should have been taken then, so that he could not have tricked you, not even had he wanted."

§ 200. N.B.—**Vivid Construction.**

In Greek sometimes the subjunctive or future indicative is found after a historic main verb (the future indicative not infrequently); the result is a gain in vividness, as, e.g., " I did this, so that (I said to myself) he *shan't* . . ."

Ἑξακοσίους λογάδας ἐξέκριναν, ὅπως τῶν τε Ἐπιπολῶν εἴησαν φύλακες, καί, ἢν ἐς ἄλλο τι δέῃ, . . . παραγίγνωνται. (Thuc. vi. 96)

" They chose 600 picked men that they might be guards of Epipolae, and that they might be at hand if needed for anything else."

Here apparently the use of subjunctive and optative is arbitrary (compare the rapid oscillation between past tenses and historic presents in many passages of Latin narrative). A case can be made out for the view that in such mixtures the subjunctive expresses a nearer and the optative a remoter end, but it is not necessary or convincing.

§ 201. In Homer the vivid subjunctive after a historic main verb is not used unless the action of the final clause is still future to the speaker :

Ἀχλὺν δ' αὖ τοι ἀπ' ὀφθαλμῶν ἕλον, ἣ πρὶν ἐπῆεν,
ὄφρ' εὖ γιγνώσκῃς ἠμὲν θεὸν ἠδὲ καὶ ἄνδρα.
(*Il.* v. 127)

" I have taken the mist from thine eyes, which before was on them, that thou mayest distinguish aright god and man."

Here ἕλον is virtually primary.

(But an optative may be used after a primary main verb to show that the purpose is remote :

. . . ἡγείσθω φιλοπαίγμονος ὀρχηθμοῖο,
ὥς κέν τις φαίη γάμον ἔμμεναι, ἐκτὸς ἀκούων.
(*Od.* xxiii. 134)

" . . . let him lead the merry dance that any man that

hears the sound from without may deem it is a marriage-feast."

N.B.—Here the occasion is quite imaginary.)

§ 202. The following examples show how free Latin can be in the use of tenses :

1. *Simul servis . . . Rubrius ut ianuam clauderent et ipsi ad foris adsisterent imperat.* (Cic. *Verr.* ii. 1. 66)

"At the same time R. orders the slaves to shut the door and to stand by . . ."

2. *Mago nuntios Carthaginem mittit qui hortentur ut auxilia mitterent.* (Liv. xxviii. 31)

"M. sends envoys to Carthage to urge that reinforcements should be sent."

3. *Haec ait et Maia genitum demittit ab alto,*
Ut terrae utque novae pateant Carthaginis arces
Hospitio Teucris, ne fati nescia Dido
Finibus arceret. (V. *Aen.* i. 299)

"So he speaks and sends down from heaven the son of Maia, that the land and towers of young Carthage might open in welcome to the Trojans, nor Dido, unwitting of Fate, bar them from her realm."

§ 203. In Greek the *Future Indicative* is sometimes used to express purpose in a dependent clause :

(i) Sometimes with ὅπως, or ὡς.

Μὴ πρόσλευσσε . . . ἡμῶν ὅπως μὴ τὴν τύχην διαφθερεῖς.
(Soph. *Ph.* 1068)

"Don't look, lest you spoil our chance."

(ii) Commonly with relative adjectives and adverbs (which in Latin may be used in all final constructions). After a historic main verb the *future optative* is natural (i.e. as in Reported Speech it represents the fut. indic. of the primary), but often the vivid future indicative of the primary is maintained. (See § 261.)

1. Ναυτικὸν παρεσκεύαζον ὅ τι πέμψουσιν ἐς τὴν Λέσβον.
(Thuc. iii. 16)

"They were getting ready a fleet to send to Lesbos."

THE SENTENCE

2. Αἱρεθέντες ἐφ' ᾧτε ξυγγράψαι νόμους, καθ' οὕστινας πολιτεύσοιντο. (X. *Hell.* ii. 3. 11)
"... on condition that they should compile laws by which they were to govern."

§ 204. (N.B.—The *Subjunctive* found in Attic Greek after *relatives*, in a final sense, is deliberative :

... τοῖς μέλλουσιν ἕξειν ὅ τι εἰσφέρωσιν.
(X. *Oec.* 7. 20)
"... who are to have something to contribute.")

CONSECUTIVE CLAUSES

§ 205. " He is so stupid that he does not know...." Here Greek and Latin constructions differ widely, being based on different ideas.

In **Greek** the result is expressed in the *infinitive* introduced by one of the particles ὥστε, ὡς or by οἷος, ὅσος, ἐφ' ᾧ, ἐφ' ᾧτε (negative μή); or in the indicative when special stress is laid on the actuality of the result. Ὥστε μὴ εἰδέναι = " in such a way as not to know "; ὥστε οὐκ οἶδεν = " that he is actually ignorant ". This infinitive is an example of the infinitive's dative force (see § 163) : it gives the result as the indirect object of the action. This infinitive may also express purpose, e.g. Example 3. Homer usually has the simple infinitive, which makes the dative force of the infinitive clearer.

Examples :
1. ... εἰσὶ καὶ οἵδε τάδ' εἰπέμεν. (*Il.* ix. 688)
" And here are these also to tell these things."
2. Σὺ δὲ σχολάζεις, ὥστε θαυμάζειν ἐμέ. (Eur. *Hec.* 730)
" But thou, to my surprise, dost tarry."
3. Πᾶν ποιοῦσιν ὥστε δίκην μὴ διδόναι.
(Plat. *Gorg.* 479 c)
" They do everything to avoid paying the penalty."
4. Οὕτως ἐναργές ἐστιν, ὥσθ' εὑρήσετε ...
(Aeschin. i. 128)
" It is so clear that you will actually find ..."

As ὥστε has no influence on the moods of the verb it

may take other constructions that might be found in an independent sentence.

"Ὥστε, εἰ μακρὰ ἡ περίοδος, μὴ θαυμάσῃς.
(Plat. *Phaedr.* 274 A)
". . . so don't be surprised if it is a long way round."

§ 206. In Latin the subjunctive is used introduced by *ut* (negative *ut non*, as opposed to *ne* which is the negative of the final clause); e.g. *ut non sciat*. The subjunctive implies, not that the result is unreal, but that it is *causally connected* and logically subordinate to the main clause. (We have already seen instances of the way in which Latin uses the subjunctive in subordinate clauses to express causal relation.) Latin is keen on this point just as it is keen on strict time relations.

Examples:

1. *Ea est causa, ut veteres cloacae nunc privata passim subeant tecta.* (Liv. v. 55)
 "That is the reason that at the present day old sewers everywhere pass under private houses."

2. *Vulneribus confectus ut iam se sustinere non posset.*
 (Caes. *B.G.* ii. 25)
 ". . . so weakened by his wounds that he could no longer hold himself up."

In the following examples the sequence is varied according to the sense required.

(i) After a historic main verb the present is used of actions that apply to the present time:

Siciliam ita vexavit ut restitui nullo modo possit.
(Cic. *Verr.* i. 4)
"He has so ravaged Sicily that it can be in no way restored."

(ii) The perfect subjunctive is used to stress the actuality of the result *or* to express a result completed only at the time of writing:

Adeo turbati erant . . . ut quosdam consul manu ipse reprenderit et . . . in hostem verterit.
(Liv. xxxiv. 14)
"So demoralized were they that the consul himself

actually laid hands on some of them and turned them round to face the enemy."

Aemilius Paullus tantum in aerarium pecuniae invexit ut unius imperatoris praeda finem attulerit tributorum. (Cic. *Off.* ii. 22)

". . . brought so much money into the treasury that the spoil taken by one general did away with war-taxes."

(i.e. for all time following up to the present; *afferret* would mean that it put an end to them immediately at that time.)

§ 207. Also the Latin use of the relative adjective in causal consecutive usage (mentioned below, § 250) should here be noted.

1. *Me miserum qui non adfuerim.* (Cic. *Fam.* iii. 11)
   "Alas, that I should not have been there."

2. *Ex antiquissimis philosophis Xenophanes unus qui deos esse diceret divinationem funditus sustulit.*
   (Cic. *Div.* i. 3)
   "X., the only one of the early philosophers while asserting the existence of gods wholly to do away with divination."

Sometimes, as in Example 2. (especially with *qui quidem*), this use is *limitative*.

§ 208. *Abnormal Negative in Greek.* Sometimes we find οὐ used in an ὥστε + Infinitive construction.

Ὑμᾶς εἰδέναι ἡγοῦμαι τοῦτον οὕτω σκαιὸν εἶναι ὥστε οὐ δύνασθαι μαθεῖν τὰ λεγόμενα. (Lys. x. 15)
"I suppose you know he is so stupid that he can't grasp what is said."

The Direct form underlying this is οὕτω σκαιός ἐστιν ὥστε οὐ δύναται and the οὐ is retained in the Indirect. The advantage is that in this way the stress can still be kept on the actuality, which would be lost if ὥστε μή were used. (Perhaps οὐ negatives a single word; cp. §§ 296, 299.)

Most instances of this ὥστε οὐ + Infinitive are, like this,

in Indirect Speech. But there are instances where this explanation does not easily apply, e.g.

οὐ μακρὰν γὰρ τειχέων περιπτυχαί,
ὥστ᾽ οὐχ ἅπαντά σ᾽ εἰδέναι τὰ δρώμενα.
(Eur. Ph. 1357)
"The circuit of the walls is not so large that you do not know all that is being done," i.e. "the city is so small that you know all . . ."

Goodwin (*Moods and Tenses*, p. 229) observes that in all such instances as this " the thought could be expressed equally well by ὥστε + infinitive and ὥστε + finite verb. . . . We can therefore easily suppose a mixture of two constructions . . . instead of ὥστε μὴ εἶναι or ὥστε οὐκ ἐστιν . . . we have ὥστε οὐκ εἶναι. This occasional confusion would be made easier by familiarity with ὥστε οὐ + infinitive in indirect discourse."

§ 209. The Consecutive clause may also express *terms or conditions* on which the action of the main verb depends : in Greek ὥστε, ἐφ᾽ ᾧ, ἐφ᾽ ᾧτε with the infinitive, or ἐφ᾽ ᾧ, ἐφ᾽ ᾧτε with a future indicative are used ; in Latin *ut* with the subjunctive, often with an antecedent *ita.* Cp. English " I charge ye so that ye tell no man ".

1. Αἱρεθέντες ἐφ᾽ ᾧτε ξυγγράψαι νόμους.
(X. *Hell.* ii. 3. 11)
" Elected on the condition that they compiled laws."

2. Ἐπὶ τούτῳ δὲ ὑπεξίσταμαι τῆς ἀρχῆς, ἐφ᾽ ᾧτε ὑπ᾽ οὐδενὸς ἄρξομαι. (Hdt. iii. 83)
"On this condition I abdicate my rule—that I shall be ruled by none."

3. *Certe malet existimari vir bonus, ut non sit, quam esse, ut non putetur.* (Cic. *Fin.* ii. 22)
"Certainly he will prefer to be thought a good man without being one to being a good man without being thought one."

§ 210. The Greek *Parenthetic Infinitive* (ὡς ἔπος εἰπεῖν, ἐμοὶ δοκεῖν κτλ.) is also a consecutive usage. See § 166.

1. Καὶ ἔργου, ὡς ἔπος εἰπεῖν, ἢ οὐδενὸς προσδέονται ἢ βραχέος πάνυ. (Plat. *Gorg.* 450 D)
'And they require, in a manner of speaking, little or no work."

THE SENTENCE 111

2. Ἀλλ', ἐμοὶ δοκεῖν, τάχ' εἴσει. (Aesch. Pers. 246)
"But soon methinks wilt thou know."

These infinitives are limitative or apologetic; difficult to explain, but best regarded, like the consecutive infinitive proper, as datives of purpose: ἐμοὶ δοκεῖν = "for my thinking", ὡς ἔπος εἰπεῖν, ἑκατόν = "for the giving of a round figure (as we say "for convenience"), a hundred."

From the use of the infinitive in such expressions developed the use in ὀλίγου δεῖν, μικροῦ δεῖν:

... πολλῶν λόγων γιγνομένων ὀλίγου δεῖν καθ' ἑκάστην ἐκκλησίαν. (Dem. ix. 1)

"... when many speeches are being made in almost every assembly."

("almost", literally "so as to want a little".)

DEFINITE RELATIVE AND TEMPORAL SENTENCES

§ 211. Relative clauses may be introduced by relative pronouns and adjectives or by relative adverbs of *time, place* and *manner*. Thus strictly they include all temporal clauses: conditional sentences, too, are strictly a species of relative sentences (εἰ and *si* being probably in the first place relative adverbs meaning "in which way"; see § 226). But εἰ and *si* soon lost this relative flavour and conditional usages came to form a well-marked syntax of their own.

§ 212. The relative clause developed thus. A demonstrative pronoun, Greek ὅ, German *der*, English "that", comes to be regarded in the light of something previously mentioned in the sentence; e.g. "I found a book that was good" was originally "I found a book; it (that) was good". Here "that" introduces a clause which is logically subordinate and which, therefore, comes to be considered as syntactically subordinate. So too in *Od*. xv. 310

καὶ ἅμ' ἡγεμόν' ἐσθλὸν ὄπασσον,
ὅς κέ με κεῖσ' ἀγάγῃ

meant originally "Grant me a good guide; let him lead me thither". Ὅς τε in Homer shows an intermediate stage.

Notice too that the interrogative pronoun in Greek and Latin is also the indefinite (τίς, τις, *quis, quis*), and compare

"Who knows this ? " (τίς τοῦτο οἶδε; *quis hoc scit ?*) with "Does anyone know this ? " (τοῦτο οἶδέ τις; *hoc scit quis ? ecquis hoc scit ?*). In Latin, then, *quam pecuniam habeo servo* may well have grown out of *quam pecuniam habeo ? eam pecuniam servo*. When the pronoun has become merely relative the order of the clauses is varied at pleasure ; cp. English "who" (relative), which has developed out of the interrogative "who ? "

§ 213. Relative and Temporal Sentences may be divided into two great classes : I. Those in which the antecedent of the relative or the time referred to is *Definite* ; II. Those in which it is *Indefinite*. (See §§ 245 ff.)

Definite Relative and Temporal Sentences : i.e. referring to particular things, occasions, etc. Negatives οὐ, *non*.

The clause has its verb in the indicative, unless influenced by Oratio Obliqua or Attraction.

1. Τίς ἐσθ' ὁ χῶρος δῆτ' ἐν ᾧ βεβήκαμεν;
(Soph. *O.C.* 52)
"What is this place in which we have set foot ? "

2. Ἕως ἐστὶ καιρός, ἀντιλάβεσθε τῶν πραγμάτων.
(Dem. i. 20)
"Now, while the chance holds, tackle the situation."

3. *Stellas quas Graeci cometas vocant.* (Cic. *N.D.* ii. 5)
"The stars which the Greeks call comets."

4. *Pompeius ut equitatum suum pulsum vidit, acie excessit.*
(Caes. *B.C.* iii. 94)
"When Pompey saw his cavalry beaten back, he left the battle-line."

Causal Clauses

§ 214. Causal sentences express the cause given for the statement or for some part of the statement contained in the main sentence, e.g. "He would not walk in Judaea, because the Jews sought to kill him ", where the causal clause explains " not in Judaea " (St. John vii. 1).

Causal clauses both in Greek and Latin regularly take the indicative, both in primary and historic sequence, with the introductory *causal* particles ὅτι, διότι, διόπερ, ὡς, οὕνεκα, ὁθούνεκα ("because", "in that", "as"); ἐπεί,

THE SENTENCE 113

ἐπειδή, ὅτε, ὁπότε, εὖτε (" seeing that ", " since ") ; Latin *quia, quod* (" because ", " in that ") ; *quoniam* (=*quom*, i.e. *cum, iam,* " now that "), *quando, quandoquidem* (" since ").

It will be seen that these particles fall into two classes :

(i) *Relative :* i.e. English " in *that* ", Greek ὅτι, Latin *quod* (both neuter acc. sing. used adverbially), etc. (*Quia* is probably a form of the acc. neut. plur. of the relative.)

(ii) *Temporal.*

Examples of true causal usage :

1. Δημοβόρος βασιλεύς, ἐπεὶ οὐτιδανοῖσιν ἀνάσσεις.
   (Hom. *Il.* i. 231)
   " Folk-devouring king, seeing that thou rulest men of nought."

2. Κήδετο γὰρ Δαναῶν, ὅτι ῥα θνήσκοντας ὁρᾶτο.
   (*ibid.* 56)
   " He was anxious for the Danaans, for that he saw them dying."

3. *Quia natura mutari non potest idcirco verae amicitiae sempiternae sunt.* (Cic. *Am.* 32)
   " Because nature cannot change therefore are true friendships everlasting."

4. *Torquatus filium suum quod is contra imperium in hostem pugnaverat necari iussit.* (Sall. *C.* 52)
   " T. ordered his son to be executed because he had fought against the enemy contrary to orders."

Temporal conjunctions used in causal clauses generally follow the rules for temporal clauses.

§ 215. When cum in Latin is used as a causal particle it takes the *subjunctive*. This has already been noticed under Temporal Sentences.

Dionysius cum in communibus suggestis consistere non auderet contionari ex turri alta solebat.
(Cic. *T.D.* v. 20)
" Since D. did not dare to stand on the public platforms he used to make his speeches from a high tower."

In Latin usage the chief distinction is between temporal clauses expressing mere time and those expressing purpose or causal connexion between the verbs of the temporal clause and the main sentence. To express simple fact the temporal clause has the indicative. So *dum, donec, quamdiu, quoad* (= "while") are used with present indicative in indefinite sentences to express mere fact. So too *cum, ubi,* etc., with all tenses of the indicatives.

N.B.—(i) Occasional use of present indicative for the future; cp. Example 4. below.

(ii) The strictly completed tenses.

When there is *causal connexion* the subjunctive is used.

1. *Quae cum ita sint, Catilina, perge quo coepisti.*
(Cic. *Cat.* i. 5)
"Since this is so, Catilina, pursue the course you have begun."

   Cum haec leges consules habebimus. (Cic. *Att.* v. 12)
"By the time you are reading this we shall have our consuls."

2. *Exspecta, dum Atticum conveniam.* (Cic. *Att.* vii. 1)
"Wait till I meet A."

   Dum anima est spes esse dicitur. (Cic. *Att.* ix. 10)
"While there is life they say there is hope."

3. *Cum in ius duci debitorem vidissent, undique convolabant.*
(Liv. ii. 27)
"When (i.e. because) they saw the debtor led off to judgement they started to rush together from every quarter."

   Cum Placentiam consul venit, iam moverat Hannibal.
(Liv. xxi. 39)
"When the consul reached P., H. had already moved."

4. *Antequam pro L. Murena dicere instituo, pro me ipso pauca dicam.* (Cic. *Mur.* 1)
"Before I begin to speak for L. Murena, let me say a little in my own defence."

   Antequam veniat, litteras mittet. (Cic. *Agr.* ii. 20)
"Before he arrives, he will send a letter."

In Silver Latin the subjunctive is found in a sentence where there is no idea of causal connexion :

Pugnatum incerto Marte donec proelium nox dirimeret.
(Tac. *H.* iv. 35)
" The fight went on indecisively till night broke it off."

The use of the subjunctive shows that its action is regarded as logically and grammatically subordinate to the action of the main sentence. If we had *quod . . . non audebat . . . solebat*, this subordination would not be so marked. *Quod non audebat . . . solebat* is built on the line of thought, " He used to . . . that is (*quod*) he did not dare ", where the relative is the merest connective between two main verbs expressing fact. (See under Relatives, § 212.)

§ 216. The subjunctive may also be used in Latin with *non quod, non quia*, to express a *rejected reason* : " Though he will not rise and give him because he is his friend, yet because of his importunity he will arise and give . . ." (St. Luke xi. 8). Here the subjunctive serves to mark a rejected reason, which, as fact, may be true.

Pugiles . . . ingemiscunt non quod doleant . . . sed quia profundenda voce omne corpus intenditur.
(Cic. *T.D.* ii. 23)
" Prize-fighters groan not because they are in pain but because by thus giving vent their whole body is exerted."

§ 217. *Alleged Reason.*

When it is implied by the speaker that the cause is given by some other person the rules of Indirect Speech are brought into play. In Greek after a primary main verb no change of mood is made, but after a historic main verb the optative is used.

Οἶσθα ἐπαινέσαντα αὐτὸν τὸν Ἀγαμέμνονα, ὡς βασιλεὺς
εἴη ἀγαθός. (X. *Symp.* 4. 6)
". . . because (as he said) he was a good king."

This gives Homer's reason for praising Agamemnon ; ἦν would mean that Xenophon gave the reason as he himself conceived it. As it is, we may understand " because he said that . . ." to get the strict sense, i.e. the ὡς sentence is virtually in Indirect Speech.

In Latin the rule that all subordinate clauses take the

subjunctive in Indirect Speech has a similar application to causal clauses which give an alleged reason.

> *Aristides nonne ob eam causam expulsus est patria quod praeter modum iustus esset ?* (Cic. *T.D.* v. 36)
> "Was not Aristides exiled for this reason—that he was excessively upright ?"

Concessive Clauses

§ 218. All clauses which contain the idea "though . . ." are usually called concessive: in Greek "though"-clauses are usually expressed by a participial construction with καίπερ, περ (see above, § 178), sometimes by means of a conditional clause ("even if"—e.g. κἄν = καὶ ἐάν); in Latin "though"-clauses are usually introduced by *quamquam, quamvis, quamlibet, licet*; these conjunctions, with the exception of *quamquam*, usually take the concessive subjunctive (§ 187). The formation of these words is obvious: *quamquam* is the fem. acc. sing. of the reduplicated *quis-*, "however" (*quam*, sc. e.g. *viam*, adverbial accusative = in which way; cf. τῇδε, sc. ὁδῷ), "however much", *quamvis, quamlibet* = "how you please", *licet* = "it is allowed", "granted". When the concession is put in conditional form, *etsi* ("even if") is generally used.

1. Πιθοῦ γυναιξί, καίπερ οὐ στέργων ὅμως.
   (Aesch. *Sept.* 712)
   "Hearken to women though you like them not."

2. *Nihil agis, dolor ; quamvis sis molestus, numquam te esse confitebor malum.* (Cic. *T.D.* ii. 25)
   "It's no good, Pain; be troublesome as much as you like, I will never acknowledge you an evil."

3. *Licet faciant quos volent consules . . . videbis brevi tempore magnum . . . Catonem.* (Cic. *Att.* ii. 9)
   "(It is allowed)—let them make whomever they like consuls . . . soon you will see Cato great . . ."

These subjunctives, irrespective of the conjunctions, are concessive subjunctives, and are there in their own right before the conjunctions are added. *Quamvis, quamlibet, licet* are used with this subjunctive; *quamquam* in classical

Latin is not used with this subjunctive, it is used with the simple indicative.

> Quamquam itinere et proelio fessi erant, tamen . . . procedunt. (Sall. J. 53)
> "However tired they were (as a matter of fact) . . ."

Quamvis essent fessi would mean literally " Let them have been tired, as much as you like . . ."

Conditional Sentences

§ 219. A conditional sentence is a sentence containing a *supposition*, usually introduced by "if"—εἰ, *si*. It consists of two clauses : (i) a dependent clause (*protasis* = "premiss") which expresses the condition ; (ii) a main clause (*apodosis* = "consequence") which states what follows from that condition and therefore naturally comes after it in order of time.

The *protasis* is dependent and expresses an imaginary happening ; the *apodosis* is the principal clause and expresses an idea which, if the protasis is realized, is stated as a fact. Therefore the regular negative of the protasis is μή and that of the apodosis οὐ. Where οὐ is found in protasis it usually negatives a particular word rather than the clause ; e.g.

> Εἰ τοὺς θανόντας οὐκ ἐᾷς θάπτειν . . .
> (Soph. *Aj.* 1131)
> "If thou forbiddest the dead to be buried . . ."

(But Homer sometimes has οὐ negativing a whole protasis. Possibly in early Greek any indicative in protasis took οὐ, the negative of the indicative as the mood of fact.) (See § 296.)

> Εἴπερ γάρ τε καὶ αὐτίκ' Ὀλύμπιος οὐκ ἐτέλεσσεν,
> ἔκ τε καὶ ὀψὲ τελεῖ. (*Il.* iv. 160)
> "For even if the Olympian has not brought about the fulfilment forthwith, yet doth he fulfil at the last . . ."

The adverb ἄν (epic κε, κεν) is regularly used (i) in the protasis when the verb is subjunctive, (ii) in the apodosis with the optative and with historic indicatives in unfulfilled conditionals.

§ 220. Conditional sentences may be distinguished in three ways : (i) according to whether they refer to past, present, future ; (ii) according to whether anything is implied about their fulfilment or non-fulfilment; (iii) according to whether they are particular or general conditions.

§ 221. *Past and Present Conditions expressed openly.* Indicative in both halves : e.g. " If you want a drink, you can get it here ", " If you were in the room, you saw what was going on ". The choice is left quite open—" you may have been there, you may not have been there " ; no suggestion of probability or remoteness.

>Present : εἰ τοῦτο ποιεῖς, ἁμαρτάνεις.
>si hoc facis, erras.
>
>Past : εἰ τοῦτο ἐποίησας, ἥμαρτες.
>si hoc fecisti, erravisti.

(Or with any historic tense of the indic.)

There are many varieties of such conditions and many combinations of tenses (e.g. εἰ τοῦτο πεποίηκας, ἁμαρτάνεις and εἰ τοῦτο ποιεῖς, ἥμαρτες), according to the shade of meaning required.

§ 222. *Unfulfilled Past and Present Conditions.* " If you were now doing this (i.e. you are actually not), you would be doing wrong ", " If you had done this (i.e. actually you did not), you would have been wrong ".

>Present : εἰ τοῦτο ἐποίεις, ἡμάρτανες ἄν.
>si hoc faceres, errares.
>
>Past : εἰ τοῦτο ἐποίησας, ἥμαρτες ἄν.
>si hoc fecisses, errasses.

Greek here uses the indicative, though the actions are merely imagined and cannot be said to be stated as facts, merely to mark *time* distinctions which the optative cannot do. The unreality is given by ἄν—". . . *in that case* you did wrong."

Homeric Usage.

In Unfulfilled Present Conditions the present optative is usually used even in apodosis :

Εἰ μὲν νῦν ἐπὶ ἄλλῳ ἀεθλεύοιμεν Ἀχαιοί,
ἦ τ' ἂν ἐγὼ τὰ πρῶτα λαβὼν κλισίηνδε φεροίμην.
(Il. xxiii. 274)

"If in some other man's honour we Achaeans were now holding our games, verily I myself would win first prize and bear it to my hut."

In Unfulfilled Past Conditions the imperfect indicative is found (which in Attic is used for *present* unfulfilled):

Καί νύ κε δὴ ξιφέεσσ' αὐτοσχεδὸν οὐτάζοντο,
εἰ μὴ κήρυκες, Διὸς ἄγγελοι ἠδὲ καὶ ἀνδρῶν,
ἦλθον . . . (Il. vii. 273)

"And now would they have been smiting each other hand to hand with their swords, had not the heralds, messengers of gods and men, come . . ."

Here the use of the imperfect is helped out by the idea of continuance in οὐτάζοντο.

Also, in this type of conditional, an aorist optative is used in the apodosis:

Καί νύ κεν ἔνθ' ἀπόλοιτο ἄναξ ἀνδρῶν Αἰνείας,
εἰ μὴ ἄρ' ὀξὺ νόησε . . . (Il. v. 311)

"Then would he have perished, the lord of men, Aeneas, had not she quickly spied . . ."

So in a potential sentence:

Ἐμοὶ δὲ τότ' ἂν πολὺ κέρδιον εἴη. (Il. xxii. 108)
"More gain had it then been for me."

§ 223. *Vivid Future Conditions.* "If you fall into the river you will get wet." Future indicative in both halves; or in Greek the protasis may be in the subjunctive expressing the action not so much as a future event as a possibility. This subjunctive always takes ἄν, usually in the forms ἐάν, ἤν, ἄν (all = εἰ ἄν).

$\begin{Bmatrix} εἰ\ τοῦτο\ ποιήσεις, \\ ἐὰν\ τοῦτο\ ποιῇς, \end{Bmatrix}$ ἁμαρτήσει.

si hoc $\begin{Bmatrix} facies, \\ feceris. \end{Bmatrix}$ *errabis.*

N.B. the completed tense (fut. perfect) in Latin, which is very accurate on time-distinctions.

In Vivid Future Conditions Homer uses the subjunctive in protasis, future indicative in apodosis, as in Attic : εἴ κε is commoner than εἰ ἄν, ἤν. Notice that we find sometimes—

(a) Subjunctive with ἄν, κε in both protasis and apodosis :

Εἰ δέ κε μὴ δώῃσιν, ἐγὼ δέ κεν αὐτὸς ἕλωμαι.
(*Il.* i. 324)
" But if he will not give, then I myself will take her."

(b) Εἰ without ἄν or κεν : usually in general sayings, but there are exceptions :

Εἴπερ γάρ σε κατακτάνῃ, οὔ σ' ἔτ' ἔγωγε
κλαύσομαι ἐν λεχέεσσι . . .   (*Il.* xxii. 86)
" For if he shall slay thee, no more will I bewail thee on a couch . . ."

§ 224. *Remoter Future Conditions.* " If you were to try it you would soon find out." In Greek optative in both halves, apodosis with ἄν. Latin has in both present (more rarely perfect) subjunctive :

εἰ τοῦτο ποιοίης ἁμαρτάνοις ἄν.
si hoc facias, erres.
si hoc feceris, erraveris.

In Remoter Future Conditions in Homer κεν is found in both apodosis and protasis :

Εἰ τούτω κε λάβοιμεν, ἀροίμεθά κε κλέος ἐσθλόν.
(*Il.* v. 273)
" If (*then,* as I propose) we take these, we should win glorious renown."

§ 225. All the above examples apply to Particular Conditions, i.e. conditions which are true of a single occasion : " If they catch him, they will shoot him " ; " If you are passing by, please leave this note " ; " If I don't eat my breakfast, I shall be hungry before lunch ".

But *General Conditions* are indefinite in their application ; *whenever* the protasis holds good the apodosis follows on : " If I sleep, I dream " ; " If ever he went to London, he stayed at the Ritz " ; both these sentences refer to an indefinite group of actions. (Cp. §§ 245 ff.)

For *Present* Indefinite Conditions Greek has ἐάν + Subjunctive, followed by an indicative in the apodosis, and for *Past* Indefinite εἰ + Optative, followed by the Imperfect indicative. Latin, as above, has indicative throughout.

1. Ἢν ἐγγὺς ἔλθῃ θάνατος, οὐδεὶς βούλεται θνῄσκειν.
(Eur. *Alc.* 671)
"When death comes near, no one is (ever) willing to die."

2. Εἴ τις ἀντείποι, εὐθὺς τεθνήκει. (Thuc. viii. 66)
"If anyone objected, he was a dead man at once."

Incompletely expressed Conditional Sentences.

§ 226. *Protasis Obscured or Suppressed.*

Sometimes the protasis is expressed by means of a participle, or implied in an adverb or in an ablative absolute, etc.

1. Τοιαῦτα τἂν γυναιξὶ συνναίων ἔχοις. (Aesch. *S.* 195)
"Such troubles wouldst thou have if thou lived with women."

2. Διά γ' ὑμᾶς πάλαι ἂν ἀπολώλειτε. (Dem. xviii. 49)
"If it had depended on you you would long since have been ruined."

3. *Illius impulsu . . . moenia mota forent.*
(Ov. *M.* iii. 61)
"Had he striven at them . . . the walls would have been moved."

Often the verb of the protasis is omitted as in the phrases ὡς εἰ, πλὴν εἰ (where πλήν = εἰ μή):

Οὐδὲ τὰ ὀνόματα οἷόν τε αὐτῶν εἰδέναι, πλὴν εἴ τις κωμῳδοποιὸς τυγχάνει ὤν. (Plat. *Ap.* 18 c)
"Nor is it possible even to know their names—if one doesn't know if one happens to be a comic poet."

In Homer there is a common ellipse with εἰ δ' ἄγε:

Εἰ δ' ἄγε τοι κεφαλῇ κατανεύσομαι, ὄφρα πεποίθῃς.
(*Il.* i. 524)
"Come now, I will bow my head for thee, that thou mayest trust."

Here, apparently, the verb of the protasis is omitted, i.e. "if (you like)". But very possibly εἰ ἄγε is purely interjectional = Latin *eia*. This may be the origin of the use of εἰ in introducing conditionals—to draw attention to them by an exclamation : e.g. " Look here ! I will stand. You can sit down " = " If I stand, you can sit down ". (Some scholars suggest that εἰ was originally a temporal particle— εἰ : εἶτα :: ἐπεί : ἔπειτα—see Monro, p. 292.)

Sometimes a protasis is expressed in an imperative (see § 194, " Seek and ye shall find "). This suggests an early paratactic stage of the conditional sentence in which the protasis is stated as an independent validity. (See above.)

   1. Λαβέ καὶ εἴσει.   (Plat. *Theaet.* 154 c)
     " Take it and you will know."
   2. *Lacesse, iam videbis furentem.*   (Cic. *T.D.* iv. 54)
     " Arouse him and you will find him a Tartar."

§ 227. When the protasis is completely omitted, the sentence is called potential (i.e. it expresses a possibility, usually, but not necessarily, dependent upon an assumed condition). This is common where the supposition is contrary to fact in past and present conditions, or—in future conditions—where the supposition is remote.

Potential of Unfulfilled Condition :
   1. Ἐβουλόμην ἂν αὐτοὺς ἀληθῆ λέγειν.   (Lys. xii. 22)
     " I should have liked them to speak the truth."
   2. *Crederes victos* . . .   (Liv. ii. 43)
     " You would think them beaten men."

Potential of Remote Future :
(Common as a polite request and as a polite command : " Would you mind passing the cream ? " " You might close the door ".)

   1. Τὸν μάλιστα ἐπιτιμῶντα . . . ἡδέως ἂν ἐροίμην . . .
                                                     (Dem. xviii. 64)
     " But I would gladly ask my critic."
   2. Κλύοις ἂν ἤδη, Φοῖβε.   (Soph. *El.* 637)
     " Hear now, Phoebus."
   3. *Caedi discipulos minime velim.*   (Quint. i. 3. 13)
     " I should not like pupils to be beaten."

§ 228. From this potential indicative with ἄν must be distinguished the iterative use of imperfect and aorist indicative with ἄν to denote customary action. This probably developed from the use of the past indicative to express what was likely to happen in past circumstances. Thus ἐποίησεν ἄν, meaning, in the first place, " he, under certain past conditions, would have done ", came to have an iterative sense, " he would have done, under all conditions or whenever there was occasion ".

1. Εἴ τις ἀντιλέγοι . . ., ἐπὶ τὴν ὑπόθεσιν ἐπανῆγεν ἄν πάντα τὸν λόγον. (X. *Mem.* iv. 6. 13)
"... he always brought the discussion back to the main point."
2. Διηρώτων ἄν αὐτοὺς τί λέγοιεν. (Plat. *Ap.* 22 B)
" I used to ask them what they meant."

Apodosis Obscured or Suppressed.

§ 229. The Apodosis may be contained in a participle:

1. Οἶμαι ἐγὼ ταῦτα λέγειν ἔχειν, μὴ κωλύων εἴ τις ἄλλος ἐπαγγέλλεταί τι. (Dem. iv. 15)
" That, I think, is what I have to say, but I do not object if anyone else has any proposal."
2. *Peditum acies videbatur, si iusta . . . pugna esset, haud . . . impar futura.* (Liv. xxii. 28)
"... though it would not have been uneven if it had been a regular battle."

§ 230. Or in a substantive which has the force of a verb:

1. . . . ὡς ὄντ' ἀναστατῆρα Καδμείων χθονός, εἰ μὴ θεῶν τις ἐμποδὼν ἔστη δορί. (Aesch. *Sept.* 105)
"... as being the ravager of the land of the Thebans had not one of the gods withstood his spear."
2. *Omnium consensu capax imperii nisi imperasset.*
(Tac. *H.* i. 49)
" By common consent a man who would have made a good emperor—if only he had not reigned."

§ 231. Sometimes the verb of the apodosis is omitted when it can be easily supplied, especially in similes after ὥσπερ εἰ, ὥσπερ ἄν εἰ, *tamquam, quasi,* etc.

1. Οἱ δ' οἰκέται ῥέγκουσιν· ἀλλ' οὐκ ἂν πρὸ τοῦ.
    (Ar. *Nub.* 5)
   "The domestics are snoring; but they wouldn't have been in the old days."
2. Διεπορεύθησαν ὥσπερ ἂν εἰ προπεμπόμενοι.
    (Isoc. iv. 148)
   ". . . marched as if they were under escort."
3. *Restat ut in castra Sexti, aut, si forte, Bruti nos conferamus.* (Cic. *Att.* xiv. 13)
   "It remains for us to betake ourselves to the camp of Sextus, or, if it so happens, to Brutus's."
4. *Tamquam si claudus sim, cum fusti est ambulandum.*
    (Plaut. *Asin.* 427)
   "I've got to walk with a stick, as though I were lame."

In 1. πρὸ τοῦ represents the protasis—" they would not be . . . if they were living in the old days "; 2. has an ellipse of the verbs of both protasis and apodosis—as they would *have marched* if they *had been* under escort. In 4. full would be *tamquam ambulem si claudus sim.*

There is a similar ellipse in Homer in similes with ὡς εἰ:
 . . . καί μ' ἐφίλησ' ὡς εἴ τε πατὴρ ὃν παῖδα φιλήσῃ.
    (*Il.* ix. 481)
   "He loved me as a father (will love) if he loves his son."

In τῶν νέες ὠκεῖαι ὡσεὶ πτερὸν ἠὲ νόημα (*Od.* vii. 36) the conditional substructure is forgotten and ὡς = εἰ (simply) " like ".

§ 232. The Apodosis may be completely left to the imagination when it is easily supplied from the context:

Εἰ μὲν ἐγὼ ὑμᾶς ἱκανῶς διδάσκω οἵους δεῖ πρὸς ἀλλήλους εἶναι· εἰ δὲ μή, καὶ παρὰ τῶν προγεγενημένων μανθάνετε. (X. *Cyr.* viii. 7)
"If my teaching of how you should behave to one another is adequate—(well and good); if it is not, then you must learn too from those who lived before you."

§ 233. Sometimes the protasis contains the idea of a suppressed apodosis, especially with εἴ πως, ἐάν πως, *si forte.*

Clauses introduced by these phrases convey the idea of purpose.

1. Πατρὸς ἐμοῦ κλέος . . . μετέρχομαι, ἤν που ἀκούσω.
(Hom. *Od.* iii. 83)
i.e. " that I may hear of him if perchance I shall."
2. *Tentata res est si primo impetu capi Ardea posset.*
(Liv. i. 57)
i.e. " that they might take Ardea if it could . . ."

The true explanation is by the ellipses indicated; the apparent dependent question then disappears.

Mixed Conditionals.

§ 234. These are sentences combining different forms of protasis and apodosis (perhaps rather more common in Greek). When such a combination is found it is usually due to a *need for a special shade of meaning*. Anyhow there is always some point in the abnormality, some gain in meaning. The following are the commonest mixed constructions : of these

A and B merely have a bolder verb in the apodosis;
C has a cramped apodosis ; D and E cramped protasis ;
F has an extended form of apodosis.

§ 235. A. The **Protasis a Remote Future Condition.**
The **Apodosis Present or Future Indicative.**

(i) Apodosis—Future :

1. εἴ τίς μοι ἀνὴρ ἅμ᾽ ἕποιτο καὶ ἄλλος
μᾶλλον θαλπωρὴ καὶ θαρσαλεώτερον ἔσται.
(Hom. *Il.* x. 222)
" And if any other man should come with me, then will there be the greater cheer and comfort."
2. *Si fractus illabatur orbis*
Impavidum ferient ruinae. (Hor. *C.* iii. 3. 7)
" If the world should be shattered and fall upon him, its fall shall strike him unafraid." (Cp. Henley's " the menace of the years finds and shall find him unafraid ".)

Here the event that follows from the condition is stated with great confidence as a future fact, not merely a possibility ; i.e. between the two halves of the sentence the speaker gains in confidence and makes the tone of the whole more vivid.

N.B. in 1. there is precisely the same lack of symmetry in the English.

§ 236. (ii) Apodosis—Present :
1. Οὔ μοι θέμις ἔστ' οὐδ' εἰ κακίων σέθεν ἔλθοι,
ξεῖνον ἀτιμῆσαι. (Hom. *Od.* xiv. 56)
"It is not right for me, not even if a meaner man than thou were to come, to dishonour a stranger."
2. *Mulieribus . . . par ad honesta, libeat, facultas est.*
(Sen. *Dial.* vi. 16)
"Women, if they but choose, have equal opportunity of doing good."

Here the protasis gives a hypothetical instance, the apodosis expresses a certain truth which extends beyond the limit implied in the protasis. Strictly the thought of the protasis requires a slightly different form of apodosis, the idea of which is included in the thought of the whole sentence. The full thought of 1. is "It is not right for me to dishonour a stranger, no, and it would not be right even if a meaner man than you should come". But the general truth "It *is* not right" includes and even strengthens the more particular truth "It would not be right". Cp. ἀλλ' ὃν πόλις στήσειε τοῦδε χρὴ κλύειν, § 241.

§ 237. B. The Protasis an Unfulfilled Past Condition.
The Apodosis expressing vividly as a Fact what would have followed.

This is merely a rhetorical exaggeration. For obvious reasons (see § 238) not found in Greek.
1. *Pons Sublicius iter paene hostibus dedit, ni unus vir fuisset.* (Liv. ii. 10)
"The Sublician bridge all but let the enemy in—had it not been for one man."
2. *Me truncus illapsus cerebro*
Sustulerat nisi Faunus ictum
Dextra levasset . . . (Hor. *C.* ii. 17. 28)
"A tree-trunk fell on my head and had killed me had not Faunus lightened the blow with his hand."

(N.B. the English "had killed me" for "would have . . .", which, if rather archaic, is a similar usage to the Latin. Notice the effect of the usage: "It *had killed me*, had not . . .". Cp. *Romeo and Juliet*: "An I might live to see thee married once, I have my wish ".)

§ 238. C. The **Protasis** an Unfulfilled Past or Present Condition.
The **Apodosis** an Actual Fact.

Here the combination is not strictly logical and the explanation is that the real apodosis is omitted. This would seem to be confined to Latin, as in Greek it would be indistinguishable from Conditionals of the type εἰ τοῦτο ἐποίησας ἥμαρτες, because in a past unfulfilled condition εἰ τοῦτο ἐποίησας has also to do duty for "If you had done this".

 1. *Memini numeros, si verba tenerem.* (V. *Ecl.* ix. 45)
  "I remember the tune, if I had the words."
 2.   *iam tuta tenebam,*
 Ni gens crudelis ferro invasisset . . . (V. *Aen.* vi. 358)

Cp. from *The Times Lit. Sup.*: "She has collected the material for a good book, if only the execution had been up to the mark".

In 1. the idea is "I remember the tune, and I should have the complete song if . . ."; in 2. "I was grasping safety and should have been safe, had not a savage tribe assailed me with the sword"; but possibly refer to § 230.

The gain is in conciseness and vividness.

§ 239. D. The **Protasis** an Open Condition.
  The **Apodosis** giving a more remote or an unrealized result.

 1. Εἰ δέ τις ἀθανάτων γε κατ' οὐρανοῦ εἰλήλουθας,
  οὐκ ἂν ἔγωγε θεοῖσιν ἐπουρανίοισι μαχοίμην.
         (Hom. *Il.* vi. 128)
 2. Εἰ γὰρ ὀρθῶς ἀπέστησαν, ὑμεῖς ἂν οὐ χρεὼν ἄρχοιτε.
         (Thuc. iii. 40)
 3. *Epistulam misissem, nisi tam subito fratris puer proficiscebatur.* (Cic. *Att.* vii. 1)
 4. *Peream male si non optimum erat.* (Hor. *S.* ii. 1. 6)

Each clause in these combinations seems to have its proper force. But, considered strictly, the protasis in each case expresses an established fact independent of the apodosis, and the apodosis takes its shade of meaning from another protasis which is understood. Thus:

1. " You have come : if a god came, I should not fight with a god " (i.e. potential).
2. " They revolted :—if with justice, it would follow that your empire is unjustified " (cautious, tactful apodosis).
3. "My brother's servant was (i.e. is) starting out; if he had not started so soon, I would have sent the letter."
4. " It was excellent; if what I say is not true let me perish." (Not strictly parallel, but similar.)

§ 240. E. Sometimes in Greek a **Protasis of an Open Condition** contains a potential optative or indicative with ἄν.

1. Οὗτοι, οὐδ' εἰ μὴ ποιήσαιτ' ἂν τοῦτο . . ., εὐκαταφρόνητόν ἐστιν. (Dem. iv. 18)
 " Nor, even if you were to fail to do this, is it easily to be despised."
2. Τίς οὐκ ἂν ἀπέκτεινέ με δικαίως, εἰ . . . καταισχύνειν ἐπεχείρησ' ἄν; (id. xviii. 101)

'Ἐπεχείρησ' ἄν is really the apodosis of an understood protasis, e.g. " if I had been able " : the full sense of Demosthenes' sentence is, " If I would (under any circumstances) have attempted to disgrace . . .", and the true protasis is " If it is true that I would have . . ."

§ 241. F. The **Protasis an Unfulfilled Condition.**
The **Apodosis**—an Indicative of a verb expressing " must ", " ought ", " could ", etc. + an infinitive.

1. Ἐν αὐτῇ τῇ δίκῃ ἐξῆν σοι φυγῆς τιμήσασθαι, εἰ ἐβούλου. (Plat. *Crit.* 52 c)
 " During the trial itself you could have assessed the penalty at banishment, had you wished."
2. Ἐμὲ εἰ ἠδίκησεν ἰδιώτην ὄντα, ἰδίᾳ καὶ δίκην προσῆκε διδόναι. (Dem. xxi. 33)
 " If he had injured me as a private person, he should have given satisfaction in a private suit."

3. *Antoni gladios potuit contemnere si sic
   Omnia dixisset.* (Juv. x. 123)
   " He could have despised the swords of Antony if all
   his utterance had been like this."

In these sentences the stress is laid on the *infinitive*: the infinitive, not the main verb, represents the apodosis. In fact the verb + infinitive are a sort of periphrasis. In 1. ἐξῆν τιμήσασθαι roughly = ἐτιμήσω ἄν. N.B. the English " you were able to assess ", " you would have assessed " are equally in place. So in 3. *potuit* is a sort of auxiliary: *potuit contemnere = contempsisset*. Cp. ἀλλ' ὃν πόλις στήσειε τοῦδε χρὴ κλύειν (Soph. *Ant.* 666), for 2.: χρῆν and χρή because the obligation is ever-present, not conditional—"Whomever the city might appoint (see § 192), him we *must* obey."

N.B.—If the stress is laid on the actual necessity, possibility, etc., of the act, ἄν must be used.

Εἰ γὰρ . . . τὰ δέοντα οὗτοι συνεβούλευσαν, οὐδὲν ἂν ὑμᾶς ἔδει βουλεύεσθαι. (Dem. iv. 1)
" If these had given you the right counsel, there would be no need for you to take counsel now."

§ 242. Lastly we may consider the protasis with εἰ to express the object of emotion after, e.g., θαυμάζω, αἰσχύνομαι, where a causal clause might be expected.

Θαυμάζω εἰ μηδεὶς . . . ἐνθυμεῖται. (Dem. iv. 43)
" I am surprised that no one considers . . ."

Doubtless the original effect of such sentences was one of tentativeness or politeness, i.e. the statement is expressed hypothetically, not as a fact. Demosthenes means " Nobody notices . . . and I'm surprised ", but he says, " If nobody notices, then I'm surprised ". But with certain verbs the usage has become stereotyped and this tentative flavour is lost.

ADDENDA TO CONDITIONALS

§ 243. Δέ in Apodosis.

Μέν and δέ are properly used only with clauses that are strictly co-ordinate, i.e. of precisely the **same status in the** sentence; further, their presence binds together the two clauses, so that δέ constitutes a conjunction; in translating we need not translate μέν, which is merely a particle, but δέ (which often appears without an antecedent μέν) must be translated by "and", "but", etc.

Yet we occasionally find in early Greek conditional sentences in which the apodosis is introduced by δέ (sometimes ἀλλά, αὐτάρ), as though the apodosis were co-ordinate with the protasis. The usage is also found, but rarely, in Attic.

1. Εἰ δέ κε μὴ δώωσιν, ἐγὼ δέ κεν αὐτὸς ἕλωμαι.
(Hom. *Il.* i. 137)
"But if they give it not, then I myself will take one."

2. Εἰ ὑμῖν ἐστι τοῦτο μὴ δυνατὸν ποιῆσαι, ὑμεῖς δὲ ἔτι καὶ νῦν ἐκ τοῦ μέσου ἡμῖν ἕζεσθε. (Hdt. viii. 22)
"If it is not possible for you to do this, still, even so, just keep out of the fight."

This δέ cannot be rendered in English; if we put in a "then" or "yet", these are merely adverbs, not conjunctions.

The effect of this δέ is to stress the contrast between the two halves of the sentence; the logical importance of the protasis raises it above its grammatical status; the δέ depends upon the idea that the if-clause is a self-contained sentence.

Compare the use of ἀλλὰ νῦν ("now at least") in Attic:

. . . εἰ μή τι, ἀλλὰ τὴν περὶ τὸν ἥλιον ὁμοιότητα . . . διεξιών. (Plat. *Rep.* 509 c)
". . . at all events going over your similitude of the sun."

(Εἰ μή τι = "if you do nothing else".)

This irregular δέ is found also in sentences other than conditional (though the usage is generally known as "δέ in Apodosis").

1. Οἵη περ φύλλων γενεή, τοίη δὲ καὶ ἀνδρῶν.
(Hom. *Il.* vi. 146)
"As is the generation of leaves, so is the generation of man."

THE SENTENCE 131

2. Ἐπεί τε ὁ πόλεμος κατέστη, ὁ δὲ φαίνεται καὶ ἐν τούτῳ
προγνοὺς τὴν δύναμιν. (Thuc. ii. 65)
"And when the war broke out, it seems that in this
too he rightly gauged her power."

Here it is used to point the contrast: sometimes it is used, after an involved or protracted subordinate clause, to indicate the beginning of the main sentence. (Cp. Thuc. i. 11.)

§ 244. **The Ideal Second Person in Latin.**
The second person, indicating an indefinite subject, is commonly found in Latin in the subjunctive. It is most common in conditional sentences, especially in potential. (This idiom is, of course, very common in colloquial English.) It is also found with *ne* in the present subjunctive in prohibitions.

1. *Iniurias fortunae, quas ferre nequeas, defugiendo relinquas.*
(Cic. *T.D.* v. 41)
"Turn your back on the blows of Fortune which you cannot bear."

2. *Putasses eius luctus aliquem finem esse debere.*
(Sen. *Dial.* vi. 13)
"You would have thought there should be some limit to that grief."

3. *Mens quoque et animus, nisi tamquam lumini oleum instilles, exstinguuntur senectute.* (Cic. *Sen.* 11)
"Mind and spirit, too, unless you feed them like a lamp, die out in old age."

4. *Proinde ubi se videas hominem indignarier ipsum . . .
Scire licet non sincerum sonere . . .* (Lucr. iii. 870)
"So if you see a man complaining . . . you can know that he does not ring true."

N.B.—This indefinite imaginary person takes a subjunctive where usually a definite person would have an indicative.

INDEFINITE RELATIVE AND TEMPORAL CLAUSES

§ 245. **Indefinite Relative and Temporal Clauses.**
A relative with an indefinite antecedent gives a conditional force to its clause and may be called a conditional

relative; e.g. ὅ τι λέγεις ἀκούω = εἴ τι λέγεις . . ., ὅ τι ἂν λέγῃς ἀκούσομαι = ἐάν τι λέγῃς . . ., ὅ τι μὴ ἔλεξας, οὐκ ἂν ἤκουσα = εἴ τι μὴ ἔλεξας . . . and so on.

It will be simplest in our consideration of these conditional relatives to follow them through the four groups of the conditional sentence (see § 220). They will be seen to follow the same rules as conditionals proper.

§ 246. (i) *Present or Past Open Condition*:

1. Ἐπίσταμαι
ὁρᾶν θ' ἃ δεῖ με, κοὐχ ὁρᾶν ἃ μὴ πρέπει.
(Eur. *Ino*, fr. 417)
"I know how to see the things I should see and not see the things I should not see."

2. Ἐνεβίβασαν τῶν σκευῶν ὅσα μὴ ἀνάγκη ἦν ἔχειν.
(X. *An.* v. 3)
"They put on board such equipment as was unnecessary."

3. *Quicumque is est, ei me profiteor inimicum.*
(Cic. *Att.* x. 31)
i.e. "Even if he is . . . I profess myself his enemy."

4. *Quoscumque de te queri audivi quacumque potui ratione placavi.* (Cic. *Q. fr.* i. 2)
"If I heard any complaining about you I appeased them as best I could."

§ 247. (ii) *Present and Past Unfulfilled*:

1. Ὁπότερον τούτων ἐποίησεν, οὐδενὸς ἂν ἧττον Ἀθηναίων πλούσιοι ἦσαν. (Lys. xxxii. 23)
"Whichever of these he had done, they would still be as rich as any Athenian."

2. Ὁπηνίκα ἐφαίνετο ταῦτα πεποιηκώς, ὡμολογεῖτ' ἂν ἡ κατηγορία τοῖς ἔργοις αὐτοῦ. (Dem. xviii. 14)
"If he ever appeared to have done this, his accusation would agree with his acts."

3. *Quaecumque vos causa huc attulisset, laetarer.*
(Cic. *Or.* ii. 4)
"Whatever reason had brought you here, I should be glad."

4. *Qui videret equum Troianum introductum, urbem captam diceret.* (Cic. *Verr.* iv. 23)
"Whoever saw the Trojan horse brought in would say that the city was taken."

§ 248. (iii) *Vivid Future Condition* :
1. Τάων ἥν κ' ἐθέλωμι φίλην ποιήσομ' ἄκοιτιν.
(Hom. *Il.* ix. 397)
"Of them whomsoever I wish I will make my wife."

So in Homer without ἄν or κεν :
Ἀλλὰ μάλ' εὔκηλος τὰ φράζεαι, ὅσσ' ἐθέλῃσθα.
(*Il.* i. 554)
"But in comfort contrive what thou wilt."

2. *Fortunam, quaecumque accidat, experiantur.*
(Caes. *B.G.* i. 31)
". . . whatsoever fortune may fall to them."

§ 249. (iv) *Remote Future Condition* :
1. Τί ἂν παθεῖν (δύναιτο) ὃ μὴ καὶ ὑφ' αὑτοῦ πάθοι;
(Plat. *Lys.* 214 E)
"What would he suffer that he did not suffer at his own hands ? "

2. *Haec . . . qui videat nonne cogatur confiteri deos esse ?*
(Cic. *N.D.* ii. 4)
"Would not anyone who saw this be forced to admit that there are gods ? "

All the above examples, it will be seen, follow precisely the conditional constructions.

§ 250. N.B.—A Generic clause in Latin takes the subjunctive instead of the indicative (e.g. in class (i)) when, as well as being generic, i.e. marking an indefinite class, it is *also causal or consecutive*, e.g. :

1. *Peccasse mihi videor qui a te discesserim.*
(Cic. *Fam.* xvi. 1)
"I think I have made a mistake in leaving you," i.e. because . . .

2. *Hospes, qui omnia cuperet rite facta, descendit ad Tiberim.*
(Liv. i. 45)
"The stranger, since he wanted everything to be done in perfect order, went down to the Tiber."

Obviously these sentences are relative conditionals but much more, especially in 2. where the *qui* more clearly expresses a characteristic and contains a hidden consecutive idea. The Latin for " All who love their country " is *omnes qui patriam amant* (merely generic) ; but *sunt qui patriam ament* is generic *and* consecutive, stating the characteristic of the subject of *sunt* (literally, " there are (men) who are so disposed as to love). (See § 206 under " Consecutive ".)

When the relative clause in Latin has the indicative it expresses nothing but simple fact ; but a subjunctive shows the presence of something subtler than fact, e.g. causal connexion between the verb of the main clause and the verb of the subordinate.

§ 251. General Relative Sentences.

Sometimes the verb of the antecedent clause expresses a customary or repeated action or a general truth, and the relative clause itself refers to any act or acts in a certain group, e.g. " I pay for what I buy ".

In Greek the subjunctive with ἄν is used in the dependent clause in primary sequence ; the optative without ἄν in historic. In Latin the indicative is used in these sentences for mere indefinite frequency (though the subjunctive is found in late Latin) ; cp. Conditionals in which Greek has ἐάν + subjunctive, Latin the indicative.

1. Καὶ γὰρ συμμαχεῖν τούτοις ἐθέλουσιν ἅπαντες, οὓς ἂν ὁρῶσι παρεσκευασμένους. (Dem. iv. 6)
   " All wish to have as allies those whom they see prepared."

2. Οὓς ἴδοι εὐτάκτως ἰόντας . . . ἐπῄνει.
   (X. *Cyr.* v. 3. 55)
   " It was his custom to give a word of praise to all whom he saw marching in good order."

3. *Imitamur quoscumque visum est.* (Cic. *Off.* i. 32)
   " We copy whomsoever we please."

4. *Quisquis erat qui aliquam partem in meo luctu sceleris Clodiani attigisset, quocumque venerat, damnabatur.*
   (Cic. *Sest.* 31)
   " Whoever had been such as to share C.'s crime in my dark hour, wherever he went, used to be condemned."

THE SENTENCE

§ 252. The subjunctive in the relative clause in Latin suggests causal connexion between the main and subordinate verbs, though in late Latin the subjunctive is found without any such reason.

> Ut cuiusque legionis tentoria accessissent, superbe agebant . . . (Tac. H. ii. 27)
> i.e. " They went round the lines boasting . . ."

§ 253. **Indefinite Temporal Sentences.**

Naturally most temporal clauses marking a definite point of time are past : " When he had left the room, I went on with my work ". But in reported speech of a past action which is past to the reporter but future to the subject of the action the time will become indefinite : " He said that when the other had left the room he would go on with his work ". Thus English is insensitive to the difference to which Latin particularly is sensitive. Most future temporals are indefinite, but distinguish " When he arrives I shall go " from " When the clock strikes I shall go ".

In Greek the temporal clause has

(i) ἄν + Subjunctive when main verb is Primary.
(ii) Optative when main verb is Historic.

> (i) Ἐπειδὰν διαπράξωμαι ἃ δέομαι, ἥξω.
> (X. An. ii. 3. 29)
> " When I have finished what I want to do I will come."
> (ii) Ἐπειδὴ δὲ ἀνοιχθείη, εἰσῄειμεν. (Plat. Phaed. 59 D)
> " Each day when the prison was opened, we used to go in."

Sometimes in Attic this subjunctive is used without ἄν :

> 1. . . . Μηδένα ἐκβῆναι μέχρι πλοῦς γένηται.
> (Thuc. i. 137)
> " That no one should disembark before the time for sailing."
> 2. . . . Ἕως ἀνῇ τὸ πῆμα . . . σῴζ' αὐτά.
> (Soph. Ph. 764)
> " Keep them until the sickness lets me go."

§ 254. ΠΡΙΝ has a special usage : originally it was an adverb which came to be used as a preposition with the infinitive ; this is the prevailing construction in Homer, even where later Greek would have the finite moods, e.g.

> Οὐ λήξω πρὶν Τρῶας ἅδην ἐλάσαι πολέμοιο.
> (*Il.* xix. 423)
> "I will not cease before I give the Trojans their surfeit of war."

In Homer there are six instances of πρίν with the subjunctive and one with the optative ; it is never found with the indicative.

In Attic the general usage of πρίν is—

(i) After an *affirmative* main sentence it is constructed with the infinitive (dative inf. " beforehand for . . ."—see § 166).

(ii) After a *negative* main sentence it is used in the same way as other temporal particles.

But the infinitive is used when πρίν means simply " before " not " until ".

> Οὐ πρὶν πάσχειν, ἀλλ' ἐπειδὴ ἐν τῷ ἔργῳ ἐσμέν, τοὺς ξυμμάχους . . . παρεκαλέσατε. (Thuc. i. 68)
> "You have called together the allies, not before the blow fell, but now that we are in the thick of it . . ."

A typical example of πρίν with the indicative, referring simply to a definite past action, is—

> Οὐ πρότερον ἐπαύσαντο ἐν ὀργῇ ἔχοντες αὐτόν, πρὶν ἐζημίωσαν. (Thuc. ii. 65)
> "They did not cease to hold him in wrath till they fined him."

Πρίν with the indicative after an affirmative main clause is rare :

> Ἐπὶ πολὺ διῆγον τῆς ἡμέρας πειρώμενοι ἀλλήλων, πρὶν δὴ Ἀρίστων πείθει τοὺς ἄρχοντας. (Thuc. vii. 39)
> "They spent most of the day feinting at each other, until Ariston persuaded the commanders . . ."

But here the " until " meaning of πρίν is stressed by the continuation of the action expressed by the imperfect, and the feeling of the sentence is virtually the same as that in the example before. (Cp. Soph. *O.T.* 775.)

When πρίν takes the subjunctive (+ ἄν) or optative, it

THE SENTENCE

is only after negative sentences; the only two apparent exceptions to this rule (Lys. xxii. 4, Isoc. iv. 16) occur in sentences that are virtually negative.

Αἰσχρὸν δ' ἡγοῦμαι πρότερον παύσασθαι, πρὶν ἂν ὑμεῖς ὅ τι ἂν βούλησθε ψηφίσησθε. (Lys. xxii. 4)

i.e. "I refuse to stop before you have voted whatever you want."

When the πρίν clause refers to a result not fulfilled in the past, i.e. depends upon a condition not realized, πρίν takes a past indicative. N.B. the main clause is negative or virtually negative. E.g.

Χρῆν Λεπτίνην μὴ πρότερον τιθέναι τὸν νόμον, πρὶν τοῦτον ἔλυσε. (Dem. xx. 96)

". . . before he had repealed this law."

Object Clauses

I. *Modal Clauses.*

§ 255. These are the clauses that follow verbs of striving, providing, planning, effecting, etc.—"See to it that it is done". Whereas the final clause answers the question "Why?" the object clause answers the question "What?" and gives the object of the main verb. *Efficit ut transeat = transitum efficit*, and *ut transeat* is as much an object of the verb as *transitum*. Sometimes these clauses are called "modal", i.e. they express the way in which the action is done: ὅπως = "how." Example 1. = "You must see to it how (in the way in which) things shall be well". The regular construction in these object clauses is in Greek ὅπως, ὅπως μή + future indicative; but the optative and subjunctive are found. In Latin the final rules apply.

1. Σοὶ δὴ μέλειν χρὴ τἄλλ' ὅπως ἕξει καλῶς.
(Eur. *I.T.* 1051)
"For the rest it should be your care that all is well."

2. Ἔπρασσον ὅπως βοήθεια ἥξει. (Thuc. iii. 4)
"They were trying to get help."

3. Ἐπεμέλετο αὐτῶν ὅπως ἀεὶ ἀνδράποδα διατελοῖεν.
(X. *Cyr.* viii. 1. 44)
"He took care that they should remain slaves for ever."

In Attic subjunctives + ὅπως ἄν are found in such clauses. (See under ἄν, § 288.)

Σκόπει, ὅπως ἂν ἀποθάνωμεν ἀνδρικώτατα.
(Ar. *Eq.* 80)

II. *Clauses expressing Fear.*

§ 256. We have seen above how the final construction grew out of a parataxis. In " fearing " clauses this is still more obvious, because independent subjunctives expressing fear survive in classical Greek. Homer (*Il.* xvi. 128) has μὴ δὴ νῆας ἕλωσι, " perchance they may take the ships " (μή, because I don't want them to; literally, " let them not take . . ."). So Plato has μὴ ἀγροικότερον ᾖ, " perhaps it is too rude " : this is a more sophisticated usage : the speaker puts forward his view cautiously or with an excess of politeness ; he says, " Let this not be too rude, but I think it is ". This is sometimes called the subjunctive of cautious assertion. (It is clear that this usage is not to be explained by saying that a verb of fearing is omitted ; the phrase may be the equivalent of a statement of fear, but it is not such a thing itself in form.) (See § 309.)

Other examples :

1. Μή τι κακὸν ῥέξωσι. (Hom. *Od.* xvi. 381)
" Perchance they may do some mischief."
2. . . . μὴ σοὺς διαφθείρῃ γάμους. (Eur. *Alc.* 315)
" She may ruin your marriage."
3. Μὴ φαῦλον ᾖ καὶ οὐ καθ' ὁδόν. (Plat. *Crat.* 425 B)
" Perhaps it is bad and not in the right way."

Μὴ φαῦλον ᾖ = " I think it will be bad " ; if it is needed to negative this, " I think it will not be bad ", we have μὴ οὐ—φαῦλον ᾖ. In all such sentences the οὐ simply negatives some word in the clause, e.g.

Ἀλλὰ μὴ οὐ τοῦτο ᾖ χαλεπόν, θάνατον ἐκφυγεῖν.
(Plat. *Ap.* 39 A)
" I suspect that it is not this, the avoidance of death, that is the difficulty."

Here again Greek has to use the indicative tenses to mark the *fear* of a *present* or *past* occurrence.

THE SENTENCE

1. Μὴ γὰρ τοῦτο τόν γε ὡς ἀληθῶς ἄνδρα ἐατέον ἐστί.
   (Plat. *Gorg.* 512 D)
   "Perhaps the true man should disregard this."

2. Ἀλλὰ μὴ τοῦτο οὐ καλῶς ὡμολογήσαμεν.
   (Plat. *Men.* 89 c)
   "But perhaps we have not fairly conceded this."

§ 257. Out of this independent use arose the μή and μὴ οὐ clauses after verbs of fearing. The Latin connectives are *ne, ne non, ut*. In Latin too this construction developed out of a parataxis: *timeo—ne veniat*. So with *ut*, which in this usage was originally "how". *Ne* (= lest) shows that the negative ("let him not come") is wished and the positive ("that he will come") feared; *ut* (*ne non* especially when the principal sentence is negatived) gives the opposite effect: *timeo ut veniat* = "I fear—how may he come?" (deliberative).

The rules for sequence and tense are the same as in Final. Greek uses indicative for present and past fears, and for future events sometimes μή and ὅπως μή with the future. The use of subjunctive and optative shows that the person fearing looks upon the event feared as future. In Latin fears for the present and future take present subjunctive (and imperfect when the main verb is historic); past tenses take the perfect and pluperfect subjunctive.

Examples:

1. Δέδοικα μὴ οὐδ᾽ ὅσιον ᾖ ἀπαγορεύειν.
   (Plat. *Rep.* 368 B)
   "I am afraid that it may not be righteous to refuse."

2. Ὑποπτεύσας μὴ τὴν θυγατέρα λέγοι, ἤρετο.
   (X. *Cyr.* v. 2. 9)
   "He asked, suspecting that he might mean his daughter."

3. *Timeo ne laborem augeam.* (Cic. *Leg.* i. 4)
   "I fear that I shall make the work more."

4. *Unum illud extimescebam ne quid turpius facerem, vel dicam, iam effecissem.* (Cic. *Att.* ix. 7. 1)
   "I had this one terror, that I was doing, or rather, had already done, some more disgraceful thing."

With the Indicative in Greek :

1. Δέδοικα μὴ λελήθαμεν (τὴν εἰρήνην) ἐπὶ πολλῷ ἄγοντες.
(Dem. xix. 99)
". . . that we have been unwittingly enjoying peace borrowed at high interest."

2. Τοῦ δαίμονος δέδοιχ᾽ ὅπως μὴ τεύξομαι κακοδαίμονος.
(Ar. *Eq.* 112)
" I fear that the luck I shall get will be bad luck."

ORATIO OBLIQUA

§ 258. If I say " That is what I like ", another person, reporting my words later, may report them either directly or indirectly. He may say either " He said ' That is what I like ' ", or " He said that that was what he liked ", in the second case making my original words conform to the structure of his own sentence. When the original words are thus transformed they are said to be in Oratio Obliqua, i.e. indirect speech. Similarly we may say " He thought that . . .", " He hoped that . . .", " He knew that . . .", etc.

Greek, being a more vivacious language, makes far less use of O.O. than Latin.

Now just as in English we can say either " I declare that he is innocent " or, perhaps less commonly, " I declare him to be innocent ", so in Greek we can say either λέγω ὅτι οὐκ ἀδικεῖ or λέγω αὐτὸν οὐκ ἀδικεῖν. In Latin we have only the accusative and infinitive construction : *dico eum insontem esse.* Also in Greek there is the participial construction after verbs of sensation—αἰσθάνομαι αὐτὸν ἀδικοῦντα.

In the first construction we have two simple statements linked together by a particle : " I declare ; he is innocent ", λέγω—οὐκ ἀδικεῖ, becoming for greater clearness, " I declare *that* he is innocent ", λέγω ὅτι οὐκ ἀδικεῖ (notice that colloquially we preserve a parataxis—" I declare he is innocent "). In the second construction we have a rather more complex approach, and the label Accusative and Infinitive is misleading. In Homer we find examples of this construction in which the accusative can only have been constructed with the main verb :

λαοὺς δ᾽ Ἀτρεΐδης ἀπολυμαίνεσθαι ἄνωγε. (*Il.* i. 313)

THE SENTENCE

Here λαούς is the direct object of ἄνωγε and the infinitive is merely explanatory : " He gave an order to the people— for the purifying of themselves " (infinitive as dative of purpose). But in such a sentence as

βούλομ' ἐγὼ λαὸν σῶν ἔμμεναι   (*Il.* i. 117)

a further step is marked because λαόν in itself *cannot* be considered the object of βούλομαι : here the object is rather the state indicated by the infinitive phrase ; λαόν supplies the subject of the infinitive phrase and makes the predication. After this the accusative comes to be joined with an infinitive quite mechanically to express an object clause of verbs of saying, thinking, etc., verbs which cannot of themselves take a normal direct accusative. (Inasmuch as this construction, as opposed to the ὅτι construction, stresses the subordination of the object clause to the main verb, it is not surprising that it has predominated in Latin.)

§ 259. Usually in Greek when the subject of the infinitive is the same as the subject of the main verb, either it is not expressed or is expressed in the *Nominative*, and similarly any predicate-noun or adjective. The reason is a natural attraction : what is predicated of the subject is by the very gist of the sentence part of the subject at the outset. Some Latin poets have this use, perhaps in imitation of the Greek.

1. Οἴεσθε Χαλκιδέας τὴν Ἑλλάδα σώσειν, ὑμεῖς δ' ἀποδράσεσθαι . . .   (Dem. ix. 74)
   " . . . that the Ch. will save Hellas and you will escape."

2. *Phaselus ille quem videtis, hospites,*
   Ait fuisse navium celerrimus.   (Catull. 4. 1)
   " That yacht ye see there, my friends, says it has been the fleetest of craft."

But note that we do find e.g.

Οἶμαι ἐμὲ πλείω χρήματα εἰργάσθαι ἢ ἄλλους . . .
(Plat. *Hipp. maj.* 282 E)
" . . . that I have made more money . . ."

§ 260. The *Accusative and Infinitive* Construction.

In **Greek** all independent sentences in O.R. may go into the infinitive construction in O.O.

In **Latin** likewise, BUT Second Person questions and Commands take the subjunctive in O.O.

1. Τὰς μὲν ἐπιστολὰς ... ἀνέγνωσαν, ἐν αἷς ... κεφάλαιον ἦν ... οὐ γιγνώσκειν ὅ τι βούλονται· πολλῶν γὰρ ἐλθόντων πρέσβεων οὐδένα ταὐτὰ λέγειν· εἰ οὖν τι βούλονται σαφὲς λέγειν, πέμψαι ... ἄνδρας ὡς αὐτόν. (Thuc. iv. 50)

   "They read the letters of which the gist was that he did not understand what they wanted; many envoys had come but none had said the same as any other; if they want to make their meaning clear they should send men to him ..."

2. *Quare ne committeret ...* (Caes. *B.G.* i. 13)
   (O.R. *ne commiseris.*)
   "Therefore (he said) let him not allow it ..."

3. *Quid esse ... turpius ?* (*ibid.* v. 28)
   (O.R. *Quid est turpius ?*)
   "(He asked) what was more disgraceful ? "

4. *Litteras ad senatum misit ... quid de praeda faciendum censerent ?* (Livy)
   (O.R. *Quid censetis ?*)
   "He sent a letter to the senate (to ask) what they thought should be done about the booty."

Commands quoted in the infinitive are much more common in Latin. Usually in such cases Greek prefers to insert δεῖν or χρῆναι with the infinitive, the command thus being converted into statement about what *ought* to be done, or else a verb of commanding is introduced. (But see Thuc. ii. 24. 2.)

With quoted questions Greek prefers to insert a verb of asking, thereby turning them into indirect questions.

(N.B.—*Quid esse turpius ?* is a *quoted* question; *rogat quid sit turpius* is called an *indirect* question. See below, § 272.)

§ 261. *The* ὅτι, ὡς *Construction in Greek.*

After primary main verbs the mood and tense of the O.R. are retained.

After Historic main verbs the verb of the O.R. goes into the Optative (a future is represented by fut. optat.) *or* (vivid construction) may be left as in Primary sequence.

BUT N.B. Past Indicatives must remain in the Indicative,

THE SENTENCE

because, if they were changed, we could not distinguish them from Optatives standing for primary indicatives.

In a few cases, however, where there is no ambiguity, the Present Optative does stand for a Past Indicative of O.R.

> καί μοι πάντες ἀπεκρίναντο ὅτι οὐδεὶς μάρτυς παρείη, κομίζοιτο δὲ λαμβάνων καθ' ὁποσονοῦν δέοιτο Ἄφοβος παρ' αὐτῶν. (Dem. xxx. 20)
>
> "They all replied that no witness had been present and that Aphobus had received the money from them, taking it in such amounts as he happened to want."
>
> (The O.R. would be οὐδεὶς μάρτυς παρῆν, ἐκομίζετο δὲ λαμβάνων καθ' ὁποσονοῦν δέοιτο.)

§ 262. *Complex Sentences in Oratio Obliqua.*

"He said that he would post the letter when he had written it", ". . . if he remembered it", etc.

In **Latin** the verbs of dependent clauses in O.O. go into the Subjunctive.

In **Greek** after a primary main verb the mood and tense of the direct are retained; after a historic main verb the verb is changed to the Optative or (vivid use) may be left as in primary sequence.

BUT (as with the ὅτι, ὡς construction) a past tense of the Indicative must remain in the indicative (see previous paragraph), though again, in a few instances, where there is no ambiguity, the general principle may be observed; compare the following two sentences:

> Ἐπιστεῖλαι δὲ σφίσιν αὐτοῖς τοὺς ἐφόρους (ἔφασαν) εἰπεῖν, ὡς ὧν μὲν πρόσθεν ἐποίουν μέμφοιντο αὐτοῖς.
> (X. *Hell.* iii. 2. 6)
>
> ". . . that the Ephors instructed them to say that they blamed them for what they had done."
>
> (The O.R. would be . . . ὧν πρόσθεν ἐποιεῖτε μεμφόμεθα ὑμῖν),

and

> Εἶχε γὰρ λέγειν ὡς Λακεδαιμόνιοι διὰ τοῦτο πολεμήσειαν αὐτοῖς, ὅτι οὐκ ἐθελήσαιεν μετ' Ἀγησιλάου ἐλθεῖν . . . οὐδὲ θῦσαι ἐάσειαν αὐτὸν ἐν Αὐλίδι.
> (X. *Hell.* vii. 1. 34)
>
> ". . . that the L. had made war on them because they

had not consented to go with Agesilaus and had not allowed him to sacrifice at Aulis."

(O.R. ἐπολέμησαν ἡμῖν, ὅτι οὐκ ἠθελήσαμεν . . . οὐδὲ . . . εἰάσαμεν.)

The normal usage is as follows :

O.R. Ἐὰν τοῦτο λάβω, εὖ πράξω.
O.O. Ἔφη, εἰ . . . λάβοι, εὖ πράξειν.
O.R. Εἰ τοῦτ' ἔλαβον, εὖ ἂν ἔπραξα.
O.O. Ἔφη, εἰ . . . ἔλαβεν, εὖ ἂν πρᾶξαι.

§ 263. *Abnormalities of the* ὅτι, ὡς *Construction.*

(i) The occasional use of ὅτι, ὡς with an Imperfect or Pluperfect standing for the present or perfect of O.R., after a historic verb of saying, even in Attic :

1.   οὐ γάρ οἵ τις ἐτήτυμος ἄγγελος ἐλθὼν
ἤγγειλ' ὅττι ῥά οἱ πόσις ἔκτοθι μίμνε πυλάων.
(Hom. *Il.* xxii. 438)
"For no true messenger had come to her to tell that her lord abode without the gates."

2. . . . ὃς ἡμᾶς διεδύετ' | ἐξαπατῶν καὶ λέγων | ὡς φιλαθηναῖος ἦν καὶ | τἀν Σάμῳ πρῶτος κατείποι.
(Ar. *Vesp.* 283)
". . . saying that he was a friend of the Athenians and that he first gave warning of the trouble in Samos."

Here we can only say that the ὅτι clause stands in looser relation than usual to the main sentence, and that its message is given by the speaker a past existence of its own, as in English usage : " He abode without the gates : none had come to tell her " ; " He was a friend . . . : he said he was a friend ". Certainly it seems a less sophisticated usage than the regular Attic, and it prevails in Homer, where it reminds us of so many other paratactic usages.

§ 264. (ii) Omission of ὅτι with Optative when it is clear that a thought, etc., is being expressed :

1. Ἔλεγον ὅτι παντὸς ἄξια λέγοι Σεύθης· χειμὼν γὰρ εἴη . . .   (X. *An.* vii. 3. 13)
"They said that Seuthes's words were all-important; for (they said) it was winter . . ."

2. Ἀλλὰ γὰρ οὐδέν τι μᾶλλον ἦν ἀθάνατον ... καὶ ταλαιπωρουμένη τε δὴ τοῦτον τὸν βίον ζώη καὶ τελευτῶσα ... ἀπολλύοιτο. (Plat. *Phaed.* 95 D)

". . . but that it was none the more immortal for that . . . and lives in toil through this life and finally perishes."

The last is an extreme instance : Plato, as is suggested by the " philosophic " ἦν (see § 131), is stating the theory of others.

§ 265. (iii) οἶδ' ὅτι without following verb ("I am sure").

Πάρειμι δ' ἄκων οὐχ ἑκοῦσιν, οἶδ' ὅτι.
(Soph. *Ant.* 276)

"And I am here against my will and against your will, I am sure."

Here οἶδ' ὅτι is an afterthought, but, logically, to make sense, may be taken at the beginning : " I am sure that I am here . . .". So with δηλόνοτι, in which the ὅτι usage has disappeared and which is used as an ordinary adverb ; so to-day we hear, e.g., " It's a game, sort of ".

§ 266. *The Greek Participial Construction.*

Verbs of perceiving, knowing, etc., take an Accusative and Participle where Latin would have Acc. and Infinitive. So, too, in Nominative attraction a Nom. and Participle is found.

1. . . . πυθόμενοι Ἀρταξέρξην νεωστὶ τεθνηκότα.
(Thuc. iv. 50)
". . . hearing that A. had just died."

2. Νῦν δ' ἐννοοῦμαι φαῦλος οὖσα. (Eur. *Hipp.* 435)
" I know well that I am weak."

In this construction the thing perceived of the object has a closer connexion with it than in the infinitive construction, i.e. the action is given as the attribute of the object. Compare λέγω αὐτὸν μικρὸν εἶναι with αἰσθάνομαι αὐτὸν μικρὸν ὄντα.

This construction is found with verbs meaning " to see ", " hear ", " learn ", " perceive ", " know ", " be ignorant of ", " remember ", " forget ", " show ", " prove ", " acknowledge ", " appear ", and also with ἀγγέλλω. With the infinitive verbs of knowing, etc., mean knowing *how* to do a thing (literally *for* the doing; it is the dat. inf., § 164).

> Οἶδ' ἐπὶ δεξιά, οἶδ' ἐπ' ἀριστερὰ νωμῆσαι βῶν.
> (Hom. *Il.* vii. 238)
> "I know how to wield to right, I know how to wield to left my oxhide shield."

§ 267. In Latin whenever an indicative appears in an O.O. passage it expresses an aside by the reporter :

> *Diogenes dicere solebat Harpalum (qui temporibus illis praedo felix habebatur) contra deos testimonium dicere.* (Cic. *N.D.* iii. 34)
> "Diogenes used to say that Harpalus (who at that time was generally thought the happy plunderer) was a witness against gods."

We have already considered *Alleged Reasons* (Virtual O.O.) (see § 217).

§ 268. Some sentences in Latin have this subjunctive of alleged reason *unnecessarily*.

> *Litteras quas me sibi misisse diceret recitavit homo.*
> (Cic. *Phil.* ii. 3)
> "The fellow read out letters which he alleged I had sent to him."

Cicero could say what he wanted to say by either *Litteras quas me sibi misisse dicebat* or *quas ego sibi misissem* ; he combines both, thereby doubling the force of his repudiation and adding to his scorn.

§ 269. Here may be mentioned, as perhaps due to the influence of O.O. constructions, the Latin usage of putting into the subjunctive any verb *dependent on an infinitive* :

> 1. *Pigri est ingenii contentum esse iis quae sint ab aliis inventa.* (Quint. x. 2. 4)
> "It is the mark of a backward mind to be satisfied with the discoveries of others."
>
> 2. *Sapiens non dubitat, si ita melius sit, migrare de vita.*
> (Cic. *Fin.* i. 19)
> "The wise man does not hesitate to die, if it is better so."

THE SENTENCE

§ 270. Reported Conditions sometimes have their apodosis not expressed but implied in the main verb of the sentence :

1. Τὸν Εὐηνὸν ἐμακάρισα, εἰ ὡς ἀληθῶς ἔχει ταύτην τὴν τέχνην. (Plat. *Ap.* 20 B)
"I congratulated E. (told him he was blessed) if he really had this art."

2. *Nisi restituissent statuas, vehementer minatur.*
(C. *Verr.* ii. 67)
"He made violent threats if they did not restore the statues."
(*minatur = dicit se puniturum*; O.R. *puniam nisi restitueritis.*)

§ 271. Both in Greek and Latin dependent clauses in O.O. are sometimes attracted into the accusative and infinitive construction, in Latin only such clauses as are introduced by a relative, where *qui* stands for no more than *et is*.

1. . . . ὡς δ' ἀκοῦσαι τοὺς παρόντας θόρυβον γενέσθαι.
(Dem. xix. 195)
"And that when the bystanders heard a great din arose . . ."

2. *Mundum censent regi numine deorum . . . ex quo illud consequi ut . . .* (Cic. *Fin.* iii. 19)
"They think the world is ruled by the power of the gods and that therefore . . ."

§ 272. *Indirect (Reported) Questions.*

The difference between an Indirect Question and a "Quoted" Question (see above, § 260) is this : the Indirect Question is introduced by a special verb of *asking* (e.g. "He asked what his name was" for the direct "What is your name ? ") ; whereas the "Quoted" Question occurs in the middle of a reported speech without a special verb of asking to introduce it, and in fact depends upon the verb of saying with which the reported speech began (e.g. "He said that he had no right to be there : he was trespassing : what was his name ? . . .").

N.B. in English the Indirect Question does not need an interrogation mark because the introductory verb of asking is enough, but the "Quoted" Question does need one, to show that it is a question and not a statement.

Indirect Questions can be introduced by a variety of verbs, e.g. " see ", " find ", " consider ", " wonder ", etc. etc.—" I wanted to see what the garden was like ". (Direct, " What is the garden like ? ")

Greek. After a Primary main verb, mood and tense of the Direct are kept ; after a Historic main verb (i) the Optative is used on O.O. rules, or (ii) the mood and tense of the Direct are kept (vivid use).

Latin. The Subjunctive is used of the verb in the question.

§ 273. The following are anomalous uses in Indirect Question:

Greek. *Indirect Deliberative Questions*: εἰ is used with a subjunctive ; ἐάν has usually only a conditional force and rarely means "whether". (Aesch. *F.L.* 7 has σκέψασθε δ' ἂν ὑμῖν εἰκός τι πρᾶγμα δόξω πάσχειν.)

> Τὰ δὲ ἐκπώματα οὐκ οἶδ' εἰ Χρυσάντᾳ δῶ.
> (X. *Cyr.* viii. 4. 16)
> " I don't know whether I am to give the cups to C."

§ 274. **Latin.** (i) A re-echoed question goes into the subjunctive, because it is regarded as an indirect question, the verb of asking being understood.

> Th. *Quid faciundum censes ?* Tr. *Egon quid censeam ?*
> (Plaut. *Most.* 556)
> " What do you think should be done ? " " (You ask) what do I think ? "

(ii) N.B. such direct forms as

> *Dic quaeso, num te illa terrent ?* (Cic. *T.D.* i. 5)
> " Tell me, do those things frighten you ? "

as opposed to *dic num terreant*. So in English we say either " Tell me, what is it ? " or " Tell me what it is ". These direct forms are common in Plautus and Terence, as are so many other paratactic idioms.

> *Nunc cuius iussu venio et quam ob rem venerim dicam.*
> (Plaut. *Amph.* 17)
> " Now at whose bidding do I come and why I came I will tell you."

A similar usage is found in such phrases as *mirum quantum profuit, nescio quis venit.*

§ 275. *Indirect Commands and Wishes.*

"He charged them not to depart from Jerusalem" (Direct, "Do not depart . . .").

Here, again, the difference from "Quoted" commands is that Indirect commands have a special introductory verb of commanding, whereas the "Quoted" command appears thus : "He said that he had no right to be there : he was trespassing : what was his name ? let him clear off before . . .". (See above, § 272.)

Indirect Commands.

Greek. Accusative and Infinitive.

Latin. Accusative and Infinitive with some verbs (e.g. *iubeo*) ; usually dependent jussive subjunctive or final subjunctive.

There is no real difference between these subjunctives, but the final is marked by the introduction of *ut* or *ne.*

1. Παρήγγειλαν . . . πάντας ἀναπαύεσθαι.
   (X. *An.* iii. 5. 18)
   "They passed the word along for all to rest."

2. . . . συγγνώμην κελεύων ἔχειν αὐτόν.   (Hdt. i. 116)
   ". . . begging him to have pardon."

3. *Iugurtha oppidanos hortatur moenia defendant.*
   (Sall. *J.* 56)
   "J. urges the townsmen to defend the walls."

4. *Quam mallem vinctos mihi traderet.*   (Liv. xxii. 49)
   "How I should have preferred him to hand them over bound !"

Use of *Final Construction.*

1. Πάνακτον ἐδέοντο ὅπως παραδώσουσι Λακεδαιμονίοις.
   (Thuc. v. 36)
   "They asked them to hand over Panactum to the L."

2. *Verres rogat et orat Dolabellam ut ad Neronem proficiscatur.*   (Cic. *Verr.* i. 29)
   "V. asks and implores D. to go to N."

§ 276. *Note on the Tenses of the Latin Subjunctive.*

We have seen the various uses of the four tenses of the Latin subjunctive. Of these it is easy to understand why the perfect and pluperfect subjunctives express different degrees of *past* unreal action. But why does *videam* refer to the future, not to the present ? It is because " I may see " = " I am not now seeing, but perhaps I shall see ", and looks forward, just as οὐδὲ ἴδωμαι in Homer means " nor shall I see ". And why does *viderem* refer to the present ? This is a problem. It is to be noted that English and Greek similarly use a past form (even in " I wish I were " the subjunctive is a form shared with the plural of the past tense). Is it because the past time is the only certain time of established fact ?—that in, e.g., *di facerent sine patre forem,* the speaker wants hereafter to look back—" I wish I could say (hereafter) ' I was fatherless ' " ? Or is it because the present subjunctive looks forward at the passing moment while the imperfect looks back at it ? It is hard to say.

ˮAN *AND* KEN

(The following account is derived mainly from Monro's *Homeric Grammar*, pp. 327 ff.)

§ 277. **Origin and Meaning.**
First, the use of ἄν and κεν (*Aeolic*) in Homer. There κεν is used about four times as often as ἄν, though they appear to be used to mean much the same thing, e.g. in potential sentences:

1. Ἄλλον μέν κεν . . . ῥεῖα κατευνήσαιμι.   (*Il.* xiv. 244)
   " Easily would I send to rest another . . .ˮ
2. Τίς ἄν τάδε γηθήσειεν;   (*Il.* xxiv. 367)
   " Who would rejoice at these things ? ˮ

§ 278. (i) *The force of these particles* may be seen by contrasting apparently similar sentences that contain or do not contain them. We notice that they are used in Conditional Sentences, e.g. which point to a definite future occasion; but that they are not used in sentences, e.g. similes and proverbial sayings, which imply frequent or indefinite occasions.
Examples:

1. Κέκλυτε δὴ νῦν μευ, Ἰθακήσιοι, ὅττι κεν εἴπω.
   (*Od.* ii. 25)
   "Hearken to me now, Ithacans, to the word I shall utter.ˮ
2. . . . ἀστέρ' ὀπωρινῷ ἐναλίγκιον, ὅς τε μάλιστα
   λαμπρὸν παμφαίνῃσι.   (*Il.* v. 5)
   ". . . like unto the autumn star which shines exceeding bright.ˮ

So in similes introduced by ὡς ὅτε κτλ. the subjunctive is

usually used without ἄν or κεν, because these are strictly general relative clauses.

1. Ὣς ἔφατ'· Ἀργεῖοι δὲ μέγ' ἴαχον, ὡς ὅτε κῦμα
ἀκτῇ ἐφ' ὑψηλῇ, ὅτε κινήσῃ Νότος ἐλθών.
(*Il.* ii. 394)

"So he spake, and the Argives shouted aloud, even as a wave upon a steep shore, when the South wind comes and stirs it."

2. Ὡς δ' ὅτ' ἄν ἐκ πόντοιο σέλας ναύτῃσι φανήῃ
καιομένοιο πυρός . . . (*Il.* xix. 374)

"And as when to seafarers on the sea there appears the light of a blazing fire . . ."

So in the following pair 1. is indefinite, 2. refers to a present occasion:

1. Ὣς ἀπόλοιτο καὶ ἄλλος ὅτις τοιαῦτά γε ῥέζοι.
(*Od.* i. 47)

"So perish another who should do the like."

2. Δῶρον δ' ὅττι κέ μοι δοίῃς, κειμήλιον ἔστω.
(*Od.* iv. 600)

"Whatever gift thou shouldst give, let it be an heirloom."

So in *Final* Sentences the insertion of ἄν or κεν marks reference to a definite occasion or condition: the absence of ἄν or κεν shows that the reference is to indefinite time:

1. . . . δῶρα δ' Ἀχιλλῆϊ φερέμεν τά κε θυμὸν ἰήνῃ.
(*Il.* xxiv. 119)

". . . and to bear gifts to Achilles that may soften his heart."

2. . . . τιμὴν δ' Ἀργείοις ἀποτινέμεν ἥν τιν' ἔοικεν,
ἥ τε καὶ ἐσσομένοισι μετ' ἀνθρώποισι πέληται.
(*Il.* iii. 286)

". . . and to pay to the Argives the recompense that is fitting, such as shall abide among men that shall be hereafter."

It seems, then, that ἄν and κεν denote reference to a particular time, and mean something like "then", "in that case".

§ 279. (ii) *A difference in shade of meaning* may be noticed between ἄν and κεν.
(a) ἄν is preferred to κεν in negative clauses.
(b) ἄν is especially used in the second of two parallel clauses.

Ἀλλὰ χρὴ τὸν μὲν καταθάπτειν ὅς κε θάνῃσι . . .
ὅσσοι δ' ἄν πολέμοιο περὶ στυγεροῖο λίπωνται . . .
(*Il.* xix. 228)

" It is right to bury the man who dies, but as many as are left of hateful war . . ."

Ἄν, then, appears to be stronger than κεν. Where κεν points out, ἄν may correct. Ἄν, then, is used as an adversative particle. That is why it is preferred in negative clauses, the negative being a contrast to the implied positive.

Monro (*Homeric Grammar*, p. 333), quoting οὐκ ἄν τοι χραίσμῃ κίθαρις, translates " the lyre will not avail you (viz. in battle)—whatever it may do elsewhere" (*Il.* iii. 54).

Lastly, notice that where κεν is an enclitic, ἄν as the stronger particle is accented (just as, while τε is an enclitic, δέ is accented).

§ 280. Ἄν is probably of the same origin as the Latin *an*, the root-meaning of both being " in that case ". For in early Latin *an* is often used to introduce an alternative in a double question : e.g. *non ignoscis ? an non credis ?* (Sen. R.C. vii. 16) (" Won't you forgive ? or don't you believe it ? "). Used with single questions *an* implies that the question is an alternative : *Quid ais ? an venit Pamphilus ?* (Ter. Hec. 346). Here *an* means " well then ", " in that case ".

§ 281. **Ἄν in Attic.**
There are two principal uses.

Ἄν *in Potential Sentences* (main).
The force of ἄν here is to limit the possibility expressed to conditions either stated explicitly (i.e. when the protasis is given—the complete conditional sentence) or left implicit (merely potential).

When such sentences are put into O.O. the ἄν is retained with the infinitive or participle ; or even in direct speech the potential clause being subordinate may be expressed in a participle.

1. Οἶμαι γὰρ ἂν οὐκ ἀχαρίστως μοι ἔχειν.
(X. *An.* ii. 3. 18)
"I think it would not be a thankless work for me."

2. Πόλλ' ἂν ἔχων ἕτερ' εἰπεῖν περὶ αὐτῆς παραλείπω.
(Dem. xviii. 258)
"Though I could say much else on the subject I leave it on one side."

The following idioms deserve special notice:

§ 282. (i) *Omission of verb* in potential clauses with ἄν, where the verb is easily understood from the context:

Οἱ δ' οἰκέται ῥέγκουσιν· ἀλλ' οὐκ ἂν πρὸ τοῦ.
(Ar. *Nub.* 5)
"The domestics are snoring, but they wouldn't have been in the old days."

Here the ἄν obviously points to the potential indicative understood. This elliptical use is especially common with κἄν and ὥσπερ ἂν εἰ.

§ 283. (ii) *Omission of* ἄν with the second of two verbs, where it is easily supplied:

Τί ἐποίησεν ἄν; ἢ δῆλον ὅτι ὤμοσεν; (Dem. xxxi. 9)
"What would he have done ? isn't it obvious that he would have . . . ?"

§ 284. (iii) *Repetition of* ἄν for emphasis or, in a long sentence, for clearness:

1.   ὅταν δέ τις θεῶν
βλάπτῃ, δύναιτ' ἂν οὐδ' ἂν ἰσχύων φυγεῖν.
(Soph. *El.* 696)
"But when a god thwarts, not even the strong could escape."

2. Ὑμεῖς δ' ἴσως τάχ' ἂν ἀχθόμενοι, ὥσπερ οἱ νυστάζοντες ἐγειρόμενοι, κρούσαντες ἄν με, πειθόμενοι Ἀνύτῳ, ῥᾳδίως ἂν ἀποκτείναιτε. (Plat. *Ap.* 31 A)
"But you perhaps might be angry like people awakened from a nap and might slap me and, as Anytus advises, easily kill me."

§ 285. (iv) Notice that some clauses with ὅπως, ὡς with the optative with ἄν look like Final clauses, but are really potential with ὅπως, ὡς as relative adverbs of manner:

Τὰς πρῴρας κατεβύρσωσαν, ὅπως ἂν ἀπολίσθανοι ἡ χείρ.
(Thuc. vii. 65)
"They covered the bows with hides, so that the grappling-iron when thrown on might slip off."

§ 286. **Ἄν with the Subjunctive in Subordinate Sentences.**
Here the force of ἄν seems changed, being used in sentences of indefinite application. But N.B. (a) the ἄν always clings to the conjunction; (b) it is the *subjunctive* that gives the indefiniteness. The combination represents something like our "in *the event* of" (which introduces an indefinite contingency but suggests that a definite occurrence is necessary to give validity to the meaning of the sentence).
The only idioms to notice:
(i) *Omission of ἄν*: not infrequent in Sophocles, found in Thucydides, but otherwise rare in prose.

1.   Δυστάλαινα τἄρ' ἐγὼ
εἰ σοῦ στερηθῶ.   (Soph. *O.C.* 1442)
"Unhappy me, if I shall be bereft of thee!"

2. Σωφρόνων δὲ ἀνδρῶν οἵτινες τὸν πόλεμον νομίσωσι
μεταχειρίζειν ...   (Thuc. iv. 18)
"They are wise who reckon to conduct war ..."

§ 287. (ii) Ἄν retained with optative as a remoter variant on the indefinite subjunctive, as if the writer in changing over had accidentally left in the ἄν: but the usage may be potential as that in § 285.

1. Ἀναγκαῖον αὐτοῖς διαλέγεσθαι παρ' ὧν ἂν λάβοιεν τὸν
μισθόν.   (X. *Mem.* i. 2. 6)
"... talk with those from whom they received their pay."

2. ... τὸ φάρμακον ... σῴζειν ἐμέ,
ἕως ἂν ἀρτίχριστον ἁρμόσαιμί νιν. (Soph. *Tr.* 685)
"... until I should apply it freshly spread."

§ 288. (iii) Ἄν in final clauses proper with ὅπως, ὡς (distinguish from the use in § 285) is common in Attic, especially in the formal language of inscriptions. Here ἄν, apparently, retains its old force, restricting to defined circumstances:

1. Καὶ φάτε αὐτὸν τοιοῦτον εἶναι, ὅπως ἂν φαίνηται ὡς
κάλλιστος.   (Plat. *Symp.* 199 A)
"And say that he is such that he may appear as beautiful as possible."

2. Οὐκ ἄπιθ', ὅπως ἂν οἱ Λάκωνες . . . ἀπίωσιν;
(Ar. *Lys.* 1223)

"Aren't you going, so that the Laconians can go away?"

1. may be merely an indefinite relative clause (= " in whatever way he may . . . ") ; but 2. is purely final.

§ 289. Ἄν is not used with the primary tenses of the indicative (except with the future, and that rarely).

Sometimes it would appear to be used with the present indicative, but is really thrown forward for emphasis and clearness. A good example is :

Ἐγὼ . . . οὐκ ἂν ἡγοῦμαι Φίλιππον, οὔτ' εἰ τὰ πρῶτα βιασθεὶς ἄκων ἔπραξεν, οὔτ' ἂν εἰ νῦν ἀπεγίγνωσκε Θηβαίους, τοῖς ἐκείνων ἐχθροῖς συνεχῶς ἐναντιοῦσθαι. (Dem. vi. 16)

"I think that neither if he had acted at first under compulsion, nor if he were now renouncing the Thebans, would Philip consistently oppose their enemies."

The ἄν, repeated for emphasis, belongs to ἐναντιοῦσθαι: ἂν ἐναντιοῦσθαι stands for ἂν ἐναντίοιτο of O.R.

§ 290. Ἄν is found with the future indicative and, consequently, with the future participle and infinitive. The use is rare and, though modern editors have done their best to get rid of the anomaly by changing the tense or cutting out ἄν, well-authenticated.

Ὁ δὲ δῆμος τῶν Ἀργείων . . . νομίζων μέγιστον ἂν σφᾶς ὠφελήσειν, τειχίζει μακρὰ τείχη ἐς θάλασσαν.
(Thuc. v. 82)

"The Argive democracy, thinking to do great service to them (the Athenians), built long walls down to the sea."

. . . λέγων πρὸς ὑμᾶς ὡς, εἰ διαφευξοίμην, ἤδη ἂν ὑμῶν οἱ υἱεῖς . . . πάντες παντάπασι διαφθαρήσονται.
(Plat. *Ap.* 29 c)

". . . saying that if I were acquitted your sons would all be utterly ruined."

Καὶ ἢ ἀφίετε ἢ μὴ ἀφίετε, ὡς ἐμοῦ οὐκ ἂν ποιήσοντος ἄλλο, οὐδ' εἰ μέλλω πολλάκις τεθνάναι.
(Plat. *Ap.* 30 B)
"Acquit me or condemn me, knowing that I shall not change my ways even if I am to die many times over."

Ἄν is often found with the future indicative in Homer: typical examples are

1. Εἰ δ' ἄγε, τοὺς ἂν ἐγὼν ἐπιόψομαι, οἱ δὲ πιθέσθων.
(*Il.* ix. 167)
"Well then (in that case) whomsoever I appoint let them obey."

2. Ἀλλ' ἴθ', ἐγὼ δέ κέ τοι Χαρίτων μίαν ὁπλοτεράων δώσω ὀπυιέμεναι. (*Il.* xiv. 267)
"Come now and I will (would) give thee one of the younger Graces to wife . . ."

and the usage, which makes the future more tentative in tone than it usually is (it is a sort of mixture of the simple future and the optative with ἄν), survives in Attic.

§ 291. The main difference between Homeric usage and Attic is that Attic is more restricted, e.g. in subordinate clauses Attic has mostly lost the distinction between general and definite expressions. Of the four distinct Homeric constructions, ὃς ἔλθῃ, ὃς ἂν ἔλθῃ, ὃς ἔλθοι, ὃς ἂν ἔλθοι, two are lost to Attic, and ἄν, always attending the subjunctive and never the optative, has become meaningless and stays as an ornament.

THE NEGATIVES

§ 292. The Greek negative adverbs are οὐ (οὐκ, οὐχ before vowels, οὐκί, οὐχί emphatic forms, cp. οὗτος, οὑτοσί) and μή: οὔτε, μήτε, οὐδέ, μηδέ are conjunctions.

The Latin negatives are *non, nē, haud, nĕ, ni*. There was probably in early Latin a *ne* with varying quantity *nĕ* like *prŏ-*. *Ne* is a negative prefix as, e.g., in *nequeo, nefas, nemo* (= *ne homo*), *neuter*, etc. *Non* is the old Latin *noenum* (= *ne unum*). *Haud* is probably connected with οὐ (through Indo-European *ăwĕ*); the *h*, it is suggested, is added to prevent confusion with *aut*. *Ne* and *ni* were originally the same, in the form *nei*; in later Latin *ni* survives in *nimirum, quidni*. *Nec*, the negative conjunction, originally had the sense of *non* (cp. *negotium* (= *nec otium*), *necopinans*). (See Lindsay, *The Latin Language*; Thompson, *Attic Syntax*, p. 447.)

§ 293. *Comparison of* οὐ, μή *with* non, ne.

ΟΎ { is definite, is objective, negatives facts, simple statements.

ΜΉ { is indefinite, is subjective, negatives conceptions, contingencies (i.e. jussive, final, consecutive clauses, indefinite relative and temporal if-clauses).

NON { negatives facts, simple statements.

NE { negatives *only* jussive and final clauses.

Types of Negatived Sentences.

§ 294. *Jussive* and *final* sentences (negatives μή, *ne*) as opposed to statements of fact (οὐ, *non*).

THE NEGATIVES

1. Ἐγὼ θρασὺς οὔτ' εἰμί, μήτε γενοίμην. (Dem. viii. 68)
 "I am not, nor may I ever be, foolhardy."
2. Τί μ' οὐκ . . . ἔκτεινας ὡς ἔδειξα μήποτε . . . ;
 (Soph. O.T. 1391)
 "Why didst thou not kill me that I might never have shown . . ."
3. *Quem non amat, non amat.* (Petr. S. 37)
 "Whom he dislikes, he dislikes."
4. *Tu ne cede malis.* (V. Aen. vi. 95)
 "Yield thou not to ills."
5. *Non vereor ne tua virtus . . . non respondeat.*
 (Cic. Fam. ii. 5)
 "I have no fear that your qualities will fail to correspond."

§ 295. There are some independent sentences in Homer and Aristophanes in which μή is found with an indicative:

1. Ἴστω νῦν τόδε γαῖα . . .
 μὴ δι' ἐμὴν ἰότητα Ποσειδάων ἐνοσίχθων | πημαίνει.
 (Il. xv. 329)
 "Earth be my witness . . . not by my will does earth-shaking P. hurt him."
2. Μὰ γῆν . . . μὴ 'γὼ νόημα κομψότερον ἤκουσά πω.
 (Ar. Av. 194)
 "By Earth herself, . . . never yet have I heard a cleverer idea!"

In each of these sentences there is a negative oath of denial which makes it something more than a mere statement. The assertion is in each case dependent upon the oath formula, and possibly it may be this dependence which is responsible for the μή, i.e. in 1. the idea is "Let Zeus be my witness . . . (so) that no man . . .". But even so, as we see from the other examples, there is a confusion between this idea of dependence and straightforward assertion.

§ 296. *Conditional Clauses*: negatives μή, Latin introduced by *nisi* (= *ne-si*) or *si . . . non* where a particular word is to be negatived.

The If-clause states something assumed or imagined: negative μή.

THE NEGATIVES

The Apodosis (the protasis being assumed) states a fact: negative οὐ.

In Homer οὐ is found in the protasis when the protasis verb is in the Indicative. Monro (*Homeric Grammar*, § 316, following Vierke) suggests that originally open indicative conditions were regularly negatived by οὐ, and later came to take μή on the analogy of clauses which had subjunctive and optative.

In classical Greek οὐ is sometimes found in protasis negativing a particular word (cp. Latin *si . . . non . . .*).

1. Οὐκ ἂν νήσων ἐκράτει, εἰ μή τι καὶ ναυτικὸν εἶχεν.
    (Thuc. i. 9)
    "He would not have mastered the islands unless he had had a fleet."

2. Εἰ δ' οὐ κείνου γ' ἐσσὶ γόνος . . . (Hom. *Od.* ii. 274)
    "But if thou art not his son . . ."

3. Εἰ τοὺς θανόντας οὐκ ἐᾷς θάπτειν . . .
    (Soph. *Aj.* 1131)
    "If thou sufferest not the dead to be buried," i.e. forbiddest.

4. *Si futurum est fiet ; si non est futurum, non fiet.*
    (Sen. *N.Q.* ii. 37)
    "If it is to be it will be ; if it is not to be it will not be."

§ 297. *Relative and Temporal Clauses :*
Definite—οὐ, *non*
Indefinite—μή, *non*

1. Ἦν δέ τις . . . Ξενοφῶν, ὃς οὔτε στρατηγός, οὔτε λοχαγός, οὔτε στρατιώτης ὢν συνηκολούθει.
    (X. *An.* iii. 1. 4)
    ". . . who had gone with them, not as general, captain, or soldier."

2. . . . λέγονθ' ἃ μὴ δεῖ. (Soph. *Ph.* 583)
    ". . . *such things as* one should not."

3. προσημαίνουσιν ἅ τε χρὴ ποιεῖν καὶ ἃ οὐ χρή.
    (X. *Cyr.* i. 6. 46)
    "They *define* the things one must do and the things one must not do."

Refer back to § 245. In the following example the actuality apparently needs more stress than the generality.

THE NEGATIVES 161

Οἱ δὲ πολλοὶ τῶν ἱκετῶν ὅσοι οὐκ ἐπείσθησαν . . .
(Thuc. iii. 81)
" The majority of the suppliants as many as were not persuaded . . ."

§ 298. *The Infinitive*: negatives μή (except in O.O. where οὐ is retained from the O.R.), *non*. (It is interesting to note that in the oldest Sanskrit the negative particles are used only with finite verbs : with Infinitive, Participles, Nouns, a negative prefix was used.)

Μή naturally negatives the Infinitive, because the Infin. is the abstract mood (νικᾶν expresses the general idea of " winning " without reference in itself to any particular person's winning).

1. Αἰσχρὸν μὴ ἀληθεύειν.
2. Εἰκὸς σοφὸν ἄνδρα μὴ ληρεῖν. (Plat. *Theaet.* 152 B)

So with *Consecutive Clauses* :

Actual consequence—οὐ + Indic., *non*
Natural consequence—μή + Infin., *non*

Μή indicates a consequence not necessarily fulfilled but the logical result, οὐ a consequence fulfilled but not necessarily the logical result.

Naturally, too, μή is used with Infin. after verbs of commanding, wishing, because it represents a μή clause of the direct speech, e.g. ἀπαγορεύω μὴ ποιεῖν implies the command μὴ ποιεῖτε and ἐβούλοντο μὴ προέσθαι implies μὴ προιώμεθα.

Thus verbs of promising, hoping, swearing, admitting, persuading, attesting, normally have an infinitive negatived by μή, because they imply μή in the direct, e.g.

Προωμολόγηται μηδὲν μᾶλλον μηδ' ἧττον ἑτέραν ἑτέρας ψυχὴν ψυχῆς εἶναι, (Plat. *Phaed.* 93 D)
" It has been previously admitted that one soul is no more or less a soul than another,"

where the original concession " let it not be . . ." is implied. These verbs all contain an effort of thought or will, and so take a jussive μή.

Other examples:

1. Ἔλεγον αὐτοῖς μὴ ἀδικεῖν. (Thuc. ii. 5)
"They told them *not* to do wrong."
2. Ὤμνυε μηδὲν εἰρηκέναι. (Dem. xxi. 119)
"He swore that he had said nothing."
3. Ἠγγυᾶτο μηδὲν αὐτοὺς κακὸν πείσεσθαι.
(X. An. vii. 4. 13)
"He guaranteed that they would suffer no harm."

§ 299. Where such verbs, e.g. of swearing, are found with οὐ and the infinitive they are regarded as merely making an assertion:

Ὀμώμοκεν οὐ χαριεῖσθαι . . . (Plat. Ap. 35 c)
"He has sworn that he will not do favours . . ."

Where οὐ is found with the infinitive when μή would be normal, it is usually because οὐ negatives some single word:

Δοκεῖς χαιρήσειν ἢ οὐκ ἀποθανεῖσθαι; (Andoc. i. 101)
"Do you think you will get off free or escape death?"

§ 300. Sometimes μή is found with the Infinitive in Indirect Statement even when no extenuation (e.g. that it contains the idea of an oath, as in ἀπεκρίνατο μηδενὸς ἥττων εἶναι, X. Hell. ii. 3. 11) can be made. It may be because μή and Infinitive was so common a usage; just as one hears people say "between you and I" just because the phrase "you and I" is so much more common and "you and me" is thought to sound wrong (Goodwin, *Moods and Tenses*, § 685).

Ἀντέλεγον μὴ δικαίως σφῶν καταδεδικάσθαι.
(Thuc. v. 49)
"They replied that they had not justly condemned them."

Προὔλεγον μὴ ἂν γίγνεσθαι πόλεμον. (Thuc. i. 139)
"They warned them that war would not break out . . ."

§ 301. *Participles, Adjectives, Nouns.* Latin always *non*.
(i) Participle in Indirect Statement in Greek. Negative οὐ (as with infinitive in O.O.).

Τοῖς γὰρ ἐπιχειρήμασιν ἑώρων οὐ κατορθοῦντες.
(Thuc. vii. 47)
" For they saw that they were not succeeding in their attempts."

But verbs of perception sometimes take μή, just as we find μή with the infinitive in O.O.

Εὖ ἴσμεν μὴ ἂν ἧσσον ὑμᾶς λυπηροὺς γενομένους.
(Thuc. i. 76)
" We are sure that you would not have become less tiresome "
(for οὐκ ἂν ἐγένεσθε of the O.R.).

(ii) The οὐ Participle may be causal: οὐκ ἀληθεύων, " since (as a matter of fact) he does not tell the truth ", i.e. οὐ = *definitely* not.
The μή Participle may be conditional: μὴ ἀληθεύων " *if* he does not tell the truth ", i.e. μή = *hypothetically* not.

1. Θρασὺς . . . ἀνὴρ
κακὸς πολίτης γίγνεται, νοῦν οὐκ ἔχων.
(Eur. *Bac.* 270)
" The reckless man makes a bad citizen, since he has no wit."

2. Οὐκ ἂν δύναιο, μὴ καμών, εὐδαιμονεῖν. (Eur. fr. 464)
" Thou couldst not be happy if thou didst not work."

(iii) Similarly Participles with the Article have negative

οὐ when *particular*,
μή when *general*.

1. Ἐθορυβεῖτε ὡς οὐ ποιήσοντες ταῦτα. (Lys. xii. 73)
" You clamoured, as not intending to do this."

2. Ὁ μὴ δαρεὶς ἄνθρωπος οὐ παιδεύεται. (Men. *Mon.* 422)
" Whoever is not beaten is not educated."

§ 302. *Negatived Adjectives* follow the same rules: οἱ μὴ δίκαιοι (general), " all who are not just "; αἱ οὐκ ὀρθαὶ πολιτεῖαι αὗται, " *these* wrong forms of government."

THE NEGATIVES

An alleged anomaly is (see Goodwin, p. 270; Thompson, p. 446):

Οἱ Λακεδαιμόνιοι . . . ὄντες καὶ πρὸ τοῦ μὴ ταχεῖς ἰέναι . . .   (Thuc. i. 118)
" The L. who were even in the old days not quick to go to war."

But, as the context shows, Thucydides writes because he wants to express a general cause : a people who had been slow before would naturally be backward now : the generalization about Lacedaemonian slowness depends upon past instances. (Goodwin has a fantastic explanation : Postgate suggested that in many places μή is written for οὐ to avoid an ugly sound such as τοῦ οὐ . . .)

So in ὁ μηδὲν εἰδὼς Οἰδίπους ἔπαυσά νιν (Soph. O.T. 397) the idea is consecutive—" I who am such that I could have known nothing " (ironical).

§ 303. *Negatived Nouns* similarly :

1. Ὁ μὴ ἰατρός.   (Plat. *Gorg.* 459 B)
" The non-physician."

2. . . . Διὰ τῆς Λευκάδος τὴν οὐ περιτείχισιν.
                                            (Thuc. iii. 95)
" . . . owing to the unfortified state of Leucas ", " to the *fact* that L. was not fortified ".
(literally " the non-fortification ").

§ 304. Οὐ *and* μή *contrasted in the same sentence.*
Note the difference between them in the lines

Κατθανὼν δὲ πᾶς ἀνὴρ
γῆ καὶ σκιά· τὸ μηδὲν εἰς οὐδὲν ῥέπει.
                                            (Eur. *Mel.* fr. 20)
" Every man at death is earth and shade ; that which is as nought goes back to nothingness."

It is difficult to convey this difference in translation ; it can be done only by paraphrase ; the sense is " What was conceived to be nothing now turns out to be actually nothing ". Thompson (*Attic Syntax*, p. 377) aptly quotes from the Epitaph on Gay :

Life is a jest, and all things show it ;
I thought so once, but now I know it.

THE NEGATIVES

This is just the sense of the Greek :
>   μή = imagined, indefinite, conceptual nothing.
>   οὐ = actual, definite nothing.   (Cp. Soph. *Aj.* 1231.)

§ 305. *Negatives in Questions.*

>   οὐ; expects answer YES.   Latin *nonne ?*
>   μή; expects answer No.   Latin *num ?*

Οὐ expects the answer YES because οὐ definitely negatives a statement, but the interrogative form is a form of doubt or denial and cancels the οὐ negation, so that the two negatives make a positive. This is seen more clearly with the Latin *nonne*: a neutral question is introduced by *-ne*, suggesting that the question is equivalent to a negative, and when this is added to a negation it cancels it and an affirmative tone is left.

Μή expresses an apprehension which is similarly cancelled by the query and so the answer No is expected. *Num* originally meant " now " (Greek νυν: *nunc = num-ce*). So in the *num* sentence there is merely the negative tone implied in the interrogative form.

Actual examples need not be given. But the theory is:

Οὐ τοῦτο ἄριστόν ἐστι; { Surely it is not that this
Nonne hoc optimum est?   isn't best ? i.e.   It is.
                          { This is best, isn't it ?   Yes.

Μὴ τοῦτο ἄριστόν ἐστι; { Surely it is not that this
Num hoc optimum est?   may be best ? i.e.   It is not.
                          { Now *is* this best ?   No.

§ 306.
But the following type of sentence requires notice because it has occasioned so much controversy :

>   Οὐ θᾶσσον οἴσεις, μηδ' ἀπιστήσεις ἐμοί;
>   (Soph. *Tr.* 1183)
>   " Wilt thou not give me thy hand and not distrust
>   me ? "

The simplest explanation is Goodwin's, that here are two separate questions : " You will join hands, won't you ? " (YES). " You won't distrust me, will you ? " (No). Μηδέ for μή simply joins the two questions as part of the same thought and does away with the need for a question-mark after οἴσεις.

(Jebb argues that the μηδέ shows that the οὐ is carried on to the μή of the second clause to form an οὐ μή construction, i.e. expressing strong prohibition. This οὐ μή construction, he says, is in essence interrogative: οὐ καταβήσει; = " will you not come down ? " i.e. " you will come down, won't you ? " When this positive command is negatived, μή (marking the negative force of the prohibiting verb) is inserted to negative the verb—οὐ μὴ καταβήσει; = " will you not not-come down ? " i.e. " do not come down ".)

§ 307. *The Combination* οὐ μή.

In classical Greek οὐ μή is found—
  (i) with the aorist subjunctive (less commonly present);
  (ii) with future indicative.

These constructions express *strong negation* or *strong prohibition*.

Negation :

1. Οὔτοι σ᾽ Ἀχαιῶν, οἶδα, μή τις ὑβρίσῃ.
   (Soph. *Aj.* 560)
   " Never, I know, shall one of the Achaeans insult thee."

2. Τοὺς πονηροὺς οὐ μή ποτε βελτίους ποιήσετε.
   (Aeschin. iii. 177)
   " You will never reform the criminal ! "

Prohibition :

1. Οὐ μὴ ληρήσεις.   (Ar. *Nub.* 367)
   " Oh don't talk rot ! "

2. Οὐ μὴ γυναικῶν δειλὸν εἰσοίσεις λόγον.
   (Eur. *And.* 757)
   " For goodness' sake don't talk in that frightened way like a woman ! "

§ 308. Since the meanings are interchanged between the two constructions we should find the same general principle to explain both.

Goodwin's explanation of the οὐ μή constructions is as follows.

An independent μή + subjunctive is found from Homer onwards to express an apprehension: μὴ δὴ νῆας ἕλωσι

(*Il.* xvi. 128) = " may they not take the ships, as I suspect they may "; similarly μὴ σοὺς διαφθείρῃ γάμους (Eur. *Alc.* 315) and μὴ φαῦλον ᾖ (Plat. *Crat.* 425 B) = " may it not prove bad, as I fear it may ", i.e. " (I suspect) it may prove bad ".

Μὴ πάθῃς τόδε, then, means " perhaps you may suffer this " ; οὐ is added to negative this apprehension : οὐ (μὴ πάθῃς τόδε) (Soph. *El.* 1029) = " there is *no* chance or fear about your suffering this ", i.e. " you *shall not* suffer this ".

Sometimes this added οὐ, where sense requires, negatives, not the whole sentence, but some particular word ; in which case it is prefixed to that word. So we get the μὴ οὐ or μὴ . . . οὐ of cautious assertion so common in Plato.

Μὴ οὐ τοῦτο ᾖ τὸ μαντήιον. (Hdt. v. 79)
" I suspect that the oracle may mean not this . . ."

From this, οὐ μή with the future developed thus :
The future could regularly be used to express commands and prohibitions (πάντως δὲ τοῦτο δράσεις, Ar. *Nub.* 1352 ; χειρὶ δ' οὐ ψαύσεις ποτέ, Eur. *Med.* 1320) (see § 134) : " thou shalt not steal " came to mean " do not steal ".

So the stronger future-expression οὐ μὴ σκώψῃς, " thou shalt not jest ", came to mean " do not jest ".

Further, οὐ μή considered as a strong negative came to be used more commonly with the future in a Second Person prohibition (as οὐ in οὐ ψαύσεις), e.g. οὐ μὴ ληρήσεις, " don't talk nonsense ". The following sentences prove that in time οὐ μή came to be regarded as merely a strong negative since it is used in O.O. :

1. Εὖ γὰρ οἶδα σαφῶς ὅτι ταῦθ' . . . οὐ μὴ ἐπιλάθῃ.
(Ar. *Pax* 1302)
" For I am perfectly sure that . . . you will never forget."

2. Εἶπεν ὅτι ἡ Σπάρτη οὐδὲν μὴ κάκιον οἰκιεῖται (αὐτοῦ ἀποθανόντος). (X. *Hell.* i. 6. 32)
" He said that Sparta would be none the less well governed when he was dead."

Alternatively, the extension of οὐ μή to constructions with the future indicative may well have been made because μή with the future indicative might well at one time have expressed an apprehension. This, on the principle that φοβοῦμαι μὴ νῆας ἕλωσι is developed from the simple μὴ νῆας ἕλωσι, is suggested by such a sentence as ὥστ᾽ εἰκὸς μὴ βραδύνειν ἐστί, μή τις ὄψεται (Ar. *Ec.* 495), which must be based on the simple apprehension μή τις ὄψεται. If so, οὐ μὴ λέξεις is as natural as οὐ μὴ λέξῃς.

(The above account of οὐ μή is based on the discussion in Goodwin's *Moods and Tenses*, pp. 389-397. Its chief weakness is the weakness of authority for the usage οὐ ψαύσεις = " don't touch me ! " Also it requires that in one usage οὐ μή should cancel each other, in another that they should be taken as a single negative. Those who are interested may pursue the inquiry by reference to Thompson's *Attic Syntax*, pp. 435 ff. ; Riddell's *Digest*, p. 177 ; and Sonnenschein's article in *Classical Review*, 1902, pp. 165-168.)

§ 309. The old explanation of the Negation use was that of an ellipse of a verb of fearing, that, e.g., οὐ μὴ γένηται (" it shall not be ") depended on the idea, e.g. οὐ (δέος ἐστὶ) μὴ γένηται. (Thus, e.g., Elmsley, *Quarterly Review*, 1812.)

But this (i) puts the cart before the horse in explaining a simple sentence by a complex ; we saw above how, e.g., the final sentence developed from the simple jussive, and the fact is that μὴ γένηται is logically and historically prior to δέος ἐστὶ μὴ γένηται ; (ii) cannot explain the οὐ μή Prohibition even if it explains the οὐ μή Negation. And those who hold this view have to turn to another, usually that mentioned above, i.e. that the οὐ μή Prohibition is interrogative.

§ 310. *The Combination* μὴ οὐ.

(i) In sentences expressing *apprehension* or *tentative statement*.

In this usage, as we have seen, οὐ negatives some particular word. Μὴ τοῦτο ἀληθὲς ᾖ = " perhaps this is true " ; μὴ τοῦτο οὐκ ἀληθὲς ᾖ = " perhaps this is not-true ".

Further examples :

1. Ἀλλὰ μὴ οὐ τοῦτο ᾖ χαλεπόν, θάνατον ἐκφυγεῖν.
(Plat. *Ap.* 39 A)
" But it is not this, the avoidance of death, that is the difficulty."

THE NEGATIVES 169

2. Ἀλλ' ἀκέουσα κάθησο, ἐμῷ δ' ἐπιπείθεο μύθῳ,
μή νύ τοι οὐ χραίσμωσιν ὅσοι θεοί εἰσ' ἐν Ὀλύμπῳ.
(Hom. *Il.* i. 565)

"But sit thou silent and hearken to my word, lest all the gods as many as are in Olympus avail thee not."

2. shows the extension of the use to the complex (final) sentence. N.B. οὐ goes closely with χραίσμωσιν. So we have regularly later, e.g.

Ὑποπτεύομεν καὶ ὑμᾶς . . . μὴ οὐ κοινοὶ ἀπόβητε.
(Thuc. iii. 53)

"We suspect that you, too, will not prove impartial."

Compare the Latin use of *ne non*, e.g.

Timeo ne non impetrem. (Cic. *Att.* ix. 6)

"I fear that I shall not gain my request."

§ 311. In some sentences we find μή . . . μή, some distance apart, for μὴ οὐ.

ᾬήθην δεῖν ὑπείκειν, μή με σκαιὸν ἡγησάμενος φοιτητὴν μὴ προσδέχοιτο. (Plat. *Euthyd.* 295 D)

"I thought I ought to give in, lest thinking me stupid he would not receive me as his pupil."

Goodwin (*op. cit.* p. 107) remarks: "After μή had come to be felt as a conjunction and its origin was forgotten, the chief objection to μή . . . μή was probably in the sound, and we find a few cases of it where the two particles are so far apart that the repetition is not offensive".

§ 312. (ii) Μὴ οὐ in *dependent* clauses following a *negative main verb*.

Thus κωλύω σε μὴ λέγειν = (literally) "I prevent you, so as not to speak", i.e. "I prevent your speaking"; οὐ κωλύω σε μὴ οὐ λέγειν = (literally) "I do not prevent you, so as not not-to-speak", i.e. "I do not prevent your speaking".

In both cases the infinitive (strictly dative of purpose, see § 166) expresses the purpose or result. Thus to the Greek mind this negative use is quite logical.

The use is extended from verbs of hindering to others of kindred meanings, e.g. οὐδὲν ἐλλείψω . . . μὴ οὐ . . . πυθέσθαι (Soph.), οὐκ ἂν πιθοίμην μὴ οὐ τάδ' ἐκμαθεῖν (*id.*), οὐκ ἀπεσχόμην μὴ οὐκ ἐλθεῖν (Plato).

THE NEGATIVES

§ 313. This μὴ οὐ is found most commonly negativing infinitives and participles, but it is also found negativing indicative, subjunctive, optative, and also nouns.

1. Οὐ λήξω μὴ οὐ πᾶσι προφωνεῖν . . . (Soph. *El.* 104)
"I will not cease to proclaim to all . . ."

2. Οὐδ' ἂν εἷς (ἐβουλήθη) μὴ οὐ συνειδὼς ἑαυτῷ συκοφαντοῦντι. (Dem. lviii. 13)
". . . no one without being conscious of being a sycophant."

§ 314. Words not of negative form themselves but containing a negative idea are often followed by a μὴ οὐ clause:

1. Τί ἐμπόδων μὴ οὐχὶ . . . ἀποθανεῖν; (X. *An.* iii. 1. 13)
"What prevents our dying . . . ?" i.e. "There is no hindrance".

2. Δαρείῳ δεινὸν ἐδόκεε εἶναι μὴ οὐ λαβεῖν τὰ χρήματα. (Hdt. i. 187)
". . . thought it not right not to take the money."

(Here a negative is implied in δεινόν.)

§ 315. *Reinforced Negatives.*

In Greek the principle is :
(i) Where a *simple* Negative follows a previous Negative in the same clause, the two Negatives make one Positive.
(ii) Where a *compound* Negative follows a Negative (usually simpler), it continues and strengthens the former Negative.

Examples :

1. Οὐδεὶς οὐκ ἔπασχέ τι. (X. *Sym.* i. 9)
"Everyone was affected."

2. Οὐκ ἔστιν οὐδὲν κρεῖσσον ἢ φίλος σαφής.
(Eur. *Or.* 1155)
"There is nothing better than a true friend."

3. Μὴ λανθανέτω σε μηδὲ τοῦτο. (X. *Cyr.* v. 2. 36)
"And let not this escape you either."

§ 316. In Latin, as in English, Negatives cancel one another.

THE NEGATIVES

Compare the common use of *nemo non* (= " everyone "), *non nemo* (= " some one "), *nonnullus* (= " some "), *nonnumquam* (= " sometimes "), etc. Remember that *non* casts its negative force upon the word following : *nemo non amat* = " no one fails to love ", *non nemo amat* = " not-no-one, i.e. some one . . ."

But sometimes negatives are reinforced in Latin when a general negative is followed or subdivided by *neque . . . neque . . .* or *ne . . . quidem.*

1. *Nihil umquam neque insolens neque gloriosum ex ore processit.* (C. Nep. xx. 4. 2)
    "No arrogant or boastful word ever left Timoleon's mouth."

2. *Nego nec virtutes nec vitia crescere . . .*
    (Cic. *Fin.* iii. 48)
    "I say that neither good qualities nor bad grow . . ."

3. *Numquam (Scipionem) ne minima quidem re offendi . . .*
    (Cic. *Am.* 103)
    ". . . that S. was never put out by the least thing."

Cp. Shakespeare's " I will give no thousand crowns neither ". This doubling is common in English dialect, e.g. " ' I'm a-going immediate, sir—unless there's nothink I can do for you, ma'am.' ' An't there,' said Mrs. Gamp . . . '—an't there nothing I can do for you, my little bird ? ' " (Dickens).

Also Plautus has, possibly imitated from the Greek :

Neque mi haud imperito eveniet . . . (*Pers.* 535)
"Well, it won't find me unused to that sort of thing."

§ 317. *Negative Conjunctions.*

These, as their use shows little sign of abnormality, need not be considered elaborately. In Greek οὔτε, μήτε (" neither ") are usually followed by another οὔτε or μήτε. Οὐδέ, μηδέ mean sometimes " and not ", sometimes " not even ".

In Latin usage *neque*, *nec* are followed by another *neque*, *nec*; or they may follow *non* or even a positive statement. Also *neque* may stand for *ne . . . quidem* (= " not even ", Gk. οὐδέ).

THE NEGATIVES

Other Negative Uses.

§ 318. (i) Apparent ellipse of a negative after

οὐχ ὅπως, μὴ ὅπως, οὐχ ὅτι, μὴ ὅτι
non modo, non solum, nedum.   (Roby, § 1658)

These phrases often express the English "not only *not*".

1. Μὴ ὅπως ὀρχεῖσθαι ἐν ῥυθμῷ, ἀλλ' οὐδ' ὀρθοῦσθαι ἐδύνασθε.   (X. *Cyr.* i. 3. 10)
    "Not to speak of dancing in time—you could not even stand upright."

2. *Haec genera virtutum non solum in moribus nostris, sed vix in libris reperiuntur.*   (Cic. *Sen.* 17)
    "These types of virtue are not only not found in human conduct but hardly even in books."

To see the effect imagine that a verb of saying is understood: μὴ ὅπως (λέγω) ὀρχεῖσθαι = "not to speak of dancing". After οὐχ the verb implied would be in the indicative, after μή in the subjunctive or possibly imperative; but the idiom came to be used without thought of any precise verb. So in Latin *non solum in moribus* may have depended originally on the idea *non dicam solum in moribus*, "not to speak of conduct only" (*ne dicam*, final, expresses the purpose not of the action of the verb but of its mention).

Cp. the Silver use of *nedum* (which normally means "much less") in e.g.

Quae vel socios, nedum hostes victos, terrere possent.
    (Livy xlv. 29)
"... would frighten their friends, not to mention their enemies" ("... much more their enemies").

Here, too, a verb of saying seems to be implied. The usage is clearer in the Plautine parataxis:

Vix incedo inanis, ne ire posse cum onere existumes.
    (*Amph.* 330)

§ 319. (ii) *Redundant Negative* in Greek.

Such a negative, felt to be unnecessary in English, is found—

(a) In the second half of a comparative sentence when the first half is negative:

THE NEGATIVES 173

Οὐδ' εἰκὸς χαλεπῶς φέρειν αὐτῶν μᾶλλον ἢ οὐ κηπίον ...
νομίσαντας ὀλιγωρῆσαι. (Thuc. ii. 62)
" It is not right that you should fret for them rather
than count them trivial like a garden . . ."

Either μᾶλλον ἤ or οὐ would have done in this sentence—
either " it is not right to fret-rather-than-hold-light " or
" . . . to fret-and-not-hold-light ". For the doubling cp.
vulgar English : " I am stronger *nor* you ". (This implies
" You are not strong ; I am strong ".)

§ 320. (b) In O.O. clauses introduced by ὅτι or ὡς after
verbs of denying, doubting and the like.

. . . ἀρνηθῆναι ὡς οὐκ ἀπέδωκα. (Lys. iv. 1)
" . . . to deny that I have given it back."

We have already mentioned the seemingly superfluous
μή after verbs of preventing (see § 312) and explained
that the μή clause expressed the net result. This present
use is somewhat similar. The underlying thought is οὐκ
ἀπέδωκα, and the negative is retained in the complex
ἀρνηθῆναι ὡς οὐκ ἀπέδωκα. Here we may appreciate the
idiom by imagining οὐκ ἀπέδωκα in inverted commas ;
obviously it is not so closely knit in to the complex sentence
as the English " I did not " when it becomes ". . . denied
that I did ". The persistent οὐκ has the air of defiance and
strength. " You may deny that you were not the cause "
(Shakespeare, *R. III*). Cp. French : *Il parle autrement
qu'il ne pense.*

Interesting specimens of this intrusive negative are :

1.   "Ως σ' ἀπ' ἐλπίδων
    οὐχ ὧνπερ ἐξέπεμπον εἰσεδεξάμην. (Soph. *El.* 1127)
    " How far from the hopes with which I sent thee forth
    have I received thee again."

(ἀπό = " contrary to " ; οὐχ is interjected—" they are not
those with which . . ." ; for the relative attraction see § 326.)

2. Ἐρῆμος ἀνδρῶν μὴ ξυνοικούντων ἔσω. (Soph. *O.T.* 56)
" (For there can be no city and no ship) that is deso-
late of dwellers therein." (Cp. Thuc. i. 77. 3.)

§ 321. (iii) Μή instead of οὐ in answer to questions.

ΞΑ. Χαίρεις, ἱκετεύω; . . . ΑΙ. μάλλὰ πλεῖν ἢ μαίνομαι.
(Ar. *Ran.* 751)
"D'ye like that, now?" "Why, I'm more than crazy about it."

Here μάλλά = μή, ἀλλά is based on the idea μὴ (τοῦτο ἐροῦ) ἀλλ'. . . . So we might say to "Are you a Communist?" "Don't believe it!" or simply "Don't!"

Cp. Plat. *Theaet.* 177 E Μὴ λεγέτω τὸ ὄνομα. Μὴ γάρ. ("No fear!"). The μή, then, implies a negative command with the verb omitted.

§ 322. (iv) *Anticipatory Negatives.*

In Greek and Latin, as sometimes in English colloquial speech, the negative is attracted out of the dependent into the main clause of a sentence. The reason, as in the English "I don't think he will come" for "I think he will not come", is probably that it is desired to mark the negative tone of the sentence as early as possible.

1. Οὐκ ἀξιοῖ . . . φεύγοντα τιμωρεῖσθαι. (Thuc. i. 136)
"He asks him not to punish him now he is in exile . . ."
2. Sc. *Te ille deseret.* P. *Non spero.* (Plaut. *Most.* 197)
"He will leave you.—I hope not."

ATTRACTION AND ASSIMILATION

§ 323. Attraction is the process by which a word in a sentence is changed from its normal grammatical form to take upon it the form of another word near it. It is then said to be assimilated ("made like") to that other word. The underlying reason is an unreasoning tendency to make like in form words which come near each other, in fact a misguided tidiness; or it is the same sort of tendency which in copying MSS. causes the corruption known as Homoioteleuton and causes a scribe to write, e.g., τοῦτον δίκαιον τιμῶ for τοῦτον δίκαιος τιμῶ; or it is like the tendency which causes *adsimulo* to become *assimulo*.

Attraction is chiefly of genders, numbers, cases and moods.

§ 324. *Attraction of Gender.*

Demonstrative pronouns both in Greek and Latin and relatives in Greek are found attracted to the gender of the attribute:

1. . . . ὅτῳ θανεῖν μέν ἐστιν οὐ πεπρωμένον·
αὕτη γὰρ ἦν ἂν πημάτων ἀπαλλαγή. (Aesch. P.V. 754)
". . . whose fate it is not to die; for this were release from torment."

2. *Hoc opus, hic labor est.* (V. *Aen.* vi. 129)
"This is the task, and this the work."

§ 325. *Attraction of Number.*

Here the verb is made to agree with its predicate which stands nearer to it than the subject. The examples give the impression that the writer is thinking mainly of the predicate and overlooks the number of the grammatical subject.

176 ATTRACTION AND ASSIMILATION

1. Αἱ χορηγίαι ἱκανὸν εὐδαιμονίας σημεῖόν ἐστιν.
(Ant. *Tetr.* A γ 8)
"Their chorus-payments are sufficient indication of their prosperity."

Cp. the vulgarism "Those sort . . .". Sir Philip Sidney, *Apologie for Poetrie*, has " Those kinde of obiections . . ."; cp. the so-called " Schema Pindaricum ", ἔστι γὰρ ἔμοιγε βωμοί (Plat. *Euthyd*. 302 c), "I have altars "; cp. *Macbeth*, v. iii.: "SERV. There is ten thousand. MACB. Geese, villain? SERV. Soldiers, sir." Cp. ". . . few men have been loved by his fellows . . . as was David " (Helen Thomas, *World without End*).

2. *Amantium irae amoris integratiost.* (Ter. *Andr.* 555)
"Lovers' quarrels are the renewal of love."

§ 326. *Attraction of Case.*

(i) Relative attracted to Antecedent: in Greek common, especially from the accusative to the genitive or dative; in Latin less common.

1. Ἔσεσθε ἄνδρες ἄξιοι τῆς ἐλευθερίας ἧς κέκτησθε.
(X. *An.* i. 7. 3)
"You will be men worthy of the freedom which you have won."

2. . . . *iudice quo nosti populo.* (Hor. *Sat.* i. 6. 15)
". . . with your old friend the people as judge."

Notice this attraction in sentences where the antecedent is *incorporated* in the relative clause :

Ἐπορεύετο σὺν ᾗ εἶχε δυνάμει. (X. *Hell.* iv. 1. 23)

N.B. English :

"He marched with what force he had."

§ 327. (ii) The antecedent attracted to the Relative : this usage is much less common :

1. Τὴν οὐσίαν ἣν κατέλιπεν οὐ πλείους ἄξιά ἐστιν.
(Lys. xix. 49)
"The property which he left is not worth more."

2. *Urbem quam statuo vestra est.* (V. *Aen.* i. 573)
"The city which I am founding is yours."

But in ὃν θεοὶ φιλοῦσιν ἀποθνήσκει νέος (Men. fr. 128) the antecedent is left to be understood from the relative clause: so *quam urbem statuo vestra est* would be perfectly regular, as in English we say "Whatever I have is yours", the antecedent being incorporated in the relative clause. A similar incorporation is found in, e.g.,

Οὐδὲ μουσικοὶ πρότερον ἐσόμεθα οὔτε αὐτοὶ οὔτε οὓς φαμεν ἡμῖν παιδευτέον εἶναι τοὺς φύλακας.
(Plat. *Rep.* 402 B)
"Before that neither we nor the guardians whom we say we are to instruct will be truly musical."

§ 328. (iii) Note the attraction in several common idioms, as in the phrase οὐδεὶς ὅστις οὐ, which is declined throughout as a compound adjective:

Γοργίας οὐδενὶ ὅτῳ οὐκ ἀποκρινόμενος ...
(Plat. *Men.* 70 c)
(for οὐδεὶς ἦν ὅτῳ οὐκ ...).

So with θαυμαστὸς ὅσος, ὑπερφυὴς ὅσος, similarly declined, and their adverbial forms θαυμαστῶς ὡς, ὑπερφυῶς ὡς:

Ὡμολόγησε ... ταῦτα ... μετὰ ἱδρῶτος θαυμαστοῦ ὅσου.
(Plat. *Rep.* 350 c)
"He conceded this to the accompaniment of an amazing amount of perspiration."

So with οἷος, εἴ τις and similarly used phrases:

... καὶ πρὸς ἄνδρας τολμηρούς, οἵους καὶ Ἀθηναίους, τοὺς ἀντιτολμῶντας χαλεπωτάτους ἂν φαίνεσθαι.
(Thuc. vii. 21)
"... and that against daring spirits like the Athenians a daring opponent would be the most formidable."

(for ... οἷοι καὶ Ἀθηναῖοί εἰσιν).

Ἔστιν ... δικαίου ἀνδρὸς βλάπτειν καὶ ὁντινοῦν ἀνθρώπων;
(Plat. *Rep.* 335 B)
"Is it the part of a just man to injure any person whatsoever?"

(for ... τινὰ ὁστισοῦν ἐστιν).

§ 329. (iv) In Oratio Obliqua often in sentences expressing comparison, etc., what should be a nominative in the dependent clause is attracted into the case of an accusative

ATTRACTION AND ASSIMILATION

in the principal clause, when the dependent clause has no verb :

1. Ἡμεῖς δὲ μηδίσαι μὲν αὐτοὺς οὔ φαμεν διότι οὐδ' Ἀθηναίους. (Thuc. iii. 62)
   " And we say you did not medize because the Athenians did not (medize)."

2. *Suspicor te eisdem rebus, quibus me ipsum, commoveri.*
   (Cic. *Sen.* 1)
   " I suspect that you are moved by the same things as I am."

   i.e. *quibus ipse commoveor.*

§ 330. *Attraction of Moods.*

As with nouns, so, by the same tendency, verbs which are placed near each other in a sentence are often given the same termination.

(i) Attraction from the Indicative into other moods : here one may distinguish logical attraction ("assimilation") and illogical attraction.

Logical attraction may be seen in

1. βουλοίμην κ' ἐπάρουρος ἐὼν θητευέμεν ἄλλῳ,
   ἀνδρὶ παρ' ἀκλήρῳ, ᾧ μὴ βίοτος πολὺς εἴη . . .
   (Hom. *Od.* xi. 489)

2. Ἆρ' ἂν ἡγοῖο ταῦτα σὰ εἶναι, ἅ σοι ἐξείη ἀποδόσθαι;
   (Plat. *Euthyd.* 302 A)

These sentences may mean " I would rather be serf to another man who has not much substance " and " Would you consider as your own things you can sell ? " but " . . . who *had* not . . ." and ". . . which you could sell " are, logically, more accurate and as natural in English as in Greek. (The relative clause is, in fact, equivalent to a conditional protasis.)

Similarly in Indirect Questions depending on an optative, a deliberative subjunctive may be attracted into the optative.

Οὐκ ἂν ἔχοις ὅ τι χρήσαιο σαυτῷ.
(Plat. *Gorg.* 486 B)
" You would not know what to do with yourself."

§ 331. Sometimes such attraction appears to be *illogical*, e.g.

Ὄλοιο μήπω, πρὶν μάθοιμ' εἰ καὶ πάλιν
γνώμην μετοίσεις.   (Soph. *Ph.* 961)
"Perish—no, not yet before I find whether thou wilt repent."

The optative is a parasite: if the writer wants indefinite time then ἄν with the subjunctive is required; ὄλοιο expresses a present feeling, "I wish you——", and μετοίσεις is not remote. It is simple attraction, and reminds one of the common English error "I should have liked to have gone".

§ 332. In Latin any verb may go into the subjunctive because it is dependent on another verb. Such attraction is natural. *Timeo ne dum festinem cadam*: *cadam* is subjunctive because it expresses other than fact, i.e. a possibility—"I *may* fall": *festinem* is grammatically dependent upon a mere possibility and is regarded in the same light, or may mean "if I hurry". Yet, logically, the sense may be "I am hurrying: I may fall", and so *dum festinem* may mark a fact; but grammatical dependence usually wins the day in Latin. When, however, the fact needs particular stress the indicative is kept.

1. *Non committam ut dum vereare tu ne sis ineptus me esse iudices.*   (Cic. *Or.* ii. 4)
"I won't have it that in your fear that you are a fool you should think me one."

2. *Si haec contra ac dico essent omnia, tamen . . .*
                                      (Cic. *Verr.* iv. 6)
"Even if all had been contrary to what I say, nevertheless . . ."

§ 333. (ii) Attraction into the Indicative.

1. Ἀνδρὸς ἔπειτ' ὤφελλον ἀμείνονος εἶναι ἄκοιτις,
ὃς ᾔδη νέμεσιν . . .   (*Il.* vi. 350)
"Would I had been the wife of a better man who was sensitive to resentment . . ."

ATTRACTION AND ASSIMILATION

2. ... ξυνεγιγνώσκετε δήπου ἄν μοι, εἰ ἐν ἐκείνῃ τῇ φωνῇ τε καὶ τῷ τρόπῳ ἔλεγον, ἐν οἷσπερ ἐτεθράμμην.
(Plat. *Ap*. 18 A)
"I'm sure you would excuse me if I were speaking in the way of speech in which I had been brought up."

Both ἤδη and ἐτεθράμμην represent unreal actions, being dependent on unreal clauses (see § 330); but are attracted into the forms of ὤφελλον and ἔλεγον.

§ 334. (iii) Attraction into the Infinitive of sentences dependent on Infinitive. This we have already observed (see § 271).

1. ... ὡς δ' ἀκοῦσαι τοὺς παρόντας θόρυβον γενέσθαι.
(Dem. xix. 195)

2. *Mundum censent regi numine deorum ... ex quo consequi ut ...* (Cic. *Fin*. iii. 19)

§ 335. N.B.—In some sentences, usually involved sentences, unexpected forms appear that are due not to attraction but to a change of thought on the part of the writer. With attraction what would be the normal form is transformed by a sort of verbal chemistry; but where the abnormality is the result of a reaction of ideas, the process should be called *Anacoluthon* rather than Attraction, i.e. a lack of grammatical sequence, where the construction with which the sentence started is not strictly maintained.

Ἀλλ' ἢν οἱ ἡγεμόνες, ὥσπερ νῦν ὑμεῖς, κεφαλαιώσαντες πρὸς τοὺς ξύμπαντας διαγνώμας ποιήσησθε, ἧσσόν τις ἐπ' ἀδίκοις ἔργοις λόγους καλοὺς ζητήσει.
(Thuc. iii. 67)
"But if all federal leaders, as you are doing in the present instance,—if you first state briefly the facts for all concerned, and then pass sentence, there will be less seeking of fair words to cloak foul deeds."

EXAMPLES FOR EXERCISE

NOTE ON THE DISCUSSION OF SYNTAX EXAMPLES

THE following examples will suggest the lines on which examples should be approached. Remember (1) that you must have thought out your conception of the sentence before you adopt a translation; (2) that your discussion must be clearly and systematically arranged; (3) that there may be more than one point worthy of comment; (4) that you must observe proportion, not strain at a gnat and swallow a camel; (5) that in explaining a particular usage you must try as far as possible to understand the author's intention and the working of his thought.

I. *Rediit paulo post quod se oblitum nescio quid diceret.*
(Cicero)
"He returned shortly afterwards because he said he had forgotten something."

Why *diceret* ? A causal clause expressing an *alleged* reason takes the subjunctive.

The rule applied to this sentence would give us . . . *quod nescio quid oblitus esset*, which represents something like "He returned 'because he had forgotten something'".

The alternative is to show in full that the reason was merely an alleged one— . . . *quod se oblitum nescio quid dixit.*

Cicero seems to have combined both ways. The usage cannot claim to embody a conscious end—unless it may be said that Cicero wished to pour double scorn on the perfidy. But he uses it elsewhere as in *litteras quas me sibi misisse diceret recitavit homo* (Phil. ii.).

II. *Ubiis auxilium suum pollicitus est, si ab Suebis premerentur.*
(Caesar)
"He promised help to the Ubii, if they were attacked by the Suebi."

At first sight there seems to be no difficulty, as English has the same looseness of construction. But on second thought it becomes clear that "he promised" is a *fact*. What is dependent on the condition *si . . . premerentur* is not the promising but the help, i.e. the true apodosis has been absorbed into another principal sentence (which reports the condition) and is represented by *auxilium suum*.

The full expression of the meaning would be, e.g., *Ubiis se auxilium laturum pollicitus est si . . . premerentur*. His thought when making the promise was "*auxilium feram si prementur*".

Cp. Livy's *praetor aedem Diovi vovit, si eo die hostes vicisset.*

III. Ἀλλ' ὃν πόλις στήσειε τοῦδε χρὴ κλύειν.   (Sophocles)
"Whomsoever the city appoints, him we must obey."

There is a discrepancy between the moods of στήσειε and χρή: στήσειε is remote and hypothetical ("whomsoever the city were to appoint"), χρή expresses a present obligation.

Normal symmetry would require either (i) στήσῃ ἄν . . . χρή or (ii) στήσειε . . . χρείη ἄν. As it is, the sentence begins as (ii) with the air of expressing not so much a general truth as a high hypothetical law, and ends in (i)—as it were, with the reflection that such an obligation is as a matter of fact ever-present. "Whomsoever the city should appoint—we *must always* obey our rulers." This change is not uncommon with expressions of "must", "ought", etc.

Or it may be said that the emphasis is on the infinitive, that χρή is used as an auxiliary; χρὴ κλύειν = κλύοιμεν ἄν or κλύοι ἄν ὁ δίκαιος (just as *potuit contemnere* in Juvenal's line = *contempsisset*—*Antoni gladios potuit contemnere si sic Omnia dixisset*).

Cp. Χρῆν σ', εἴπερ ἦσθα μὴ κακός, πείσαντά με
γαμεῖν γάμον τόνδ'.   (Euripides)

The following example suggests a useful test :

Συντεταγμένον μὲν οὕτως ἦγε τὸ στράτευμα ὡς ἂν ἐπικουρεῖν μάλιστα ἑαυτῷ δύναιτο.   (Xenophon)

Suppose that after a brief consideration of this sentence you cannot see any particular point for comment. It seems to mean "He led the army so ordered that it might be best able to help him".

Try turning this provisional translation back into Greek. You will probably write . . . ὡς ἐπικουρεῖν μάλιστα ἑαυτῷ δύναιτο. Comparing this with the original Greek you will notice the presence of ἄν ; and you will recall that there is no mention of ἄν in the rules of the normal final construction. At least, then, it seems that ὡς ἄν . . . δύναιτο is not a *normal* final construction.

But in what sentences is ἄν with the Optative used ? Potential. That is, with a condition somehow implied. Ἄν δύναιτο = " it would be able (if there were need, if they were attacked)". The ἄν points to the condition in the background.

Putting together the immediate impression that we have here a final clause with the idea of potential usage, we can see that Xenophon is using a slightly more complex version of an ordinary final clause. " He led the army so ordered so that (literally " how ") it might be best able to help him (if there were a sudden need, etc.)."

I

(1) Ὁ δὲ ἐγκέφαλός ἐστιν ὁ τὰς αἰσθήσεις παρέχων τοῦ ἀκούειν καὶ ὁρᾶν καὶ ὀσφραίνεσθαι. (Plat. *Phaed.* 96 B)
" It is the brain that furnishes the sensations of hearing and sight and smell."

(2) Ἐβουλεύοντο εἴτε κατακαύσωσιν εἴτε τι ἄλλο χρήσωνται.
(Thuc. ii. 4)
" They were considering whether they should burn them to death or treat them in some other way."

(3) Ἀλλ' εἰ πέπαυται, κάρτ' ἂν εὐτυχεῖν δοκῶ.
(Soph. *Aj.* 263)
" Yet if he hath respite, I think all may yet be well."

(4) Ὡς ὤφελον πάροιθεν ἐκλιπεῖν βίον . . .
ὅπως θανὼν ἔκεισο τῇ τόθ' ἡμέρᾳ. (Soph. *El.* 1134)
" Would that ere I left this life . . . that thou mightest have lain in death on that day."

(5) Πότερον . . . αἰσχρόν ἐστι . . . τοῖς πονηροῖς διαφέρεσθαι;
(X. *Mem.* ii. 9. 8)
" Is it wrong to quarrel with bad men ? "

(6) Nihil *habebam* quod *scriberem* ; neque enim *novi* quicquam audieram et ad tuas omnis rescripseram pridie.
(Cic. *Att.* ix. 10)
" I have nothing to write ; I have heard no news and I answered all your letters yesterday."

(7) Ego *vapulando*, ille *verberando* . . . ambo defessi sumus.
(Ter. *And.* 213)
"We're both tired, I of being beaten, he with beating."

(8) Dies composita *gerendae rei* est. (Liv. xxv. 16)
"A day was appointed for the transaction of the affair."

(9) Partem opere in tanto, *sineret* dolor, Icare, haberes.
(V. *Aen.* vi. 31)
"Thou wouldst have a share in so great a work, Icarus, did grief allow."

10) Nullust *Ephesi* quin *sciat*. (Plaut. *Bac.* 336)
"There is nobody in Ephesus who does not know."

II

(1) Οἱ ἄρχοντες . . . οὓς ὑμεῖς εἵλεσθε ἄρχειν μου . . .
(Plat. *Ap.* 28 E)
"The commanders whom you chose to command me."

(2) Οὐ γὰρ αἰσθάνει πάλαι
ζῶντας θανοῦσιν οὕνεκ' ἀνταυδᾷς ἴσα; (Soph. *El.* 1477)
"And hast thou not perceived long since that thou hast been addressing the living as the dead?"

(3) Οὐ γὰρ ἂν ἐβλήθη ἀτρεμίζων καὶ μὴ διατρέχων.
(Ant. *Tetr.* B β 5)
"He would not have been hit had he been keeping still and not running across."

(4) Θῆκαι ὅσαι ἦσαν τεθνεώτων πάσας ἀνεῖλον.
(Thuc. iii. 104)
"They removed all the tombs of the dead that were there."

(5) Τὴν μητέρα ἐμακάριζον, οἵων τέκνων ἐκύρησε. (Hdt. i. 31)
"They counted their mother happy in being blessed with such children."

(6) Delitui, dum vela *darent*, si forte *dedissent*.
(V. *Aen.* ii. 136)
"I lay hid, till they should have sailed, if sail they would."

(7) *Referendae* ego habeo linguam natam *gratiae*.
(Plaut. *Pers.* 42)
"I have a tongue that's born for showing thankfulness."

EXAMPLES FOR EXERCISE

(8) Prodiga non sentit *pereuntem* femina *censum*.
(Juv. vi. 362)
"The extravagant woman does not see that the income is dwindling."

(9) Modum adhibendo ubi res *posceret*, priores erant.
(Liv. iii. 19)
"By using moderation when circumstances required, they were his superiors."

(10) *Nescire* quid antequam natus *sis* acciderit, id est semper esse puerum. (Cic. *Or.* 34)
"Not to know what happened before you were born is to be always a boy."

III

(1) Ἄφρων νέος τ' ἦν, πρὶν τὰ πράγματ' ἐγγύθεν σκοπῶν ἐσεῖδον. (Eur. *I.A.* 489)
"I was young and witless before I made close acquaintance with the world."

(2) Ἀλλ' ἔσθ' ὁ καιρὸς ἡμερεύοντας ξένους μακρᾶς κελεύθου τυγχάνειν τὰ πρόσφορα.
(Aesch. *Cho.* 705)
"But it is time for guests who all day have been travelling on a long journey to receive refreshment due."

(3) Χρυσᾶ χαλκείων διαμείβεσθαι νοεῖς. (Plat. *Symp.* 218 c)
"You are intending to exchange golden for bronzen."

(4) Εἰ τοὺς ἀναιτίους διώκοιμεν ... δεινοὺς ἀλιτηρίους ἕξομεν ... ἔνοχοί τε τοῦ φόνου τοῖς ἐπιτιμίοις ἐσμέν.
(Ant. *Tetr.* Γ a 4)
"If we prosecute the innocent we shall have dread avengers and we are liable to the penalties for murder."

(5) Οὐδὲ γὰρ ὧν ἔτυχεν ἦν, ἀλλ' οἷς ὁ δῆμος καταρᾶται.
(Dem. xviii. 130)
"For his acts were no ordinary acts but such as the people curse."

(6) Mea causa *causam* hanc iustam esse *animum* inducite.
(Ter. *Haut.* 41)
"For my sake persuade yourselves that this is a fair plea."

(7) Maiores nostri in dominum de servo quaeri noluerunt; non quin *posset* verum inveniri, sed quia videbatur indignum esse. (Cic. *Mil.* 59)
  "Our ancestors would not allow a slave to be questioned by torture against his master, not because the truth could not be so discovered, but because such a proceeding seemed degrading."

(8) Erant quibus appetentior *famae videretur* quando etiam *sapientibus* cupido gloriae novissima exuitur.
  (Tac. *H.* iv. 6)
  "There were some who thought him too eager for fame, since, even with the wise, ambition is the last infirmity to be shed."

(9) Dulces exuviae, dum fata deusque *sinebat*,
  Accipite hanc animam. (V. *Aen.* iv. 651)
  "Memorials, dear while destiny and heaven so willed, receive this soul."

(10) Nec vitium *duxerim*, si Cicero a Demosthene paulum in hac parte *descivit*. (Quint. ix. 4. 146)
  "Nor should I count it a fault if Cicero parted company a little with Demosthenes in this respect."

IV

(1) Φοβεῖσθε μὴ δυσκολώτερόν τι νῦν διακεῖμαι . . .
  (Plat. *Phaed.* 84 E)
  "You are afraid that I am now in a rather more irritable state."

(2) Οὐκ ἂν **φράσειας** ἥντιν' αὖ παλίντροπος
  κέλευθον ἕρπεις ὧδε σὺν σπουδῇ ταχύς;
  (Soph. *Phil.* 1222)
  "Will you not tell me on what path you are so hastily and earnestly crawling back?"

(3) Εἰ μηδένα τῶν ἄλλων ἱππεύειν εἴασαν, οὐκ ἂν δικαίως χαρίζοισθε αὐτοῖς. (Lys. xv. 8)
  "If they allowed none of the others to serve as horsemen, then you will not be justified in showing them any favour."

(4) Ἐπείθοντο, ὁρῶντες ὅτι μόνος **ἐφρόνει** οἷα δεῖ τὸν ἄρχοντα.
  (X. *An.* ii. 2. 5)
  "They obeyed, seeing that he alone had the sort of mind a commander should have."

EXAMPLES FOR EXERCISE

(5) ΠΑ. Οὐκ ἄρ' ἀποδώσεις; ΣΤΡ. οὐχ, ὅσον γέ μ' εἰδέναι.
(Ar. *Nub*. 1252)
"P. Then you won't pay it back ?—S. Not if I know it!"

(6) Aeternas quoniam *poenas* in morte timendumst . . .
(Lucr. i. 112)
"Since we must fear eternal punishment in death . . ."

(7) Tum ego te primus *hortarer* diu *pensitares* quem potissimum eligeres. (Plin. *Ep*. iv. 15)
"In that case I should be the first to advise you to weigh at leisure whom you should choose above all others."

(8) Nunc *Satyrum*, nunc agrestem *Cyclopa* movetur.
(Hor. *Ep*. ii. 2. 125)
"He dances now the Satyr, now the country Cyclops dance."

(9) Magna proponit iis qui regem *occiderint* praemia.
(Caes. *B.G.* v. 58)
"He promised handsome rewards to those who killed the king."

(10) Iugurthae omnia Romae *venum ire* in animo haeserat.
(Sall. *Jug*. 28)
"Jugurtha had got it into his head that everything at Rome was for sale."

V

(1) Ἀλλ' ἢν ἐφῇς μοι . . . λέξαιμ' ἂν ὀρθῶς. (Soph. *El*. 554)
"But if thou grantest . . . I will tell aright."

(2) Λέγεται δὲ καὶ Ἀλκμαίωνι, ὅτε δὴ ἀλᾶσθαι αὐτόν . . . , τὸν Ἀπόλλω ταύτην τὴν γῆν χρῆσαι οἰκεῖν.
(Thuc. ii. 102)
"It is said that when A. was wandering Apollo bade him by an oracle to settle in this land."

(3) Ἀλλά κε κεῖνα μάλιστα ἰδὼν ὀλοφύραο θυμῷ.
(Hom. *Od*. xi. 418)
"But having seen this thou wouldst grieve most in thy heart."

(4) Ψήφων δὲ δείσας μὴ δεηθείη ποτε
ἵν' ἔχοι δικάζειν, αἰγιαλὸν ἔνδον τρέφει. (Ar. *Vesp.* 109)
"Frightened that he might some time lack pebbles to enable him to be a juryman, he keeps a beach on the premises."

(5) Ἀτεχνῶς οὖν ξένως ἔχω τῆς ἐνθάδε λέξεως.
(Plat. *Ap.* 17 D)
"Therefore I am a complete stranger to the manner of speech used here."

(6) Rediit paulo post, quod se oblitum nescio quid *diceret*.
(Cic. *Off.* i. 13)
"He came back soon after because he said he had forgotten something."

(7) Aut *oculis* capti fodere cubilia talpae. (V. *Georg.* i. 183)
". . . or moles, bereft of sight, have dug their galleries."

(8) Maesti, *crederes* victos, in castra redeunt. (Liv. ii. 43)
". . . dejectedly—you would have thought them defeated—they return to their camp."

(9) Mamurius, *morum fabraene* exactior *artis* . . .
(Ov. *F.* iii. 383)
"M. . . . whether more precise in conduct or in handicraft . . ."

(10) Quotiens super tali negotio *consultaret*, edita domus parte utebatur. (Tac. *A.* vi. 21)
"Whenever he deliberated on such business, he used a remote part of the house."

VI

(1) Ὦ γέρον, οὔ τι ψεῦδος ἐμὰς ἄτας κατέλεξας. (Hom. *Il.* ix. 115)
"Old sir, no lie hast thou spoken of my folly."

(2) Εὖ ἐπίστασθε ὅτι οὐ μὴ λάθωμαι ὑμῶν.
(X. *Cyr.* viii. 1. 5)
"Be sure that I shall never forget you."

(3) Εἰ μὴ διὰ τὸ καὶ τὸ ἐσώθησαν ἂν οἱ Φωκεῖς.
(Dem. xix. 74)
"But for this and that the Phocians would have been saved."

(4) Καὶ ἐπίτηδές σε οὐκ ἤγειρον, ἵνα ὡς ἥδιστα διάγῃς.
(Plat. *Crit.* 43 B)
"I was careful not to wake you, so that you may have as pleasant a time as possible."

EXAMPLES FOR EXERCISE 189

(5) Τί μοι τῶν δυσφόρων ἐφίει ;   (Soph. *El.* 141)
   " Why dost thou aim at the intolerable ? "
(6) Verres *pretio*, non *aequitate* iura discribebat.
   (Cic. *Verr.* v. 11)
   " V. administered law not by equity, but by bribe."
(7) Ecquis currit pollictorem *arcessere* ?   (Plaut. *Asin.* 910)
   " Is anyone running to fetch the undertaker ? "
(8) Aram posuit *casus* suos in marmore expressam.
   (Tac. *H.* iii. 74)
   " He erected an altar with his adventures sculptured in marble."
(9) *Qui* vinum fugiens *vendat* sciens, debeatne dicere ?
   (Cic. *Off.* iii. 91)
   " Should one who sells wine that will not keep, and knows it, admit it ? "
(10) Decurrerat . . . ad prohibendos si in terram *egrederentur*.
   (Liv. xxiv. 27)
   " . . . had come down to stop them if they should land."

VII

(1) Στράτος κυρήσει νοστίμου σωτηρίας.   (Aesch. *Pers.* 793)
(2) Ἀλλ' εἴ τι μὴ φέροιμεν, ὤτρυνεν φέρειν.   (Eur. *Alc.* 755)
(3) Ἐλογιζόμην εἰ ταῦτα πρόθυμός σοι συλλάβοιμι, ὡς οἰκεῖός τέ σοι ἐσοίμην, καὶ ἐξέσοιτό μοι διαλέγεσθαί σοι ὁπόσον ἂν χρόνον βουλοίμην.   (X. *Cyr.* vii. 5. 49)
(4) Ἡ μὲν οὖν ναυμαχία τοιαύτη γενομένη ἐτελεύτα ἐς ἡλίου δύσιν.   (Thuc. iii. 78)
(5) Τίς δέ μ' ἐκφύει βροτῶν ;   (Soph. *O.T.* 437)
(6) Cur M. Brutus referente te legibus est solutus, si ab urbe plus quam decem dies afuisset ?   (Cic. *Phil.* ii. 13)
(7) Non populi gentesque tremunt . . .
   Nequid ob admissum foede dictumve superbe
   Poenarum grave sit solvendi tempus adultum.
   (Lucr. v. 1222)
(8) Ad Sullam nuntiatum mittit, conloquio diem locum tempus ipse deligeret.   (Sall. *Jug.* 108)
(9) . . . Omne cum Proteus pecus egit altos
   Visere montes.   (Hor. *C.* ii. 2. 7)
(10) Dedit mihi quantum maximum potuit, daturus amplius, si potuisset.   (Plin. *Ep.* iii. 21)

VIII

(1) Χρὴ . . . δεῖξαι ὅτι ὧν μὲν ἐφίενται πρὸς τοὺς μὴ
   ἀμυνομένους κτάσθων.   (Thuc. iv. 92)
(2) Οὐ μὴ λαλήσεις, ἀλλ' ἀκολουθήσεις ἐμοί.   (Ar. Nub. 505)
(3) Οὐδέν γε ἄλλο ἐστὶν οὗ ἐρῶσιν ἄνθρωποι, ἢ τοῦ ἀγαθοῦ.
   (Plat. Symp. 206 A)
(4) Δείδω μὴ δὴ πάντα θέα νημερτέα εἶπεν.   (Hom. Od. v. 300)
(5)   Θέλεις
   μείνωμεν αὐτοῦ κἀνακούσωμεν γόων;   (Soph. El. 81)
(6) Neque huius veritus sis feminae primariae.
   (Ter. Ph. 971)
(7) Sed ne, dum huic obsequor, vobis molestus sim.
   (Cic. Fin. v. 3)
(8) Quid tibi hunc receptio ad test meum virum ?
   (Plaut. Asin. 919)
(9) Pollio amat nostram, quamvis est rustica, musam.
   (V. Ecl. iii. 84)
(10) Nec consul Romanus tentandis urbibus, sicunde spes
   aliqua se ostendisset, deerat.   (Liv. xxvi. 38)

IX

(1) Τίνα ἂν τρόπον ἐγὼ μέγα δυναίμην καὶ μηδείς με ἀδικοῖ;
   (Plat. Gorg. 510 D)
(2) Εἴ περ γάρ τ' ἄλλοι γε περικτεινώμεθα πάντες
   νηυσὶν ἐπ' Ἀργείων, σοὶ δ' οὐ δέος ἔστ' ἀπόλεσθαι.
   (Hom. Il. xii. 245)
(3) Τὰ περὶ τοὺς ἀγῶνας κατελύθη ὑπὸ ξυμφορῶν, πρὶν δὴ οἱ
   Ἀθηναῖοι τότε τὸν ἀγῶνα ἐποίησαν.   (Thuc. iii. 104)
(4) Ἕδραν γὰρ εἶχε παντὸς εὐαγῆ στρατοῦ.
   (Aesch. Pers. 466)
(5) Ἐνδυστυχῆσαι τοὔνομ' ἐπιτήδειος εἶ.   (Eur. Bac. 508)
(6) Iuppiter, ut tristi lumina saepe manu.   (Catull. 66. 30)
(7) Continui montes ni dissocientur opaca
   Valle.   (Hor. Ep. i. 16. 5)
(8) Tribuno plebis quaestor non paruisti, cui tuus praesertim
   collega pareret.   (Cic. Fam. xv. 21)

(9) Postquam nihil usquam hostile cernebatur, Galli, viam ingressi, ad urbem Romam perveniunt. (Liv. v. 39)

(10) L. Catilina, nobili genere natus, fuit magna vi et animi et corporis, sed ingenio malo pravoque. (Sall. *Cat.* 5)

X

(1) ... ὅτῳ θανεῖν μέν ἐστιν οὐ πεπρωμένον.
αὕτη γὰρ ἦν ἂν πημάτων ἀπαλλαγή. (Aesch. *P.V.* 753)

(2) Ἄκουσον καὶ ἐμοῦ, ἐάν σοι ταὐτὰ δοκῇ. (Plat. *Rep.* 358 B)

(3) Τοιαῦτ' ἄττα σφᾶς ἔφη διαλεχθέντας ἰέναι· ἐπεὶ δὲ γενέσθαι ἐπὶ τῇ οἰκίᾳ, ἀνεῳγμένην καταλαμβάνειν τὴν θύραν. (Plat. *Symp.* 174 D)

(4) Σμικρῷ χαλινῷ δ' οἶδα τοὺς θυμουμένους ἵππους καταρτυνθέντας. (Soph. *Ant.* 478)

(5) Ἀλλ' ἄνα, μὴ τάχα ἄστυ πυρὸς δηίοιο θέρηται. (Hom. *Il.* vi. 331)

(6) Di bene fecerunt inopis me quodque pusilli
Finxerunt animi. (Hor. *S.* i. 4. 17)

(7) Si mihi nec stipendia omnia emerita essent, necdum aetas vacationem daret, tamen aequum erat me dimitti. (Liv. xlii. 34)

(8) Senseram, noram inductus, relictus, proiectus ab eis. (Cic. *Att.* iv. 5)

(9) Neque ille
Sepositi ciceris nec longae invidit avenae. (Hor. *S.* ii. 6. 64)

(10) Vellem suscepisses iuvenem regendum. (Cic. *Att.* x. 6)

XI

(1) Ὅστις μὴ αὐτάρκης ἐστίν, οὐ δοκεῖ σοι χαλεπὸς φίλος εἶναι; (X. *Mem.* ii. 6. 2)

(2) Ἡμεῖς δὲ κακοὶ πρὶν ἐν τῷ παθεῖν ὦμεν προφυλάξασθαι. (Thuc. vi. 38)

(3) Ἀμαθία αὕτη ἡ ἐπονείδιστος ἡ τοῦ οἴεσθαι εἰδέναι ἃ οὐκ οἶδε. (Plat. *Apol.* 29 B)

(4) (Ἡ Κέρκυρα) τῆς Ἰταλίας καὶ Σικελίας καλῶς παράπλου κεῖται. (Thuc. i. 36)

(5) Δεῖ γὰρ ἑνὸς οὗ μὴ τυχὼν
ἀπόλωλα. (Ar. Ach. 466)

(6) Multa me dehortantur a vobis, Quirites, ni studium reipublicae superet. (Sall. Jug. 31)

(7) Legitimumque sonum digitis callemus et aure.
(Hor. A.P. 274)

(8) Quod domi te inclusisti ratione fecisti. (Cic. Att. xii. 44)

(9) Tum e seditiosis unum vinciri iubet, magis usurpandi iuris, quam quia unius culpa foret.
(Tac. Hist. iv. 25)

(10) Hesterna tibi nocte dixeramus
Cenares hodie, Procille, mecum. (Mart. i. 27)

XII

(1) Φίλιππος Ποτίδαιαν ἑλὼν καὶ δυνηθεὶς ἂν αὐτὸς ἔχειν, εἰ ἐβουλήθη, Ὀλυνθίοις παρέδωκεν. (Dem. xxiii. 107)

(2) Βέλτιόν ἐστι σῶμά γ' ἢ ψυχὴν νοσεῖν. (Men. fr.)

(3) Παρήγγειλαν ἐπειδὴ δειπνήσειαν πάντας ἀναπαύεσθαι, καὶ ἕπεσθαι ἡνίκ' ἄν τις παραγγέλλῃ. (X. An. iii. 5. 18)

(4) Σωφρόνων ἐστιν, εἰ μὴ ἀδικοῖντο, ἡσυχάζειν.
(Thuc. i. 120)

(5) Τὸ ψήφισμα τοῦτο γράφω, ἵν' οὕτω γίγνοινθ' οἱ ὅρκοι.
(Dem. xviii. 21)

(6) Solvendo non erat Magius. (Cic. Att. xii. 10)

(7) Rex secunda vigilia, quod bene verteret, ingredi iubet.
(Curt. vii. 11)

(8) Solent subterraneos specus aperire, suffugium hieme et receptaculum frugibus. (Tac. Germ. 16)

(9) Nominandi istorum tibi erit magis quam edundi copia.
(Plaut. Capt. 852)

(10) Tantus anulorum acervus fuit ut metientibus supra tres modios explesse sint quidam auctores.
(Liv. xxiii. 12)

XIII

(1) Εἰ δέ μ' ὧδ' ἀεὶ λόγους
ἐξῆρχες, οὐκ ἂν ἦσθα λυπηρὰ κλύειν. (Soph. El. 556)

(2) Ὅπως ταῦτα μηδεὶς ἀνθρώπων πεύσεται. (Lys. i. 21)

EXAMPLES FOR EXERCISE 193

(3) Τοίγαρ σὺ δέξαι μ' ἐς τὸ σὸν τόδε στέγος
τὴν μηδὲν εἰς τὸ μηδέν. (Soph. *El.* 1165)

(4) Κρύσταλλός τε γὰρ ἐπεπήγει οὐ βέβαιος ἐν αὐτῇ ὥστ'
ἐπελθεῖν, ἀλλ' οἷος ἀπηλιώτου ὑδατώδης μᾶλλον . . .
(Thuc. iii. 23)

(5) Τὰ πάντα γάρ τις ἐγχέας ἀνθ' αἵματος
ἑνός, μάτην ὁ μόχθος. (Aesch. *Cho.* 521)

(6) Tum se ad Caietae recto fert litore portum.
(V. *Aen.* vi. 900)

(7) Exsequias Chremeti quibus est commodum ire, em tempus
est. (Ter. *Ph.* 1026)

(8) Nihil est in dicendo maius quam ut faveat oratori is qui
audiet. (Cic. *Or.* ii. 42)

(9) Domus erat aleatoribus referta, plena ebriorum.
(*id. Phil.* ii. 27)

(10) Labruscae folia, priusquam decidant, sanguineo colore
mutantur. (Plin. xiv. 37)

XIV

(1) Λέγεται δ' αὐτὸν μέλλοντα ξυλληφθήσεσθαι . . . γνῶναι
ἐφ' ᾧ ἐχώρει. (Thuc. i. 134)

(2) Τὸ λεγόμενον, κατόπιν τῆς ἑορτῆς ἥκομεν.
(Plat. *Gorg.* 477)

(3) Εἰ γὰρ οὗτοι ὀρθῶς ἀπέστησαν, ὑμεῖς ἂν οὐ χρεὼν ἄρχοιτε.
(Thuc. iii. 40)

(4) Σιγησόμεσθα κρεισσόνων νικώμενοι. (Eur. *Med.* 315)

(5) Ταῦτα ἀγαθὸς ἕκαστος ἡμῶν, ἅπερ σοφός, ἃ δὲ ἀμαθής,
ταῦτα δὲ κακός. (Plat. *Lach.* 194 D)

(6) Omnia postposui, dummodo praeceptis patris parerem.
(Cic. *Fam.* xvi. 21)

(7) Sine, priusquam amplexum accipio, sciam ad hostem an
ad filium venerim. (Liv. ii. 40)

(8) Duco mecum Ciceronem meum in ludum discendi, non
lusionis. (Cic. *Q. fr.* iii. 4)

(9) . . . At certe credemur, ait, si verba sequetur
Exitus. (Ov. *F.* iii. 351)

(10) Tantum opes creverant, ut ne morte quidem Aeneae
movere arma Etrusci aut ulli alii accolae ausi sint.
(Liv. i. 3)

XV

(1) Καταλαμβάνουσι τεῖχος, ὃ τειχισάμενοί ποτε Ἀκαρνᾶνες κοινῷ δικαστηρίῳ ἐχρῶντο. (Thuc. iii. 105)

(2) Συγγιγνώσκειν αὐτοῖς χρὴ τῆς ἐπιθυμίας.
(Plat. Euthyd. 306 c)

(3) Ἔδοξεν αὐτῷ τοῦτο ποιῆσαι, ὡς ὅτι ἥκιστα ἂν ἐπιφθόνως σπάνιός τε καὶ σεμνὸς φανείη. (X. Cyr. vii. 5. 37)

(4) Δήμητερ, εὐδαιμονεῖν με Θησέα τε παῖδ᾽ ἐμόν.
(Eur. Supp. 3)

(5) Κατηγόρεον τῶν Αἰγινητέων τὰ πεποιήκοιεν προδόντες τὴν Ἑλλάδα. (Hdt. vi. 49)

(6) Laudantur oratores veteres, quod copiose reorum causas defendere solerent. (Cic. Verr. ii. 78)

(7) Simul ad purganda crimina et questum de se Romam eos ituros comperit. (Liv. xxxiv. 62)

(8) Nec dulces occurrent oscula nati
Praeripere et tacita pectus dulcedine tangent.
(Lucr. iii. 895)

(9) Si haec non gesta audiretis, sed picta videretis, tamen appareret uter esset insidiator. (Cic. Mil. 20)

(10) Tu quoque non melius, quam sunt mea tempora, carmen Consule, Roma, boni. (Ov. Tr. iv. 1. 106)

XVI

(1) Οὐδὲ γὰρ πρὶν ἡττηθῆναι τὴν δίκην εἶχεν ὧν δικαζόμεθα.
(Isae. v. 21)

(2) Ἐπανερομένου Κτησιφῶντος εἰ καλέσῃ Δημοσθένην . . .
(Aeschin. iii. 202)

(3) Τὴν παραυτίκα ἐλπίδα οὐδενὸς ἂν ἠλλάξαντο.
(Thuc. viii. 82)

(4) Ἀλλ᾽ ἦν ἐφῇς μοι, λέξαιμ᾽ ἂν ὀρθῶς. (Soph. El. 554)

(5) Ὑπτίοις κάτω
στρέψας τὸ λοιπὸν σέλμασιν ναυτίλλεται.
(Soph. Ant. 716)

(6) Quotusquisque iuris peritus est, ut eos numeres, qui volunt esse? (Cic. Planc. 25)

(7) Omnino supervacua erat doctrina, si natura sufficeret.
(Quint. ii. 8. 8)
(8) Protinus induitur faciem cultumque Dianae.
(Ov. M. ii. 425)
(9) Quamvis est circum caesis lacer undique membris
Truncus, adempta anima circum membrisque remota
Vivit et aetherias vitalis suscipit auras. (Lucr. iii. 405)
(10) Cur, improbe, carae
Non aliquid patriae tanto emetiris acervo ?
(Hor. S. ii. 2. 104)

XVII

(1) Τῷ μὲν ἔξωθεν ἁπτομένῳ σῶμα οὐκ ἄγαν θερμὸν ἦν.
(Thuc. ii. 49)
(2) Ἀλλ' οἶσθ' ὃ δρᾶσον; τῷ σκέλει θένε τὴν πέτραν.
(Ar. Av. 54)
(3) Ἐπεί τε ὁ πόλεμος κατέστη, ὁ δὲ φαίνεται καὶ ἐν τούτῳ προγνοὺς τὴν δύναμιν. (Thuc. ii. 65)
(4) Τοιοῦτον ἔθος παρέδοσαν, ὥστε ἑκατέρους ἔχειν ἐφ' οἷς φιλοτιμηθῶσιν. (Isoc. iv. 44)
(5) Καὶ λίμνην ποιεῖ μείζω τῆς παρ' ἡμῖν θαλάττης, ζέουσαν ὕδατος καὶ πηλοῦ. (Plat. Phaed. 113 A)
(6) GE. Haec fient. AN. Ut modo fiant ! GE. Fient : me vide. (Ter. Ph. 711)
(7) Pugnatum longo agmine et incerto Marte, donec proelium nox dirimeret. (Tac. Hist. iv. 35)
(8) Periisti, si intrassis intra limen. (Plaut. Men. 416)
(9) Antiochus Ephesi securus admodum de bello Romano erat, tamquam non transituris in Asiam Romanis.
(Liv. xxxvi. 41)
(10) Ex his Bellovaci suum numerum non compleverunt, quod se suo nomine atque arbitrio cum Romanis bellum gesturos dicerent. (Caes. B.G. vii. 75)

XVIII

(1) Οὔ μ' ἐπέεσσιν ἀποτρέψεις μεμαῶτα
πρὶν χαλκῷ μαχέσασθαι. (Hom. Il. xx. 256)
(2) Ἀκούετε λεῴ . . . πίνειν ὑπὸ τῆς σάλπιγγος.
(Ar. Ach. 1000)

(3) Θαυμάζω δὲ τῇ τε ἀποκλῄσει μου τῶν πυλῶν καὶ εἰ μὴ
ἀσμένοις ὑμῖν ἀφῖγμαι. (Thuc. iv. 85)

(4) Ἀντιπαρεσκευάζετο ἐρρωμένως, ὡς μάχης ἔτι δεῆσον.
(X. Cyr. ii. 2)

(5) Οὐκ ἀνατίθεμαι μὴ οὐ καλῶς λέγεσθαι.
(Plat. Meno 89 D)

(6) Tranquillo, ut aiunt, quilibet gubernator est.
(Sen. Ep. 85. 34)

(7) Haec tibi dictabam . . .
Excepto quod non simul esses cetera laetus.
(Hor. Ep. i. 10. 50)

(8) Decemvirorum vos pertaesum est. (Liv. iii. 19)

(9) Ostendis qualis tu, si ita forte accidisset, fueris illo tempore
consul futurus. (Cic. Pis. 7)

(10) Tecto assuetus coluber succedere et umbrae
Fovit humum. (V. Georg. iii. 418)

XIX

(1) Ὁποῖα κισσὸς δρυὸς ὅπως τῆσδ' ἕξομαι. (Eur. Hec. 398)

(2) Τὴν ναυμαχίαν αὐτοὶ κατὰ μόνας ἀπεωσάμεθα Κορινθίους.
(Thuc. i. 32)

(3) Καιρὸν εἰ φθέγξαιο, μείων ἕπεται μῶμος ἀνθρώπων.
(Pind. Pyth. i. 81)

(4) Ἢν ἄρα σφαλῶσιν, ἀντελπίσαντες ἄλλα ἐπλήρωσαν τὴν
χρείαν. (Thuc. i. 70)

(5) Ὡς μὲν οὐκ ἀληθῆ ταῦτ' ἐστὶν οὐχ ἕξετ' ἀντιλέγειν.
(Dem. viii. 31)

(6) Populabundus agros ad oppidum pervenit.
(Sisenna ap. Gell. xi. 15)

(7) Servati consulis decus Caelius ad servum delegat.
(Liv. xxi. 46)

(8) Quid tua, malum, id refert ? CH. Magni.
(Ter. Phorm. 723)

(9) Gratulor tibi, cum tantum vales apud Dolabellam.
(Cic. Att. xiv. 17 a)

(10) Voconia lex te videlicet delectabat. Imitatus esses ipsum
Voconium, qui lege sua hereditatem ademit nulli.
(id. Verr. i. 42)

XX

(1) Οὗτος σύ, ποῖ θεῖς; ἐπὶ καδίσκους; Μηδαμῶς.
(Ar. Vesp. 854)

(2) Ἱκανῶς οὖν τοῦτο ἔχομεν, κἂν εἰ πλεοναχῇ σκοποῖμεν;
(Plat. Rep. 477 A)

(3) Ἀλλ' εὐδαιμονίας τε αὖ καὶ ἀθλιότητος ὡσαύτως ἢ ἄλλως κρίνεις; (Plat. Rep. 576 D)

(4) Οὐκ ἂν πιθοίμην μὴ οὐ τάδ' ἐκμαθεῖν σαφῶς.
(Soph. O.T. 1065)

(5) Ἀλλ' οὔτι μὴν ἔγωγε τοῦ λοιποῦ χρόνου
ξύνοικος εἴσειμ'... (Soph. El. 817)

(6) Rex se munitae urbi cum magna manu popularium incluserat. (Curt. ix. 8)

(7) Iura te non nociturum esse de hac re nemini.
(Plaut. Mil. 411)

(8) Praeclare viceramus, nisi Lepidus recepisset Antonium.
(Cic. Fam. xii. 10)

(9) Nec nostris praebere vacat tibi cantibus aures.
(Ov. M. v. 344)

(10) Postremo quodvis frumentum non tamen omne
Quidque suo genere inter se simile esse videbis.
(Lucr. ii. 371)

XXI

(1) Θυμὸν γένοιτο χειρὶ πληρῶσαί ποτε
ἵν' αἱ Μυκῆναι γνοῖεν ἡ Σπάρτη θ' ὅτι
χἠ Σκῦρος ἀνδρῶν ἀλκίμων μήτηρ ἔφυ. (Soph. Phil. 324)

(2) Ἐφοβεῖτο μὴ οἱ Λακεδαιμόνιοι σφᾶς, ὁπότε σαφῶς ἀκούσειαν, οὐκέτι ἀφῶσιν. (Thuc. i. 91)

(3) Οἶσθα ἐπαινέσαντα Ὅμηρον τὸν Ἀγαμέμνονα ὡς βασιλεὺς εἴη ἀγαθός. (X. Symp. 4. 6)

(4) Οὕτω νικήσαιμί τ' ἐγὼ καὶ νομιζοίμην σοφός,
ὡς ὑμᾶς ἡγοῦμαι εἶναι θεατὰς δεξίους. (Ar. Nub. 520)

(5) Ἅπαντα γάρ σοι τἀμὰ νουθετήματα
κείνης διδακτά. (Soph. El. 344)

(6) Est fons aquae dulcis, cui nomen Arethusa est, incredibili magnitudine, plenissimus piscium.
(Cic. Verr. iv. 53)

(7) Sunt qui non habeant, est qui non curat habere.
(Hor. *Ep.* ii. 2. 182)

(8) Isto bono utare dum adsit : cum absit, ne requiras.
(Cic. *Sen.* 10)

(9) Nulla pestis humano generi pluris stetit ira.
(Sen. *Ir.* i. 2)

(10) Et ni docta comes tenues sine corpore vitas
Admoneat volitare cava sub imagine formae,
Irruat et frustra ferro diverberet umbras.
(V. *Aen.* vi. 161-163)

XXII

(1) Μὴ οὐ τοιαύτην ὑπολαμβάνεις σου τὴν μάθησιν ἔσεσθαι.
(Plat. *Prot.* 312 A)

(2) Οὐ γὰρ ἂν μακρὰν
ἴχνευον αὐτός, μὴ οὐκ ἔχων τι σύμβολον.
(Soph. *O.T.* 221)

(3) Ἀμύντωρ, ᾧ τὸ ψήφισμα ἐπεδείξατο Δημοσθένης καὶ ἀνεκοινοῦτο εἰ δῷ τῷ γραμματεῖ. (Aeschin. *F.L.* 64)

(4) Οἶσθα δῆθ' ἅ μοι γενέσθω; (Eur. *I.T.* 1203)

(5) Οὐχὶ συγκλῄσεις στόμα
καὶ μὴ μεθήσεις αὖθις αἰσχίστους λόγους;
(Eur. *Hipp.* 499)

(6) Ad Appii Claudii senectutem accedebat etiam ut caecus esset. (Cic. *Sen.* 6)

(7) Unum exuta pedem vinclis . . .
Testatur moritura deos. (V. *Aen.* iv. 518)

(8) Tumultuose decurrerat multitudo ad prohibendos si egrederentur. (Liv. xxiv. 27)

(9) Sic flendus Peleus, si moreretur, erat. (Ov. *F.* v. 408)

(10) Servus est nemo qui non, quantum audet et quantum potest, conferat ad communem salutem, voluntatis.
(Cic. *Cat.* iv. 8)

XXIII

(1) Πῶς ἄν τις μὴ θυμῷ λέγοι περὶ θεῶν, (Plat. *Leg.* 887 c)

(2) Ἐπίσχετ', αὐδὴν τῶν ἔσωθεν ἐκμάθω. (Eur. *Hipp.* 567)

(3) Ὅταν γὰρ ἐν κακοῖς
ἤδη βεβήκῃς, τἄμ' ἐπαινέσεις ἔπη. (Soph. *El.* 1056)

(4) Μόλις ἄν μοι δοκοῦσιν οὐκ ἂν παντάπασιν διαφθαρῆναι.
(Thuc. vi. 37)
(5) Ἠξίουν αὐτοὺς μαστιγοῦν τὸν ἐκδοθέντα ἕως ἂν τἀληθῆ δόξειεν αὐτοῖς λέγειν. (Isoc. xvii. 15)
(6) Aeneia puppis
Prima tenet rostro Phrygios subiuncta leones.
(V. Aen. x. 157)
(7) Est quadam prodire tenus, si non datur ultra.
(Hor. Ep. i. 1. 32)
(8) Caligula vixit annis XXIX., imperavit triennio et x. mensibus diebusque VIII. (Suet. Cal. 59)
(9) At si me iubeas domitos Iovis igne Gigantas
Dicere, conantem debilitabit onus. (Ov. Tr. ii. 333)
(10) In tanta paupertate decessit, ut qui efferretur vix reliquerit. (Nep. Aristid. 3)

XXIV

(1) Εἰ οὖν ἐγὼ γιγνώσκω μήτε τὰ ὅσια μήτε τὰ δίκαια, ὑμεῖς δὲ διδάξατέ με. (X. Hell. iv. 1. 33)
(2) Κοίλαν δὲ καθιδρυνθέντες ἐς Ἀργὼ
Ἑλλάσποντον ἵκοντο, νότῳ τρίτον ἆμαρ ἀέντι.
(Theoc. xiii. 28)
(3) Πρὸς τῶν θεῶν, ἄνθρωπε, ναύφρακτον βλέπεις.
(Ar. Ach. 95)
(4) Ἀναλαμβάνων οὖν αὐτῶν τὰ ποιήματα ... διηρώτων ἂν αὐτοὺς τί λέγοιεν. (Plat. Ap. 22 B)
(5) Δαρείῳ δὲ δεινὸν ἐδόκεε εἶναι μὴ οὐ λαβεῖν τὰ χρήματα.
(Hdt. i. 187)
(6) Pacis eras mediusque belli. (Hor. C. ii. 19. 28)
(7) Tentatum domi per dictatorem, ut ambo patricii consules crearentur, rem ad interregnum perduxit.
(Liv. vii. 22)
(8) Scire tuum nihil est nisi te scire hoc sciat alter.
(Pers. i. 27)
(9) Erat sane somni paratissimi, non numquam etiam inter ipsa studia instantis et deserentis.
(Plin. Ep. iii. 5. 8)
(10) Quaeris quid agam. Ita vivam ut maximos sumptus facio.
(Cic. Att. v. 15. 2)

XXV

(1) Ἱμάτιον ἠμφίεσαι τὸ αὐτὸ θέρους τε καὶ χειμῶνος.
(X. *Mem.* i. 5. 2)

(2) Εἰ γὰρ εἶναί τι δοκοίη τὰ μάλιστ' ἐν τούτοις ἀδίκημα, οὐδέν ἐστι δήπου πρὸς ἐμέ. (Dem. xviii. 21)

(3) Μὴ δείσῃς ποθ' ὡς
γέλωτι τοὐμὸν φαιδρὸν ὄψεται κάρα. (Soph. *El.* 1309)

(4) Λέγω καθ' ἕκαστον δοκεῖν ἄν μοι τὸν αὐτὸν ἄνδρα παρ' ἡμῶν ἐπὶ πλεῖστ' ἂν εἴδη καὶ μετὰ χαρίτων μάλιστ' ἂν εὐτραπέλως τὸ σῶμα αὔταρκες παρέχεσθαι.
(Thuc. ii. 41)

(5) Ἀλλ' οὐκ ἐάσει τοῦτό γ' ἡ δίκη σε. (Soph. *Ant.* 538)

(6) Orationis operam compendi face. (Plaut. *Most.* 60)

(7) Egone ut te interpellem ? ne hoc quidem vellem.
(Cic. *T.D.* ii. 18)

(8) Hi scribendo affuerunt . . .
(*Sen. Cons. ap.* Cic. *Fam.* viii. 8)

(9) Sed, me dius fidius, multo citius meam salutem pro te abiecero, quam Cn. Plancii salutem tradidero contentioni tuae. (Cic. *Planc.* 33)

(10) Quam vellem Romae esses si forte non es.
(*id. Att.* v. 18)

XXVI

(1) Δεινὸν ἂν εἴη πρᾶγμα εἰ Σάκας μὲν δούλους ἔχομεν, Ἕλληνας δὲ οὐ τιμωρησόμεθα. (Hdt. vii. 9)

(2) Καὶ τὴν εἰρήνην τοὺς τῶν πολεμίων ἡγεμόνας, ἀλλὰ μὴ τοὺς πρέσβεις ἀπαιτεῖτε. (Aeschin. *F.L.* 73)

(3) Πέφρικα τὰν ὠλεσίοικον θεὸν . . . τελέσαι τὰς περιθύμους κατάρας Οἰδιπόδος βλαψίφρονος. (Aesch. *Sept.* 720)

(4) Αἰσχρόν ἐστι σοφίαν μὴ οὐχὶ πάντων κράτιστον φάναι.
(Plat. *Prot.* 352 D)

(5) Τίς ἂν δίκην κρίνειεν ἢ γνοίη λόγον
πρὶν ἂν παρ' ἀμφοῖν μῦθον ἐκμάθῃ σαφῶς;
(Eur. *Her.* 179)

(6) His numquam candente dies apparuit ortu,
Seu supra terras Phoebus seu curreret infra.
(Tib. iv. 1. 66)

(7) Adeono homines inmutarier ex amore, ut non cognoscas eundem esse ? (Ter. *Eun.* 225)
(8) Hanno ex Bruttiis profectus cum exercitu, vitabundus castra hostium consulesque, loco edito castra posuit. (Liv. xxv. 13)
(9) Respondit illud argentum se paucis illis diebus misisse Lilybaeum. (Cic. *Verr.* iv. 18)
(10) Metellus evocat ad se magistratus; nisi restituissent statuas vehementer minatur. (*ibid.* ii. 67)

XXVII

(1) Ὦ πάντα τολμῶν, κἀπὸ παντὸς ἂν φέρων
    λόγου δικαίου μηχάνημα ποικίλον ... (Soph. *O.C.* 761)
(2) Θεοὶ πολῖται, μή με δουλείας τυχεῖν. (Aesch. *Sept.* 253)
(3) Ἀψυχίᾳ γὰρ γλῶσσαν ἁρπάζει φόβος. (*ibid.* 259)
(4) Ἡ πόλις ἐκινδύνευσε πᾶσα διαφθαρῆναι εἰ ἄνεμος ἐπεγένετο. (Thuc. iii. 74)
(5) Ἦλθον ἐπί τινα τῶν δοκούντων σοφῶν εἶναι ... καὶ διαλεγόμενος αὐτῷ ἔδοξέ μοι οὗτος ὁ ἀνὴρ δοκεῖν μὲν εἶναι σοφός, εἶναι δ' οὔ. (Plat. *Apol.* 21 B)
(6) Sed ita forsitan decuit cum foederum ruptore duce et populo deos ipsos committere bellum. (Liv. xxi. 40)
(7) Iam mihi videor navasse operam, quod huc venerim. (Cic. *Or.* ii. 7)
(8) Tranquillissimus animus meus qui totum istuc aequi boni facit. (*id. Att.* vii. 7)
(9) Ita tigna umide haec putent non videor mihi sarcire posse aedis meas. (Plaut. *Most.* 146)
(10) Et micat interdum flammai fervidus ardor,
     Mutua dum inter se rami stirpesque teruntur. (Lucr. v. 1100)

XXVIII

(1) Ὁ παῖς εἴπερ ἑστὼς φανερὸς ὑμῖν ἐστι μὴ βληθείς, δηλοῦται διὰ τὴν αὐτοῦ ἁμαρτίαν ἀποθανών. (Ant. *Tetr.* B β 5)
(2) Μὴ ἐξαμάρτητε περὶ τὴν τοῦ θεοῦ δόσιν ὑμῖν. (Plat. *Ap.* 30 D)

(3) Βουδῖνοι δὲ οὐ τῇ αὐτῇ γλώσσῃ χρέωνται καὶ Γελωνοί.
(Hdt. iv. 109)

(4) Ἔνιοι τῶν ἀδελφῶν ἀμελοῦσιν ὥσπερ οὐ γιγνομένους φίλους ἐξ ἀδελφῶν... (X. Mem. ii. 3)

(5) Ἥκεις γὰρ οὐ κενή γε, τοῦτ' ἐγὼ σαφῶς
ἔξοιδα, μὴ οὐχὶ δεῖμ' ἐμοὶ φέρουσά τι. (Soph. O.C. 359)

(6) Ego faxi et operam et vinum perdiderit simul.
(Plaut. Aul. 570)

(7) Bacchatur vates, magnum si pectore possit
Excussisse deum. (V. Aen. vi. 78)

(8) Id a Quinctio facile impetratum non quia satis dignos eos credebat, sed quia favor conciliandus nomini Romano apud civitates erat. (Liv. xxxii. 27)

(9) Parte tamen meliore mei super alta perennis
Astra ferar. (Ov. Met. xv. 875)

(10) Reus parricidii, quod fratrem occidisset, damnatum iri videbatur. (Quint. ix. 2. 88)

XXIX

(1) Ὄλοιο μήπω, πρὶν μάθοιμ' εἰ καὶ πάλιν
γνώμην μετοίσεις. (Soph. Phil. 961)

(2) Ἡ πόλις ἦν ὠφέλιμος ξύλων τε ναυπηγησίμων πομπῇ καὶ χρημάτων προσόδῳ. (Thuc. iv. 108)

(3) Ἀρχὴ γενήσεται πρὸς Φίλιππον ἔχθρας, εἰ τῶν πρεσβευσάντων τὴν εἰρήνην καταψηφιεῖσθε. (Dem. xix. 134)

(4) Ἀλλ' ὧνπερ ἄρχεις ἄρχε καὶ τὰ σέμν' ἔπη
κόλαζ' ἐκείνους. (Soph. Aj. 1107)

(5) Ὦ Ζεῦ, ἐκγενέσθαι μοι Ἀθηναίους τίσασθαι. (Hdt. v. 105)

(6) Haec civitas in Gallia maximam habet opinionem virtutis.
(Caes. B.G. vii. 59)

(7) Nulla profecto alia gens tanta mole cladis non obruta esset.
(Liv. xxii. 54)

(8) Hanc primum ad litora classem
Conspexi venientem : huic me, quaecumque fuisset,
Addixi. (V. Aen. iii. 652)

(9) Cotidie meam potentiam invidiose criminabatur, cum diceret senatum, non quod sentiret, sed quod ego vellem decernere. (Cic. Mil. 5)

(10) Boves arandi causa rudis neque minoris trimos neque maioris quadrimos parandum. (Varr. R.R. i. 20)

XXX

(1) Ἐκεῖ σκιά τ' ἐστί, καὶ πόα καθίζεσθαι ἢ ἂν βουλώμεθα κατακλιθῆναι. (Plat. *Phaedr.* 229 A)

(2) Καίτοι σ' ὁ φύσας χἠ τεκοῦσα προὔδοσαν, καλῶς μὲν αὐτοῖς κατθανεῖν ἧκον βίου . . . (Eur. *Alc.* 290)

(3) Κλαίων οὐδέν' ὅντιν' οὐ κατέκλασε. (Plat. *Phaed.* 117 D)

(4) Καὶ νῦν ὡς ἐφ' ἃ μὲν ἤλθομεν τὸ πρῶτον καὶ τῶν στρατιωτῶν καὶ τῶν ἡγεμόνων ὑμῖν μὴ μεμπτῶν γεγενημένων οὕτω τὴν γνώμην ἔχετε. (Thuc. vii. 15)

(5) Οὐδ' οἶδ' ἂν εἰ πείσαιμι, πειρᾶσθαι δὲ χρή. (Eur. *Med.* 941)

(6) Quid faceret ? si vivere vellet, Seianus rogandus erat. (Sen. *Dial.* vi. 22)

(7) Saepe lapidum, sanguinis non numquam, terrae interdum, quondam etiam lactis imber defluxit. (Cic. *Div.* i. 43)

(8) Hinc alii spolia occisis derepta Latinis Coniciunt igni. (V. *Aen.* xi. 193)

(9) Nimis velim improbissumo homini malas edentaverint. (Plaut. *Rud.* 662)

(10) Nec consul, ut qui id ipsum oppugnatione comminanda quaesisset, moram certamini fecit. (Liv. xlii. 7)

XXXI

(1) Ἔφευγον ἔνθα μήποτ' ὀψοίμην κακῶν χρησμῶν ὀνείδη τῶν ἐμῶν τελούμενα. (Soph. *O.T.* 796)

(2) Καὶ διαλεχθείς τι πρὸς αὐτὸν οὕτως ὡς ἂν μεθύων ὥστε μὴ μαθεῖν ὅ τι λέγοι παρῆλθε πρὸς Μελίτην ἄνω. (Dem. liv. 7)

(3) Τοῦ δ' αὐτοῦ χειμῶνος οἱ Ποτιδαιᾶται . . . λόγους προσφέρουσι περὶ ξυμβάσεως τοῖς στρατηγοῖς. (Thuc. ii. 70)

(4) Ἀλλ' ὅπως μὴ οὐχ οἷός τ' ἔσομαι, προθυμούμενος δὲ γέλωτα ὀφλήσω. (Plat. *Rep.* 506 D)

(5) Οὐδὲ πελάσαι οἷόν τ' ἦν τῇ εἰσόδῳ. (X. *An.* iv. 2)

(6) . . . multa quoque et bello passus dum conderet urbem. (V. *Aen.* i. 5)

EXAMPLES FOR EXERCISE

(7) Tam te basia multa basiare
Vesano satis et super Catullost. (Catull. 7. 9)

(8) Quaesivit iterum, si cum Romanis militare liceret.
(Liv. xl. 49)

(9) Nullust hoc meticulosus aeque. (Plaut. Amph. 293)

(10) Templa . . . in nulla provincia nisi communi suo Romaeque nomine recepit. (Suet. Aug. 52)

XXXII

(1) Ὡς τοίνυν μὴ ἀκουσομένων, οὕτω διανοεῖσθε.
(Plat. Rep. 327 D)

(2) Τῆς σῆς ἀνοίας τόνδε τὸν διδάσκαλον
δίκην μέτειμι. (Eur. Bac. 345)

(3) Ἔφη, ἐπειδὴ οὗ ἐκβῆναι τὴν ψυχήν, πορεύεσθαι μετὰ πολλῶν . . . (Plat. Rep. 614 B)

(4) Θηβαῖοι; μὴ λίαν πικρὸν εἰπεῖν ᾖ, καὶ συνεισβαλοῦσιν ἑτοίμως. (Dem. i. 26)

(5) Ὦ πόλλ' ἐγὼ μοχθηρός, ὦ πικρὸς θεοῖς,
οὗ μηδὲ κληδὼν ὧδ' ἔχοντος οἴκαδε
μηδ' Ἑλλάδος γῆς μηδαμοῦ διῆλθέ που. (Soph. Phil. 254)

(6) Sed non effugies ; mecum moriaris oportet.
(Prop. ii. 8. 25)

(7) Dum intentus in eum se rex totus verteret, alter elatam securim in caput deiecit. (Liv. i. 40)

(8) Neque munitiones Caesaris prohibere poterat, nisi proelio decertare vellet. (Caes. B.C. iii. 44)

(9) Vulgi opinio est tamquam (cometes) mutationem regni portendat. (Tac. Ann. xiv. 22)

(10) Cur valle permutem Sabina
Divitias operosiores ? (Hor. C. iii. 1. 47)

XXXIII

(1) Πολλοῦ δεῖ γιγαντομαχίας τε μυθολογητέον αὐτοῖς καὶ ποικιλτέον. (Plat. Rep. 378 c)

(2) Ὦ δυσθέατον ὄμμα καὶ τόλμης πικρᾶς,
ὅσας ἀνίας μοι κατασπείρας φθίνεις. (Soph. Aj. 1004)

(3) Οὐκ ἂν οἴει με καὶ ἀσχολίας ὑπέρτερον πρᾶγμα ποιήσεσθαι;
(Plat. Phaedr. 227 B)

EXAMPLES FOR EXERCISE

(4) Οὐκοῦν ἐχρῆν σε Πηγάσου ζεῦξαι πτερόν,
ὅπως ἐφαίνου τοῖς θεοῖς τραγικώτερος; (Ar. *Pax* 135)

(5) Περὶ τῶν ἄλλων τῶν ἀδικούντων, ὅτε δικάζονται, δεῖ παρὰ τῶν κατηγόρων πυθέσθαι. (Lys. xxii. 12)

(6) Emas non quod opus est, sed quod necesse est; quod non opus est asse carum est. (*ap*. Sen. *E.M.* xciv. 27)

(7) Asiam sic obiit ut in ea neque avaritiae neque luxuriae vestigium reliquerit. (Cic. *Mur.* 20)

(8)   Nunc viribus usus,
Nunc manibus rapidis, omni nunc arte magistra.
(V. *Aen.* viii. 441)

(9) Nam ut ferula caedas meritum maiora subire
Verbera, non vereor. (Hor. *S.* i. 3. 120)

(10) Qui unum eius ordinis offendisset omnes adversos habebat.
(Liv. xxxiii. 46)

XXXIV

(1) Ὡς δυστάλαινα τῆς ἐμῆς αὐθαδίας. (Eur. *Med.* 1029)

(2) Εἰ καὶ ἠπιστάμην, ὁ βίος μοι δοκεῖ ... οὐκ ἐξαρκεῖν.
(Plat. *Phaed.* 108 D)

(3)   Ἱκέται πρὸς σὲ δεῦρ' ἀφίγμεθα,
εἴ τινα πόλιν φράσειας ἡμῖν, εὔερον. (Ar. *Av.* 120)

(4)   Ἡ δέ κ' ἔπειτα
γήμαιθ' ὅς κεν πλεῖστα πόροι καὶ μόρσιμος ἔλθοι.
(Hom. *Od.* xxi. 161)

(5) Ἀπεπέμπετο ἡ στρατιή, ὡς ἐμοὶ δοκέειν, ἐπὶ Λιβύης καταστροφῇ. (Hdt. iv. 167)

(6) Dociliora sunt ingenia priusquam obduruerunt.
(Quint. i. 12. 9)

(7) Themistocles praedixit, ut ne prius Lacedaemoniorum legatos dimitterent quam ipse esset remissus.
(Nep. ii. 7. 3)

(8) Iugurtha timebat iram senatus, ni paruisset legatis.
(Sall. *Jug.* 25)

(9) Ardua dum metuunt amittunt vera viai. (Lucr. i. 660)

(10) Non omnes possunt olere unguenta exotica.
(Plaut. *Most.* 42)

XXXV

(1) Ἔκτισαν τὸ χωρίον τοῦτο, ὅπερ πρότερον Ἐννέα Ὁδοὶ ἐκαλοῦντο. (Thuc. iv. 102)

(2) Τὸν Ὑπερείδην, εἴπερ ἀληθῆ μου νῦν κατηγορεῖ, μᾶλλον ἂν εἰκότως ἢ τόνδ' ἐδίωκεν. (Dem. xviii. 223)

(3) Ὦ γέρον, ἦ ὀλίγου σε κύνες διεδηλήσαντο. (Hom. Od. xiv. 37)

(4) Τόν γε πράττοντά τι δίκαιον οὐ προσῆκεν ἀπορεῖν ἀλλ' εὐθὺς λέγειν, ἵνα μᾶλλον ἂν ἐπιστεύετο ὑφ' ὑμῶν. (Isae. xi. 6)

(5) Δουλεύομεν θεοῖς, ὅ τι ποτ' εἰσὶν οἱ θεοί. (Eur. Or. 418)

(6) Qui fit, Maecenas, ut nemo quam sibi sortem
Seu ratio dederit seu fors obiecerit, illa
Contentus vivat ? (Hor. S. i. 1. 1)

(7) Id velim mihi ignoscas, quod invita socru tua fecerim. (Cic. Fam. xii. 7)

(8) Tum facito ante solem occasum ut venias advorsum mihi. (Plaut. Men. 437)

(9) Romanus promissa consulis fidemque senatus expectabat, cum Appius, quam asperrime poterat, ius de creditis pecuniis dicere. (Liv. ii. 27)

(10) Transadigit costas fulvaque effundit arena. (V. Aen. xii. 276)

XXXVI

(1) Μέγα τοι κλέος αἰεί, | ᾧτινι σὸν γέρας ἕσπητ' ἀγλαόν. (Pind. O. viii. 10)

(2) Τῇ πόλει προσέκειτο ... καὶ αἱρεῖ ἀφυλάκτοις τε ἐπιπεσὼν καὶ ἀπροσδοκήτοις μὴ ἄν ποτέ τινας σφίσιν ἀπὸ θαλάσσης ... ἐπιθέσθαι. (Thuc. vii. 29)

(3) ... οἳ περὶ μὲν βουλὴν Δαναῶν, περὶ δ' ἐστὲ μάχεσθαι. (Hom. Il. i. 258)

(4) Φαίην δ' ἂν ἔγωγε μηδενὶ μηδεμίαν εἶναι παίδευσιν παρὰ τοῦ μὴ ἀρέσκοντος. (X. Mem. i. 2. 39)

(5) Ὡμολόγησαν τοῖς Ἀθηναίοις τείχη τε περιελόντες καὶ ναῦς παραδόντες φόρον τε ταξάμενοι. (Thuc. i. 108)

(6) Sisennae historia cum facile omnis vincat superiores, tum indicat tamen, quantum absit a summo. (Cic. Brut. 64)

(7)   It toto turbida caelo
Tempestas telorum ac ferreus ingruit imber.
(V. *Aen.* xii. 283)

(8) Si volebas tibi omnia licere, ne convertisses in te ora
omnia.   (Sen. *Dial.* xi. 6. 3)

(9)   Omnia novit
Graeculus esuriens ; in caelum miseris, ibit. (Juv. iii. 78)

(10) Responde, Blaese, ubi cadaver abieceris : ne hostes quidem
sepultura invident.   (Tac. *A.* i. 22)

XXXVII

(1) Πῶς ἂν ἐγώ σε δέοιμι μετ' ἀθανάτοισι θεοῖσιν,
εἴ κεν Ἄρης οἴχοιτο χρέος καὶ δεσμὸν ἀλύξας;
(Hom. *Od.* viii. 352)

(2) Χρὴ περὶ τῶν μελλόντων τεκμαίρεσθαι τοῖς ἤδη γεγενημένοις.   (Isoc. vi. 59)

(3) Οὐκοῦν ἔτι ἐλλείπεται τὸ ἢν πείσωμεν ὑμᾶς ὡς χρὴ ἡμᾶς
ἀφεῖναι;   (Plat. *Rep.* 327 c)

(4) Τοὺς ταλαιπώρους νησιώτας καθ' ἕκαστον ἐνιαυτὸν ἑξήκοντα
τάλαντα εἰσέπραττον σύνταξιν.   (Aeschin. *F.L.* 71)

(5) Διὸ καὶ τοὺς υἱεῖς οἱ πατέρες ἀπὸ τῶν πονηρῶν ἀνθρώπων
εἴργουσιν, ὡς τὴν μὲν τῶν χρηστῶν ὁμιλίαν ἄσκησιν
οὖσαν τῆς ἀρετῆς, τὴν δὲ τῶν πονηρῶν κατάλυσιν.
(X. *Mem.* i. 2)

(6) Omnibus amicis morbum tu incuties gravem,
Ut te videre audireque aegroti sient. (Plaut. *Tri.* 75)

(7) Forsitan, infelix, ventos undasque timebas.
(Ov. *F.* ii. 97)

(8) Amisit uxorem singularis exempli, etiam si olim fuisset.
(Plin. *Ep.* viii. 5)

(9) Nunc perveni Chalcidem : video ibi hospitem Zacyntho.
(Plaut. *Merc.* 940)

(10) Tumulus erat intra castra quem qui occupasset haud dubie
iniquiorem erat hosti locum facturus. (Liv. xxii. 28)

XXXVIII

(1) . . . ὁρῶν τὸ παρατείχισμα, εἰ ἐπικρατήσειέ τις, ῥᾳδίως
ἂν ληφθέν.   (Thuc. vii. 42)

EXAMPLES FOR EXERCISE

(2) Τῆς μητρὸς ἥκω τῆς ἐμῆς φράσων ἐν οἷς
νῦν ἐστιν. (Soph. *Tr.* 1122)

(3) Νῦν δ' οὐκ ἔσθ' ὅστις θάνατον φύγῃ, ὅν κε θεός γε
Ἰλίου προπάροιθεν ἐμῆς ἐν χερσὶ βάλῃσι. (Hom. *Il.* xxi. 103)

(4) Ὥστ' εἰκὸς ἡμᾶς μὴ βραδύνειν ἐστί, μὴ καί τις ὄψεται.
(Ar. *Eccl.* 495)

(5) Καὶ οὐκ ἀξιῶ ὑμᾶς τῷ εὐπρεπεῖ τοῦ ἐκείνου λόγου τὸ
χρήσιμον τοῦ ἐμοῦ ἀπώσασθαι. (Thuc. iii. 44)

(6) Si non pertaesum thalami taedaeque fuisset,
Huic uni forsan potui succumbere culpae.
(V. *Aen.* iv. 18)

(7) Qui istinc veniunt superbiam tuam accusant, quod negent
te percontantibus respondere. (Cic. *Fam.* vii. 16)

(8) Ut iuveni primum virgo deducta marito
Inficitur teneras ore rubente genas. (Tib. iii. 4. 31)

(9) Mos est hominum, ut nolint eundem pluribus rebus
excellere. (Cic. *Brut.* 21)

(10) Nec satis exaudibam nec sermonis fallebat tamen.
(Plaut. *Ep.* 239)

XXXIX

(1) Οὐδὲ τὰ περὶ τῆς δίκης ἄρα ἐπύθεσθε ὃν τρόπον ἐγένετο;
(Plat. *Phaed.* 58 A)

(2) Σὺ δ' εἶκ' ἀνάγκῃ καὶ θεοῖσι μὴ μάχου. (Eur. *Tel.* fr. 25)

(3) Ἐβουλεύοντο εἴτε κατακαύσωσιν εἴτε τι ἄλλο χρήσωνται.
(Thuc. ii. 4)

(4) Παίουσι, κρεοκοποῦσι δυστήνων μέλη,
ἕως ἁπάντων ἐξαπέφθειραν βίον. (Aesch. *Pers.* 466)

(5) Εἰ ἦν δυοῖν τὸ ἕτερον ἑλέσθαι, ἢ καλῶς ἀπόλεσθαι ἢ
αἰσχρῶς σωθῆναι, ἔχοι ἄν τις εἰπεῖν κακίαν εἶναι τὰ
γενόμενα. (Andoc. *de Myst.* 57)

(6) Rufus . . . antiquam duramque militiam revocabat, vetus
operis ac laboris et eo inmitior, quia toleravit.
(Tac. *Ann.* i. 21)

(7) Nobis, cum semel occidit brevis lux,
Nox est perpetua una dormienda. (Catull. 5. 5)

(8) Hic, qui Romam pervenisset satisque feliciter anni iam
adverso tempore navigasset, rem ad amicos detulit.
(Cic. *Verr.* ii. 38)

EXAMPLES FOR EXERCISE

(9) Vitaque mancipio nulli datur, omnibus usu.
(Lucr. iii. 971)

(10) Et hercule ut illi naturae caelesti atque immortali cesserimus, ita curae et diligentiae vel ideo in hoc plus est, quod ei fuit magis laborandum.
(Quint. x. 1. 86)

XL

(1) Τὴν μὲν πλείστην τῆς στρατιᾶς παρέταξε πρὸς τὰ τείχη τῶν Ἀθηναίων. (Thuc. vii. 3)

(2) Αὕτη ἄρα αἰτία αὐτοῖς ἐγένετο δύο γενέσθαι, ἡ ξύνοδος τοῦ πλησίον ἀλλήλων τεθῆναι. (Plat. Phaed. 97 A)

(3) Εἰ μέν κ᾽ ἐν ποταμῷ δυσκηδέα νύκτα φυλάξω,
μή μ᾽ ἄμυδις στιβή τε κακὴ καὶ θῆλυς ἐέρση,
ἐξ ὀλιγηπελίης δαμάσῃ . . . (Hom. Od. v. 466)

(4) Οὐκ ἀναμένομεν, ἕως ἂν ἡ ἡμετέρα χώρα κακῶται.
(X. Cyr. iii. 3. 18)

(5) Καὶ τὸ πλῆθος ἐψηφίσαντο πολεμεῖν· δεδογμένον δὲ αὐτοῖς εὐθὺς μὲν ἀδύνατα ἦν ἐπιχειρεῖν ἀπαρασκεύοις οὖσιν.
(Thuc. i. 125)

(6)   Est enim leporum
Disertus puer ac facetiarum. (Catull. 12. 9)

(7) Si quid huic acciderit, quem in eius locum substituitis ?
(Vell. ii. 32)

(8) Heu, miserande puer, si qua fata aspera rumpas,
Tu Marcellus eris. (V. Aen. vi. 882)

(9) Erat autem amentis, cum aciem videres, pacem cogitare.
(Cic. Lig. 9)

(10) Dic, hospes, Spartae nos te hic vidisse iacentes,
Dum sanctis patriae legibus obsequimur.
(ap. Cic. T.D. i. 42)

XLI

(1) Βάλλ᾽ οὕτως εἴ κέν τι φόως Δαναοῖσι γένηαι.
(Hom. Il. viii. 282)

(2) Ταῦτα σκοπεῖτε, ὅτι μὴ προνοίᾳ μᾶλλον ἐγίγνετο ἢ τύχῃ.
(Ant. v. 21)

(3) Ἔσθ᾽ ὅτῳ ἄλλῳ ἢ ψυχῇ δικαίως ἂν αὐτὰ ἀποδοῖμεν καὶ φαῖμεν ἴδια ἐκείνης εἶναι; (Plat. Rep. 353 D)

EXAMPLES FOR EXERCISE

(4) Οὐκ ἔσθ' ὅστις οὐχ ἡγεῖτο τῶν εἰδότων δίκην με λήψεσθαι
παρ' αὐτῶν, ἐπειδὰν τάχιστα ἀνὴρ εἶναι δοκιμασθείην.
(Dem. xxx. 6)

(5) Ὄζειν τε τῆς χρόας ἔφασκεν ἡδύ με. (Ar. *Plut.* 1020)

(6) Nec veni nisi fata locum sedemque dedissent.
(V. *Aen.* xi. 112)

(7) Mens quoque et animus, nisi tamquam lumini oleum
instilles, extinguuntur senectute. (Cic. *Sen.* 36)

(8) Hoc satis ? an deceat pulmonem rumpere ventis,
Stemmate quod Tusco ramum millesimo ducis,
Censoremve tuum vel quod trabeate salutas ?
(Pers. iii. 27)

(9) Aeriae primum volucres te, diva, tuumque
Significant initum, perculsae corda tua vi. (Lucr. i. 13)

(10) Quod ad vos attinet, ne ego libenter experirer, quam non
plus in eis iuris quam in vobis animi esset.
(Liv. v. 9)

XLII

(1) Εἰ γὰρ ἦν ἅπασι πρόδηλα τὰ μέλλοντα γενήσεσθαι . . .
οὐδ' οὕτως ἀποστατέον τῇ πόλει τούτων ἦν.
(Dem. xviii. 199)

(2) Ἡ δὲ ἀρέσκειά ἐστι μέν, ὡς ὅρῳ περιλαβεῖν, ἔντευξις οὐκ
ἐπὶ τῷ βελτίστῳ ἡδονῆς παρασκευαστική.
(Theophr. v. 1)

(3) Ἦ μένετε Τρῶας σχεδὸν ἐλθέμεν . . .
ὄφρα ἴδητ' αἴ κ' ὕμμιν ὑπέρσχῃ χεῖρα Κρονίων;
(Hom. *Il.* iv. 247)

(4) Ἀποδοτέον οὐδ' ὁπωστιοῦν τότε, ὁπότε τις μὴ σωφρόνως
ἀπαιτοῖ. (Plat. *Rep.* 332 A)

(5) Ἔτλα δ' οὖν θυτὴρ θυγατρὸς γενέσθαι,
γυναικοποίνων πολέμων ἀρωγάν. (Aesch. *Ag.* 235)

(6) Proinde ubi se videas hominem indignarier ipsum . . .
Scire licet non sincerum sonere. (Lucr. iii. 870)

(7) Tu, quod tuo commodo fiat, quam primum velim venias.
(Cic. *Fam.* iv. 2)

(8) Quid referam ut volitet crebras intacta per urbes
Alba Palaestino sancta columba Syro . . . (Tib. i. 7. 17)

EXAMPLES FOR EXERCISE

(9) Non vanae redeat sanguis imagini,
    Quam virga semel horrida
    Non lenis precibus fata recludere
    Nigro compulerit Mercurius gregi?   (Hor. *C.* i. 24. 15)

(10) Quae audivistis modo, nunc si eadem hic iterem, inscitiast.
                                          (Plaut. *Poen.* 921)

XLIII

(1) Σχολῇ γὰρ ἄν τι ἄλλο φθορὰν μὴ δέχοιτο, εἴ γε τὸ
    ἀθάνατον ἀίδιον ὂν φθορὰν δέξεται.
                                          (Plat. *Phaed.* 106 D)

(2) Τόφρα γὰρ ἂν κατὰ ἄστυ ποτιπτυσσοίμεθα μύθῳ
    χρήματ᾽ ἀπαιτίζοντες, ἕως κ᾽ ἀπὸ πάντα δοθείη.
                                          (Hom. *Od.* ii. 77)

(3) Οὐ θᾶσσον οἴσεις, μηδ᾽ ἀπιστήσεις ἐμοί;
                                          (Soph. *Tr.* 1183)

(4) . . . οὔτε ἔστιν οὐδεμία πρόφασις ἡμῖν τοῦ μὴ δρᾶν ταῦτα.
                                          (Plat. *Tim.* 20 c)

(5) Ἀνήρετ᾽ ἄρτι Χαιρεφῶντα Σωκράτης
    ψύλλαν, ὁπόσους ἄλλοιτο τοὺς αὐτῆς πόδας.
                                          (Ar. *Nub.* 144)

(6) Cantus et e curru Lunam deducere temptat
    Et faceret, si non aera repulsa sonent.   (Tib. i. 8. 22)

(7) Cohortes Batavorum, ut cuiusque legionis tentoria acces-
    sissent, superbe agebant, ablatam Neroni Italiam
    iactantes.   (Tac. *H.* ii. 27)

(8) Gubernatorem, vellet nollet, coegi petere litus.
                                          (Sen. *Ep.* 53. 3)

(9) Ecquis homost, qui facere argenti cupiat aliquantum
    lucri?   (Plaut. *Most.* 354)

(10) Sed non dixerat omnibus puellis:
     Verum ut dixerit omnibus puellis,
     Non dixit tibi: tu puella non es.   (Mart. ii. 41. 4)

XLIV

(1) Ἀλλ᾽ ἐρέω μὲν ἐγὼν ἵνα εἰδότες ἤ κε θάνωμεν
    ἤ κεν ἀλευάμενοι θάνατον καὶ κῆρα φύγοιμεν.
                                          (Hom. *Od.* xii. 156)

(2) Εἰ δέ κεν ὄψ᾽ ἀρόσῃς, τόδε κέν τοι φάρμακον εἴη.
                                          (Hes. *Op.* 485)

(3) Καίτοι ταλάντου ταῦτ' ἔμαθεν Ὑπέρβολος.
(Ar. *Nub.* 876)

(4) Οὔτ' ἔστιν οὔτε ποτὲ γένηται κρεῖττον. (Plat. *Leg.* 942c)

(5) Κίνδυνος οὖν πολλοὺς ἀπόλλυσθαι. (X. *An.* v. 1. 6)

(6) Usque adeo prius est in nobis multa ciendum
Quam primordia sentiscant concussa animai
Semina . . . (Lucr. iii. 391)

(7) Quid habent quod morte sua servent ? "Tecta urbis"
dicat aliquis "et moenia et eam turbam, a qua urbs
incolitur". (Liv. ix. 4)

(8) Tum Cererem corruptam undis Cerealiaque arma
Expediunt fessi rerum . . . (V. *Aen.* i. 177)

(9) Venit ad nos Cicero tuus ad cenam, cum Pomponia foras
cenaret. (Cic. *Q. fr.* iii. 1. 19)

(10) Hoc video, dum breviter voluerim dicere, dictum esse a
me paullo obscurius. (*id. Or.* i. 41)

XLV

(1) Τί δὲ ἵππων οἴει ἢ τῶν ἄλλων ζῴων; (Plat. *Rep.* 459 B)

(2) Εἰ δὲ μὴ Φρυγῶν
πύργους πεσόντας ᾖσμεν Ἑλλήνων δορὶ
φόβον παρέσχεν οὐ μέσως ὅδε κτύπος. (Eur. *Hec.* 1111)

(3) Τά τ' ἄλλα πάντ' ἐθέσπισεν
καὶ τἀπὶ Τροίας πέργαμ' ὡς οὐ μή ποτε
πέρσοιεν, εἰ μὴ τόνδ' . . . ἄγοιντο. (Soph. *Phil.* 611)

(4) Ἔλεγον οὐ καλῶς τὴν Ἑλλάδα ἐλευθεροῦν αὐτόν, εἰ ἄνδρας
διέφθειρεν . . . (Thuc. iii. 32)

(5) Χεῖρας νιψάμενος πολιῆς ἁλός. (Hom. *Od.* ii. 261)

(6) Nonne vides, croceos ut Tmolus odores,
India mittit ebur, molles sua turi Sabaei . . . ?
(V. *Georg.* i. 56)

(7) O fortunatos nimium, sua si bona norint,
Agricolas . . . (*ibid.* ii. 458)

(8) Fallit enim vitium specie virtutis et umbra,
Cum sit triste habitu vultuque et veste severum,
Nec dubie tamquam frugi laudetur avarus.
(Juv. xiv. 109)

EXAMPLES FOR EXERCISE 213

(9) Clamor ad caelum volvendus per aethera vagit.
(Enn. *Ann.* 520)

(10) Nihil deinde moratus, rex quattuor milia armatorum, dum recens terror esset, Scotussam misit. (Liv. xxxvi. 9)

XLVI

(1) Τῆς μητρὸς ἥκω τῆς ἐμῆς φράσων ἐν οἷς
νῦν ἐστιν. (Soph. *Tr.* 1122)

(2) Βουλέσθω εὔελπις ὁμόσε χωρῆσαι τοῖς ἐναντίοις.
(Thuc. iv. 10)

(3)   Τεῖρε δ αὐτμὴ
Ἡφαίστοιο βίηφι πολύφρονος . . . (Hom. *Il.* xxi. 267)

(4) Μέχρι μὲν οὖν οἱ τοξόται εἶχόν τε τὰ βέλη αὐτοῖς καὶ οἷοί τε ἦσαν χρῆσθαι, οἱ δὲ ἀντεῖχον. (Thuc. iii. 98)

(5) Φαίης ἄν, εἰ παρῆσθ', ὅτ' ἠγάπα νεκρούς.
(Eur. *Supp.* 764)

(6)   Illic saltus ac lustra ferarum,
Et patiens operum exiguoque adsueta iuventus.
(V. *Georg.* ii. 471)

(7) Nam te esse Tiburtem autumant, quibus non est
Cordi Catullum laedere. (Catull. 44. 2)

(8) Optimis hercule temporibus clarissimi viri vim tribuniciam sustinere non potuerunt : nedum his temporibus sine vestra sapientia salvi esse possimus. (Cic. *Clu.* 35)

(9) At enim ne quid captioni mihi sit, si dederim tibi.
(Plaut. *Most.* 922)

(10) Sed huc qua gratia te accersi iussi ausculta.
(Ter. *Eun.* 99)

XLVII

(1) Οὐκ ἔσθ' ὃς σῆς γε κύνας κεφαλῆς ἀπαλάλκοι.
(Hom. *Il.* xxii. 348)

(2) Ἄξιον δέ ἐστιν ἐπαινεῖν τὴν μὲν πόλιν ἡμῶν τῆς προαιρέσεως ἕνεκα, τὸ προελέσθαι ὅμοια, . . . τοὺς δὲ τελευτηκότας τῆς ἀνδρείας, τὸ μὴ καταισχῦναι τὰς τῶν προγόνων ἀρετάς. (Hyper. *Epit.* 2)

(3) Ζῶντι ἔδει βοηθεῖν, ὅπως ὅ τι δικαιότατος ὢν καὶ ὁσιώτατος ἔζη τε ζῶν καὶ τελευτήσας ἀτιμώρητος ἂν ἐγίγνετο.
(Plat. *Leg.* 959 c)

(4) Διαμάχομαι μὴ μεταγνῶναι ὑμᾶς τὰ προδεδογμένα.
(Thuc. iii. 40)

(5) Μεγάλα ἐκτήσατο χρήματα ὡς ἂν εἶναι 'Ροδῶπιν.
(Hdt. ii. 135)

(6) Ad moenia ipsa Romae populabundi regione portae Esquilinae excessere. (Liv. iii. 66)

(7) Metuo ne persentiscat, aurum ubi est absconditum.
(Plaut. *Aul.* 63)

(8) Is igitur ut natus sit dicitur ab Amulio exponi iussus esse.
(Cic. *Resp.* ii. 2)

(9) Ubiis auxilium suum pollicitus est, si ab Suebis premerentur. (Caes. *B.G.* iv. 19)

(10) . . . pedibus per mutua nexis
Examen subitum ramo frondente pependit.
(V. *Aen.* vii. 67)

XLVIII

(1) Εἰλήφθω ἐπὶ τῆς AB τυχὸν σημεῖον τὸ Δ, καὶ ἀφῃρήσθω ἀπὸ τῆς ΑΓ τῇ ΑΔ ἴση ἡ ΑΕ . . . (Eucl. i. Pr. 9)

(2) . . . οὔτ' ἀνὴρ πένης γεγὼς | μὴ οὐ τέχνην μαθὼν δύναιτ' ἂν ἀσφαλῶς | ζῆν τὸν βίον. (Philem. fr. 213)

(3) Εἴ περ γάρ τε χόλον γε καὶ αὐτῆμαρ καταπέψῃ,
ἀλλά τε καὶ μετόπισθεν ἔχει κότον. (Hom. *Il.* i. 81)

(4) Οἱ πατέρες, ὅσα ἄνθρωποι, οὐκ ἀμαθεῖς ἔσονται.
(Plat. *Rep.* 467 c)

(5) Ταύτην, ἄν μοι χρῆσθε συμβούλῳ, φυλάξετε τὴν πίστιν πρὸς τοῦτον . . . καὶ μὴ βουλήσεσθε εἰδέναι . . .
(Dem. xxiii. 117)

(6) Omne tulit punctum qui miscuit utile dulci.
(Hor. *A.P.* 343)

(7) Ibo visum si domist. (Ter. *Haut.* 170)

(8) Et verba omnia et vox huius alumnum urbis oleant, ut oratio Romana plene videatur. (Quint. viii. 1. 3)

(9) Cum Maximus Tarentum recepisset, rogavit eum Salinator, ut meminisset opera sua se Tarentum recepisse; "quidni", inquit, "meminerim? numquam enim recepissem, nisi tu perdidisses". (Cic. *Or.* ii. 67)

(10) Aiunt hominem, ut erat furiosus, respondisse.
(*id. Rosc. A.* 12)

XLIX

(1) Ἐπὶ δὲ στενάχοντο γυναῖκες,
Πάτροκλον πρόφασιν, σφῶν δ' αὐτῶν κήδε' ἑκάστη.
(Hom. *Il.* xix. 302)

(2) Πολλοῦ γε δεῖ μήποτέ τις τοιαῦτα ἐργάσηται.
(Plat. *Gorg.* 517 A)

(3) Ἁλοὺς μὲν γὰρ τὴν γραφὴν τῆς μὲν οὐσίας ᾔδειν ἐκστησόμενος, τῆς δὲ πόλεως καὶ τοῦ σώματος οὐκ ἐστερούμην.
(Ant. *Tetr.* A β 9)

(4) Δεῖ σ' ὅπως εὐσχήμονος ἀλεκτρυόνος μηδὲν διοίσεις.
(Crat. fr. 108)

(5) Εἰ δὲ μὴ ταχὺ λίποι, | ἔτι γλυκυτέραν κεν ἔλπομαι | σὺν ἅρματι θοῷ κλεΐξειν.
(Pind. *Ol.* i. 108)

(6) Viden' ut expalluit! datin' isti sellam ubi assidat, cito et aqualem cum aqua? (Plaut. *Curc.* 311)

(7) Ex quo efficitur, non ut voluptas ne sit voluptas, sed ut voluptas non sit summum bonum. (Cic. *Fin.* ii. 8)

(8) Cicero, Fabia Dolabellae dicente triginta se annos habere, "verum est", inquit, "nam hoc illam iam viginti annis audio". (Quint. vi. 3. 73)

(9) Etenim fateor me, dixerit ille,
Duci ventre levem, nasum nidore supinor. . . .
(Hor. *S.* ii. 7. 37)

(10) Si tribuni me triumphare prohiberent, Furium et Aemilium testes citaturus fui rerum a me gestarum.
(Liv. xxxviii. 47)

L

(1) Μὴ οὐδενὸς ἄξιοι εἶμεν κριταί, ἢ καὶ τὰ πράγματα αὐτὰ ἄπιστα ᾖ. (Plat. *Phaed.* 88 c)

(2) Τοῖς ἄρχουσιν . . . ἐπιδείξετε πότερον χρὴ δικαίοις εἶναι.
(Lys. xxviii. 10)

(3) Ὅς τε θεοῖς ἐπιπείθηται, μάλα τ' ἔκλυον αὐτοῦ.
(Hom. *Il.* i. 218)

(4) Τοῖς πρεσβυτέροις ἀντιπαρακελεύομαι μὴ καταισχυνθῆναι ὅπως μὴ δόξει μαλακὸς εἶναι. (Thuc. vi. 13)

(5) Οὐκ ἔσθ' ὅτῳ μείζονα μοῖραν νείμαιμ' ἢ σοί.
(Aesch. *P.V.* 292)

(6) Quid faciat custos, cum sint tot in urbe theatra,
Quoque sui comites ire ventur, eat ? (Ov. *A.A.* iii. 633)

(7) Nominat iste servum, quem magistrum pecoris esse diceret;
eum dicit coniurasse et familias concitasse.
(Cic. *Verr.* v. 7)

(8) Tum demum ingemuit : "Neque", ait, "sine numine vincis". (Ov. *M.* xi. 263)

(9) Ut proximus quisque Britannico neque fas neque fidem pensi haberet olim provisum erat. (Tac. *A.* xiii. 15)

(10) Miraris, cum tu argento post omnia ponas,
Si nemo praestet quem non merearis amorem ?
(Hor. *Sat.* i. 1. 86)

"Now you talk like a reasonable child," said Humpty Dumpty, looking very much pleased. "I meant by 'impenetrability' that we've had enough of that subject, and it would be just as well if you'd mention what you mean to do next, as I suppose you don't intend to stop here all the rest of your life."

LEWIS CARROLL, *Through the Looking-Glass*

INDEX

References are to paragraphs

ABLATIVE : 76-82 ; meaning of name, 76 ; conspectus of, 76 ; of Separation, 77 ; ablative-genitive in Latin, 77 ; with prepositions, 78 ; dependent on verbs, 78 ; of Origin, 79 ; of Comparison, 80 ; of Cause, 81 ; of Agent, 82

    Locative-Ablative in Latin : see under Locative

    Instrumental-Ablative in Latin : see under Instrumental

    Ablative " Absolute " : 93

ACCUSATIVE : 14-45 ; meaning of name, 14 ; conspectus of, 15 ; general remarks, 15 ; Internal, 18-32 ; of Extent of Action of verb, 19 ; internal limiting, 20 ; cognate, 21 ; in apposition to sentence, 22 ; expressing purpose, 23 ; adverbial of manner and extent, 24 ; of Description (Latin), 24 ; of part concerned, 25 ; of Extent of Space, 26-7 ; of Extent of Time, 28-30 ; with prepositions, 31, 44 ; Acc. Absolute (Greek), 32 ; External, 33-44 ; double Acc., 33 ; after passives and middles, 34-6 ; of Whole and Part, 37 ; External Acc.—after intransitive verbs, 38 ; dependent on a phrase, 39 ; on adjective or noun, 40 ; dependent on verb unexpressed, 41 ; of Exclamation, 41 ; of End of Motion, 42-4 ; anticipatory, 45 ; Acc. of Supine, 176

Accusative and Infinitive : development, 172, 258 ; general use, 260

ACTIVE VOICE : 113

ADJECTIVES : predicative and attributive, 1, 107 ; acc. dependent on, 40 ; with predicative dat., 54 ; with descriptive genit., 68 ; with objective genit., 71, 72 ; with instrumental dat., 93-4 ; with infinitive, 165 ; representing apodosis, 230

    Verbal Adjectives, 173-6

AGENT : dative of, 51, 174 ; ablative of, 82

ʼAN, KEN : in potential sentences, 226-8, 281 ; with iterative past tenses, 228 ; origin and meaning, 277-80 ; ἄν in Attic, 280-290 ; omission of verb with, 282 ; omitted, 283 ; repeated, 284 ; in apparently final clauses, 285 ; with subj., 286 ; omitted with subj., 286 ; retained with optat., 287 ; in final clauses, 288 ; with future tenses, 289-90

    In Homer : use in future conditions, 223-4 ; with subj., 278 ; with optat., 278 ; in final clauses, 278

ANACOLUTHON : with nominative, 9 ; 335

ANTICIPATORY CASES : 45

AORIST : 141-3 ; dramatic, 142 ; gnomic, 143 ; aor. participle with ἔχω, 138 ; aor. subj. in prohibitions, 185 ; in conditional sentences, 221-2

INDEX

APODOSIS : meaning, 219 ; suppressed, etc., 229-33 ; answering a protasis of a different type, 234-41

APOSIOPESIS : in conditional sentences, 232

APPOSITION: in abnormal nominative constructions, 8 ; acc. in apposition to sentence, 22 ; in accus. Whole and Part construction, 37 ; with Homeric article, 102

ARTICLE : origin, 101 ; traces in Latin, 101 ; Homeric art., as pronoun, demonstrative adjective, relative, etc., 102 ; older uses retained in Attic, 103 ; general Attic usage, 104 ; idioms of, 105-7 ; omission of, 106 ; position, 107

ATTRACTION AND ASSIMILATION : of moods, 271, 330-3 ; explained, 323 ; of gender, 324 ; of number, 325 ; of case, 326-329 ; between relative and antecedent, 326-7 ; logical, 330 ; illogical, 331 ; of subj. in Latin, 332 ; into indicative, 333 ; into infinitive in O.O., 334 ; anacoluthon)(attraction, 335

CASES : general, 2 ; 3-7

CAUSAL SENTENCES : 214-17 ; with subj. in Latin, 215 ; rejected reason (Latin), 216 ; alleged reason, 217

COMMANDS : in future indicative, 134, 186 ; use of subj. and optat. in, 182 ; positive, 183 ; relating to past time, 184 ; negative, 185 ; commands in O.O. (" quoted "), 260 ; indirect, 275

CONCESSIVE SENTENCES : 187, 218 ; in Homer, 150

CONDITIONAL SENTENCES : general, 219 ; regular types, 220 ; in Homer, 222-4, 226, 231 ; general conditions, 225 ; with protasis suppressed, etc., potential, 226 ; with apodosis suppressed, etc., 229-33 ; mixed, 234-41 ; negatives of, 296

CONSECUTIVE SENTENCES : 205-210 ; in Homer, 205 ; with infinitive (Greek), 205, 209-10 ; with subj. (Latin), 206 ; with relatives (Latin), 207 ; expressing terms, 209

COPULA : 1 ; 118

DATIVE : 46-54 ; meaning of name, 46 ; conspectus of, 46 ; of indirect object, 47 ; of indir. obj. in local relation, 48 ; ethic, 49 ; possessive, 50 ; of Agent, 51 ; of special limitation, 52 ; of Person Judging, 52 ; expressing purpose, 53 ; predicative, 54

Locative-Dative in Greek : see under Locative

Instrumental-Dative in Greek : see under Instrumental

DEFINITE : relative and temporal sentences, 211 ; use of ἄν to mark, 278

DELIBERATIVE SENTENCES : 152 ; 191-3 ; parataxis in, 190 ; remote, 191 ; present indicative in, 192 ; indirect, 273

DEMONSTRATIVE : article as, 102, 105 ; in place of reflexive, 110 ; origin of relatives, 212

DEPONENT VERBS : as middles, 112 ; 116

DESCRIPTION : accus. of, 24 ; genit. of, 64-9

DUM : with present indicative, 124 ; moods with, 215

EPISTOLARY IMPERFECT : 132

EXCLAMATION : accus. of, 41 ; genit. of, 75 ; infinitive of, 169

EXPLANATORY INFINITIVE : 166

EXTENT : accus. of : of Action of verb, 18-22 ; of Space, 26 ; of Time, 28 ; prepositions with, 31

FEAR : object clauses of, 256

FINAL SENTENCES : origin in parataxis, 194 ; 197-204 ; meaning of particles in, 197 ; moods in, 198 ; vivid construction, 200 ; with past indicative (Greek), 199 ; with future indicative (Greek), 201 ;)(modal clauses, 255 ;)(clauses of fear, 256 ; used to express indirect commands, 275 ; in Homer, 278 ; with ἄν, 285, 288

FUTURE : 133 ; participle expressing purpose, 133 ; of Command, 134, 186, 308-9; relation to subj., 149 ; wishes, 188; indicative in final clauses, 203 ; fut. optat., 203 ; conditions, 223-4 ; 248-9 ; with ἄν, 289-90 ; with οὐ μή, 307-9

FUTURE PERFECT : 140

GENDER : apparent anomaly of, 108·; attraction of, 324
GENERAL : conditions, 225 ; relative clauses, 251
GENERIC CLAUSES : 250
GENITIVE : 55-75 ; meaning of name, 55 ; conspectus of, 55 ; possessive, 56 ; with verbs, 57 ; partitive, 58 ; partitive of Place, 58 ; with prepositions, 60, 66 ; partitive of Time, 61 ; genit. absolute, 62 ; partitive with verbs, 63 ; of Definition, 64-5 ; of Material, 67 ; of Quality, 68 ; of Value, 69 ; of Purpose, 70 ; of Relation, 71-75 ; objective, 71 ; of point in which term applied, 72 ; of Cause, 74 ; of Exclamation, 75
Ablative-Genitive in Greek : see under Ablative
GERUND AND GERUNDIVE : 173-176 ; expressing necessity, 174 ; gerund with accus. in Latin, 174 ; representing present participle passive in Latin, 175 ; expressing mere passivity, 175 ; possibility, 175
GNOMIC : perfect, 137 ; aorist, 143
GOODWIN : *Moods and Tenses*, viii, 208, 300, 302, 309, 311

HISTORIC : present, 124 ; infinitive, 170 ; sequence—in indirect questions, 261-2 ; in final clauses, 198, 200 ; historic subord. verb after primary main verb, 124, 200, 202 ; historic main verb with primary subordinate verb, 200, 206
HOMER : value of, for syntax, 16, 146, 197 ; development of prepositions in, 16 ; parataxis in, 146, 183, 197 ; subj. and optat. in, 149-50 ; jussive usages, 151, 188 ; final, 201, 278 ; consecutive, 205 ; conditional, 222-4, 226, 231, 235 ; O.O., 258, 263 ; summary of differences from Attic, 291 ; relative and temporal, 278
HYPOTAXIS AND PARATAXIS : 145, 183, 194-5, 197, 274

IDEAL : tense requirements, 120 ; second person, 244 ; conditions : see Unfulfilled
IMPERATIVE MOOD : 158 ; in dependent clause, 159 ; in positive commands, 183 ; in negative commands, 185 ; concessive use of, 187
IMPERFECT : 127-132 ; as narrative tense, 127 ; incipient, 128 ; conative, 129 ; of fact just recognized, 130 ; philosophic, 131 ; epistolary, 132 ; in conditional sentences, 222 ; imperfect subjunctive in Latin, 184, 194, 276
INCORPORATION : of antecedent in relative clause, 326
INDEFINITE : with ἄν, 228, 286-288 ; relative clauses, 245-50 ; temporal, 253 ; without ἄν, 278 ; negative, 293, 297
INDICATIVE MOOD : 147 ; historic tenses of, in place of subj. and optat. in Greek, 147, 198, 199, 222, 257 ; in conditional sentences, 221-2
INDIRECT : object, 46-9 ; in local relation, 48 ; indirect discourse (O.O.), 258-75 ; questions, 272-5 ; commands, 275
INFINITIVE : with article, 41, 70, 105 ; origin, 161 ; as dative, 162 ; with verbs and substantives, 164-5 ; of Purpose, 163 ; explanatory and limitative, 166 ; of Command, 167

of Exclamation, 169; historic, 170; as nominative, 171; as accus., 172; accus. and infin., origin and general use, 172, 258-60; consecutive, 205, 209-210; negatives of, 208, 298; parenthetic, 210; verbs dependent on, 269; attraction into, 271, 329, 333

INSTRUMENTAL CASE: 89-96; meaning, 89; conspectus, 89; of means, 90; expressing Price, 90; of Cause, 91; Sociative, 92; of Attendant Circumstances, 93; of Manner, 94; of relation, 95; of Measure, 96

INTERJECTIONS: 2; conditional particles as, 226

INTERROGATIVE: particles, 305; negatives explained, 305; οὐ μή, 306, 308

INTRANSITIVE VERBS: term explained, 113; direct accus. after, 38; 57

ITERATIVE SENTENCES: 228, 251

JUSSIVE: optat., 150, 153; subj., 151; in Homer, 151, 188; usages, 182-93; commands, 183-4; negative commands, 185-6; concession, 187; wishes, 188-90; deliberatives, 191-3; relation with final constructions, 193, 197; negatives, 294

KEN: see 'AN

LIMITATIVE: all cases limitative, 5; force of accus., 14-5; internal limiting accus., 20-2; accus. of Purpose, 23; infinitive, 166

LOCATIVE CASE: of Place, 83-5; of Value, 85; of Time, 86-7; with prepositions, 88

LOGICAL: scheme of language, 1-2;)(grammatical subject, 8-9; attraction, 330

MH:)(οὐ, 293, 304; in jussive clauses, 294; with indicative, 295; in conditional, 296; in relative and temporal, 297; in consecutive, 298; with infinitive, 298; with infinitive in O.O., 300; with participles and substantives, 301-3; in questions, 305-6; in independent sentences expressing apprehension, 308; in answer to questions, 321

MH OT: in independent sentences, 309-10; in dependent clauses, 312; exceptional uses, 313-4

MIDDLE VOICE: 112; in Latin, 35-6, 112; various uses, 114; middle and passive forms, 115

MODAL CLAUSES: 255

MONRO: *Homeric Grammar*, ix, 277, 279, 296

MOODS: 144-72; indicative, 147; subjunctive and optative, 148-57; imperative, 158-160; infinitive, 161-72

NE: in prohibitions, 185; in final clauses, 197; in clauses of fearing, 257; origins, 292;)(non, 293

NĒ: 293, 305

NEC: = non, 292; in doubled negatives, 317

NEGATIVES: forms and origins, 292; general scheme of usage, 293; in jussive sentences, 294; in conditionals, 296; in relative and temporal clauses, 297; in consecutive, 298; with infinitive, 298-300; with participles and substantives, 301-3; in questions, 305-6; οὐ μή, 307-9; μὴ οὐ, 310-14; reinforced, 315-6; conjunctions, 317; ellipse of, 318; redundant, 319-20; anticipatory, 322

NI, NISI: 292, 296

NOMINATIVE: the name, 7; Whole and Part construction, 8; "pendens", 9; in Latin, 10, 259; with infinitive in Greek, 259

OBJECT: direct, of verb, 33 ff.; indirect, 46 ff.; object clauses, 255 ff.

INDEX

OBJECTIVE GENITIVE: 71-2; with adjective, 71; expressing indirect object, 71; extension of, 72

OPTATIVE: 148-56; original meaning, 148; in Homer, 150; of wish, 153, 188-9; potential, 154, 227; development of, in historic subordinate clauses, 156; deliberative, 190; deliberative in dependent clause, 191; final, 198; expressing alleged reason, 217; conditional, 224; in relative sentences, 249, 251; in temporal, 253-4; in O.O., 261-2, 264, 272-3; attraction into, 273, 330-1; use of ἄν with, 281-5

ORATIO OBLIQUA: mood of subordinate clause in Latin, 217, 267-8; explained, 258; origin of accus. and infin. construction in, 258, 260; nominative and infin. in, 259; ὅτι, ὡς construction in, 261, 263-5; complex sentences in, 262; Greek participial construction, 266; abnormal reported conditions, 270

ΟΥ:)(μή, 293, 304; with consecutive infinitive, 208; in relative and temporal sentences, 297; in consecutive, 298; general use with infinitive, 298; with participle, 299; in questions, 305

ΟΥ ΜΗ: 307-9

PARATAXIS: origin of complex sentence, 183, 194-5, 197; in Plautus and Terence, 274

PARTICIPLE: 177-81; absolute constructions, 32, 62, 87, 93; in periphrastic perfect, 138, 181; circumstantial, 178; as verbal noun, 179; neuter as substantive, 180; expressing purpose, 178; representing apodosis, 229; in O.O., 266; negatives of, 301

PASSIVE: accus. dependent on, 35; origin of, 112, 114; forms, 115

PERCEPTION: verbs of, genitive after, 57, 79; with participial construction, 266

PERFECT: 135-8; gnomic, 137; periphrastic, 138, 181

PERSON: ideal second, 244

PLUPERFECT: 139

POTENTIAL: optative without ἄν, 150, 278; optative, 154, 227-8; subj. in Latin, 227-8; abnormalities, 281-5; in final sentences, 285

PREDICATE: 1; and use of article, 107; predicative dative, 54

PREPOSITIONS: development from adverbs, 16-17; with accus. of extent, 31; with accus. of end of motion, 44; with genitive, 60; with genit. of definition, 66; with ablative, 78; with locative, 88; special uses, proleptic, 97-9; prep. and the development of a language, 100

PRESENT: 121-6; of customary action, etc., 122; conative, 122; of action continued from the past, 123; historic, 124; in future sense, 125; of permanent result, 126

ΠΡΙΝ: 254

PROHIBITIONS: 185; with οὐ μή, 307-9

PROLEPTIC: cases, 45; prepositions, 97-99

PRONOUNS: abnormal uses, 108-111

PROTASIS: 219; obscured or suppressed, 226-8; expressing purpose, 233

PURPOSE: dative of, 53-4; genitive expressing, 70; infinitive of, 163; supine expressing, 176; participle expressing, 204; protasis expressing, 233

QUESTIONS: indirect, 272-5; disjunctive, 279; negatives in, 305-6

RECIPROCAL: reflexive pronoun in place of 108; use of middle, 114

INDEX

REFLEXIVE : in place of reciprocal pronoun, 108 ; use of middle, 114
RELATIVE : article as, 102-3 ; in final clauses, 203 ; in consecutive clauses, 207 ; development of rel. sentences, 212 ; definite rel. sentences, 213 ; indefinite, 245 ; conditions, 246-9 ; generic rel. sentences, 250 ; general rel. sentences, 251
SEQUENCE : irregularities of, 124, 200-2, 206
SUBJUNCTIVE MOOD : expressing apprehension in independent sentence, 145, 256, 309 ; Greek, 148-51 ; with future meaning in Homer, 149 ; jussive, 151, 183-4 ; deliberative, 152, 191 ; Latin, 157 ; tenses in Latin, 184, 194, 276 ; expressing wish, Latin, 188-90; final, 197-199, 201 ; in vivid sequence, 200-2 ; with relatives, 203, 207, 247 ff. ; consecutive, Latin, 206-7 ; causal, Latin, 215, 250 ; in clauses of fearing, 256-7 ; in conditional sentences, 222, 224 ; potential, 226-7 ; in O.O., Latin, 260, 262 ; with οὐ μή, 307-9
SUPINE : 176

TEMPORAL CLAUSES : definite, 213 ; with *cum*, 215 ; indefinite, 253 ; with πρίν, 254
TENSES : 117-43 ; present, 121-126 ; imperfect, 127-32 ; future, 133-4 ; perfect, 135-8 ; pluperfect, 139 ; future perfect, 140 ; aorist, 141-3 ; Tenses of subjunctive, 148, 276 ; of optative, 148, 150, 222

THOMPSON : *Syntax of Attic Greek*, 292, 304, 309
TIME : expression of time-extent, 28-30 ; during which, 61 ; time when, 86
TMESIS : of verbs compounded of prepositions, 16-17
TRANSITIVE VERBS : 33, 113

UNFULFILLED : wishes, 188, 190 ; final clauses, 199 ; conditions, 222, 247, in Homer, 222

VERBAL NOUN AND ADJECTIVE : 173-81
VERBS : with double accus., 33 ; with dative, 48, 164 ; with predicative dative, 54 ; with possessive genitive, 57 ; with partitive genitive, 63 ; with genitive of definition, 65 ; with ablative, 78-9 ; with locative, 85 ; with instrumental, 90-1 ; with infinitive, 163-4 ; with object clauses, 255 ; with object clauses of fear, 256-7 ; with participial construction, 266 ; verbs of swearing with μή and infinitive, 298-9
VIVID CONSTRUCTIONS : final, 200-2 ; vivid future conditions, 223, 248 ; vivid indicative in past unfulfilled conditions, 237 ; in O.O., 261-2
VOCATIVE : 12 ; use by attraction, 13
VOICES: passive, 35, 112, 114-16 ; middle, 35-6, 112, 114-16 ; active, 113

WHOLE AND PART CONSTRUCTION : in nominative, 8 ; accus., 37 ; dative, 37
WISHES : 188-90

THE END